www.wadsworth.com

wadsworth.com is the World Wide Web site for
Wadsworth and is your direct source to dozens of
online resources.

At *wadsworth.com* you can find out about supple-
ments, demonstration software, and student resources. You can also send email to many of our
authors and preview new publications and exciting
new technologies.

wadsworth.com
Changing the way the world learns®

CROSSROADS IN MUSIC
TRADITIONS AND CONNECTIONS

Arved M. Larsen, General Editor
Illinois State University

Paul W. Borg
Illinois State University

David Poultney
Emeritus, Illinois State University

Arthur Unsworth
Appalachian State University

Robert Washburn
Dean Emeritus, Crane School of Music, SUNY Potsdam

THOMSON

SCHIRMER ™

Australia • Canada • Mexico • Singapore • Spain
United Kingdom • United States

Music Editor: Clark G. Baxter
Assistant Editor: Julie Iannacchino
Editorial Assistant: Eno Sarris
Technology Project Manager: Jennifer Ellis
Marketing Manager: Mark Orr
Marketing Assistant: Justine Ferguson
Advertising Project Manager: Brian Chaffee
Project Manager, Editorial Production: Emily Smith
Senior Print/Media Buyer: Karen Hunt
Permissions Editor: Elizabeth Zuber
Production Service: Martha Emry

Text Designer: Rokusek Design
Photo Researcher: Catherine Nance
Copy Editor: Kevin Gleason
Autographer: Ernie Mansfield
Illustrator: Atherton Customs
Cover Designer: DiDona Design
Cover Image: © John Elk/Getty Images/Stone;
   © Royalty-Free/CORBIS
Compositor: TBH Typecast, Inc.
Text and Cover Printer: Webcom Limited

For more information about our products, contact us at:
Thomson Learning Academic Resource Center
1-800-423-0563
For permission to use material from this text, contact us by:
Phone: 1-800-730-2214
Fax: 1-800-730-2215
Web: http://www.thomsonrights.com

Library of Congress Control Number: 2002107784

ISBN 0-0-534-51634-3

Wadsworth Group/Thomson Learning
10 Davis Drive
Belmont, CA 94002-3098
USA

Asia
Thomson Learning
5 Shenton Way #01-01
UIC Building
Singapore 068808

Australia
Nelson Thomson Learning
102 Dodds Street
South Melbourne, Victoria 3205
Australia

Canada
Nelson Thomson Learning
1120 Birchmount Road
Toronto, Ontario M1K 5G4
Canada

Europe/Middle East/Africa
Thomson Learning
High Holborn House
50/51 Bedford Row
London WC1R 4LR

Latin America
Thomson Learning
Seneca, 53
Colonia Polanco
11560 Mexico D.F.
Mexico

Spain
Paraninfo Thomson Learning
Calle/Magallanes, 25
28015 Madrid, Spain

This book is dedicated to Dr. Arved M. Larsen Sr.
(this is the book he intended to write) and Nell F. Larsen —
noted music educators, musicians, and wonderful parents.

TABLE OF CONTENTS

PREFACE

INTRODUCTION

Crossroads in Music is a general introduction to all types of music available in contemporary society. We have organized the material by topic—emphasizing the "crossroads" of artistic cultures and genders—to give the student a balanced, comprehensive view of music: past and present, Western and non-Western, art music and popular trends. In order to ensure that each unit is authoritatively written, five authors teamed up to prepare the text, each with expertise and teaching experience in their respective area.

PURPOSE

Crossroads in Music is suitable for use in music appreciation, listening, or literature classes that serve students without extensive musical backgrounds. Although it is intended for use at the college level, with chapters structured to an average class time, it is also appropriate for advanced high school classes. The text was conceived for the U.S. market, but it could easily be used in any English-speaking country.

ORGANIZATION

The text evolved through several organizational structures on its way to a function-based approach borrowed from ethnomusicology. This approach allows us to discuss musics from differing styles and times in close juxtaposition, much as they might occur in the student's own life. A spiral curriculum concept is evident in the re-occurrence of concepts in various contexts and the systematic reuse of musical examples. In Parts I and II (Chapters 1–9), the musical examples are designed to use less than one minute of each piece. Later, longer portions of these same examples are heard. These practices reinforce the student's understanding of musical ideas and build familiarity with important works. Another dimension is the variety of perspectives from which each musical function is viewed. This allows the student to understand how a style may evolve from folk to pop to art music over a period of time. A key feature of the text is the *Crossroads* box, a device that makes it possible to make connections across disciplines, time periods, styles, and cultures.

OUTLINE

Part I: Introduction — Chapters 1 and 2
- Establishes a starting point for the course
- Starts slowly to allow students to become oriented

Part II: Terminology — Chapters 3 through 9
- Elements are defined broadly in order to encompass diverse styles
- Students gain a fuller understanding of terms as they are used throughout the book

Parts III through VII employ function-based organization.

Part III: Ritual Music — Chapters 10 through 15
- Chapter 10 provides an orientation to the function-based approach
- Ritual music chapters establish a definition, discuss liturgical music, and extend to church music in the concert hall

Part IV: Folk Music — Chapters 16 through 18
- Describes folk music in the United States, around the world, and as building material for concert music

Parts V and VI discuss concert music.

Part V: Large Concert Ensembles — Chapters 19 through 24
- Begins with diverse concert ensembles
- Moves to orchestra, soloists with orchestra, and opera
- Includes a chapter on band music

Part VI: Small Concert Ensembles — Chapters 25 through 28
- Covers diversity in small ensembles
- Describes small vocal and instrumental ensembles
- Includes electronic music

Part VII: Commercial/Popular Music — Chapters 29 through 35
- Opens with early popular styles in the United States
- Covers rock, soul, the musical, and film music
- Concludes with global popular music

Part VIII: Synthesis — Chapters 36 and 37
- Provides an overview of the current musical scene
- Gives suggestions for enjoying a variety of music once the course is completed

ANCILLARIES

Compact Disc Set

- Four CDs containing all of the listening selections discussed in the book

Web Site

- Includes a searchable encyclopedia of people and terms including all those discussed in the text

Online Student Guide

- Includes chapter outlines, lists of terms/personalities, listening guides, and *Crossroads* summaries
- Terms are linked to definitions in the encyclopedia
- Contains pieces linked to a computer play feature, allowing students to play a piece and follow the listening guide
- Includes *Ways to Follow Your Interest*, a feature that allows students to find more information about their favorite pieces

Online Instructor's Manual and Test Bank

ACKNOWLEDGMENTS

We would like to thank our spouses, friends, and colleagues for their help and support during the evolution of this text. Special thanks to Kristin Larsen for her diligence in preparing the student and instructor's manuals and to Noah Larsen for his help with the technological aspects of the Web site. We would also like to recognize Clark Baxter for his helpful philosophical prodding during the design phase. Thanks also to Pam Miller of the Illinois State School of Music for her clerical assistance and Dr. Janet Connelly of the ISU School of Art for her help in selecting art works. In addition, we extend our thanks to the following reviewers: Dr. Melissa Colgin Abeln, University of Texas at El Paso; Lee Jordan-Anders, Virginia Wesleyan College; Wesley A. Ball, Hope College; Walter Clark, University of Kansas; Claire Detels, University of Arkansas; Dorothy Keyser, University of North Dakota; and Floyd Slotterback, Northern Michigan University.

Arved M. Larsen
Paul W. Borg
David Poultney
Arthur Unsworth
Robert Washburn

CHAPTER

Music and Your World

1

You live in what is undoubtedly the best possible time to enjoy music. More styles of music are available in more formats than ever before. Radio, television, and computers provide us with inexpensive access to musical performances from symphony orchestras to rock concerts. For home listening, you can choose from video and audiocassette, CD, CD-ROM, MP3, or laser disc formats and order your selections over the Internet. Even moderate-size cities have significant performing arts series, providing a diverse array of popular through classical artists, and often they support local symphonies, bands, and opera companies as well.

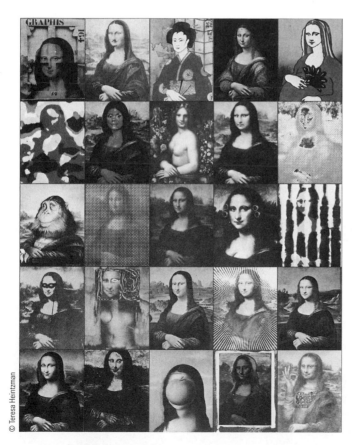

© Teresa Heintzman

Lookin' Good Mona

You not only have the optimum access to music but also the widest spectrum of styles and types of music from which to choose. For the pop fan, a small amount of effort will yield examples of popular trends in almost any country in the world. The world music enthusiast can easily find examples of authentic and popularized music from his or her country of choice. Classical music followers can keep up with the latest releases of the world's major orchestras through a variety of media. Accordingly, the primary goal of this text is to provide an understanding of the wide variety of musics that are available today. This we accomplish by introducing musical concepts (Chapters 3–9), surveying types of music according to their social and cultural function (Chapters 10–35), and concluding by describing current trends in music and ways in which you can most effectively enjoy them (Chapters 36 and 37).

At the present, we live in a *laissez-faire* musical democracy; all styles have a vote and all have the freedom to interact with other styles. Classical musicians collaborate with jazz players, rock musicians write operas, and world music is heard everywhere. Composers feel free to write in minimal, tonal, or even serial styles and mix conventional instruments with electronic sounds and other media as it suits them. Listeners are both open minded and a little fickle, selecting music from all possible offerings, making for a very diverse and competitive recording market.

"HOE DOWN" FROM *RODEO*

In this brief arrangement, Bela Fleck and the Flecktones demonstrate the diversity that is characteristic of much of the music of the present. Fleck, a New Yorker of Hungarian descent who plays a composite pop folk jazz on the banjo, is covering Aaron Copland's "Hoe Down" from his ballet *Rodeo*. An eminent American composer who was born of Jewish immigrant parents in Brooklyn, Copland was himself emulating elements of folk music of the American West in *Rodeo*. In one sense, Fleck's banjo brings "Hoe Down" full circle by returning the folk element to the music.

This performance mixes instruments of several cultures (such as the penny whistle from England and the tabla from India) with instruments that are characteristic of a variety of styles (banjo, soprano and tenor saxophone, with bassoon and the instruments of a string quartet). Electronic sounds are also represented, with Fleck playing on both acoustic and electric banjo and Future Man performing on synthe axe drumtar. Even the bassoon sound is modified through a harmonizer.

"Hoe Down," *Rodeo*, Aaron Copland, arr. Bela Fleck	LISTENING GUIDE

CD 1:1

00:00   Introduction—electric banjo and saxophone

00:16   "Hoe Down" melody

1:47   Break—improvised saxophone solo

2:18   Penny whistle enters

2:37   Bass solo (emulating sitar) with tabla

2:51   Acoustic banjo solo

3:55   "Hoe Down" melody returns

4:47   Conclusion with cha-cha-cha

YOUR PERSONAL MUSICAL CULTURE

A survey of the favorite musical style of each member of your class might surprise you with the diversity of responses. Many different popular styles are likely to be represented along with classical, jazz, and ethnic music. Although it may be obvious why a fellow student from another country has different tastes, it may be less clear why a student from a background that is similar to yours may have musical preferences that differ from your own. Several factors may help explain such differences.

The environment you grew up in undoubtedly had an impact on your musical likes and dislikes. The kind of music your family listened to may have left you with positive or negative feelings toward that particular style. Educational experiences with music in elementary or high school may also have contributed to your current musical affinities. The music available in your community has a very practical impact on your musical tastes. A large city makes many different types of music available to you, while the small town setting may provide you fewer. Also, the musical inclinations of your friends have certainly played a role in defining the kind of music you like.

At this point, you may be wondering why a sister or brother, who grew up in the same setting with many similar influences, ended up liking music you can't stand. Without question, personality traits and personal preferences affect your likes and dislikes in music.

Musical taste may also be influenced by important musical experiences. Most people can remember one or more vivid musical performances that took place early in life and probably affected later musical choices. Take a moment to identify performances that may have been important in your past. Did these events create an interest in listening to music? Did they influence your choices of styles of music?

By now you should begin to realize that your current taste in music is the result of a variety of circumstances. To expand your musical horizons, it is important to accept the fact that hearing new music is like meeting someone for the first time: those who form an opinion based on an initial experience are likely to reconsider that opinion at a later time. Since by now you probably recognize at least some of the roots and limitations of your current musical tastes, it is reasonable that you listen to a new piece of music several times before deciding if it should be added to your list for future listening.

MUSIC: A WORKING DEFINITION

Sound is all around us. To verify this fact, simply stop all activity for 30 seconds and listen to your environment. Depending on your location, you may have identified sounds of which you were not even aware. These sounds may be human made or natural and may vary in number, but inevitably some kind of sound is present.

Similarly, we find ourselves surrounded by music during many of our waking hours. In addition to more formalized concert settings, music is a frequent presence in restaurants, offices, automobiles, homes, airplanes, and shopping centers. Musics available to us represent a wide range of styles and may serve cultural, recreational, artistic, therapeutic, or educational purposes.

If both musical and nonmusical sound are part of everyday life, how can you discriminate between the two? At first this may seem like an easy question, but there are some unfamiliar styles of music that on first hearing may not sound like music at all. A key to solving this dichotomy lies in identifying the fact that humans are involved in ordering the sounds of a musical work whether it is an Indian raga, a Beethoven sonata, or an improvised jazz solo. The role of the creator of each of these works is to organize the sounds in much the same way that an author organizes words into sentences.

Another important characteristic of music is that it occurs linearly over time, like a sentence. Unlike a painting, which can be viewed at once in its entirety, music is heard a little at a time so that a composite of the musical work is formed only in the mind of the listener. Therefore, *sound organized in time* is a working definition of **music** that will allow you to identify sounds as music (without being confused by whether you like it or not).

You do not need a great deal of formal training in music to sense the organization in a musical work. One perspective on this organization is that there is a careful balance between the repetition and variation of musical materials. Repetition of musical ideas creates unity in a work by giving the listener points of reference that have become familiar from having been heard before. Since repetition does not give the sense of forward progress you hear when new or

Jazz improviser,
Paul Gonsalves

varied ideas are introduced, too much repetition may lose the listener's interest because of lack of variety. Conversely, too much variety lacks unity and may not sound "organized." These examples are all from the twentieth century, but they represent dramatically different musical styles. The questions listed below should allow you to make some basic observations about each work, in spite of the style differences.

"Mean Old Bed Bug Blues," Bessie Smith

Active Listening*
CD 1:2

Satyagraha, Act III, "Martin Luther King, Jr.," Part 3, Philip Glass

CD 1:3

The Lion's Tale (excerpt), Pauline Oliveros

CD 1:4

- Is each example organized?
- What is repeated in each example (text, musical ideas)?
- What is varied?
- In spite of the obvious differences in these pieces, does each fit the definition of music?

*Note: You may choose to play brief portions of the selections to complete the listening activities in Chapters 1–9.

2 Listening to Music

THE PLACE OF MUSIC IN CULTURE

Throughout history, music seems to have been an inevitable part of almost all cultures. This universality suggests that the human mind, with its inherent inclination to organize and synthesize, has always been naturally attracted to ordering sounds.

In each culture or society, the creation of music assumes a distinctive quality that arises from and expresses the needs and customs of the people. It has often been said that in a general sense, the arts are a reflection of the culture that created them. As can be heard in the following example, this connection can be as direct as an undeniable anthropological relationship between the characteristics of the music and a particular ethnic group.

This American Indian war dance is usually called a Grass Dance after the woven grass the dancers wore to symbolize slain enemies. Typically, men dance in costume in the center of the dance area while women participate by walking or dancing a subdued version on its periphery.

Active Listening
CD 1:5

Sioux Grass Dance, Western Plains Indians

- What type of dance steps does the music suggest?
- How detailed are the images suggested by this music?
- Does it actually suggest impressions of war or something less specific?

After several hearings you may find that you are beginning to appreciate the structure of this example independent of the obvious cultural connection. It is true that most well-constructed music can be enjoyed in an abstract manner, that is, without any extramusical connection. Nevertheless, the experience is usually enhanced by an understanding of cultural or societal relationships.

In other musical examples those relationships are less specific than the "Sioux Grass Dance" and may simply relate to a style of composing that is characteristic of a particular time and place. Mozart's *Eine Kleine Nachtmusik* was composed during the Classical Era (1750–1825), a time in Western Europe that saw a return to the ideals of balance and simplicity that characterized Greek and Roman civilizations of antiquity. These ideals became contemporary as composers sought to write clearly organized, accessible music for some of the first public (as opposed to aristocratic) audiences.

National Museum of the American Indian/Smithsonian Institute

"Grass Dancer"
at Michigan State
University powwow,
1992

Eine kleine Nachtmusik, First Movement, *Allegro*,
Wolfgang Amadeus Mozart

Active Listening
CD 1:6

- How does Mozart use silence to "punctuate" his melodies?
- How does he achieve the sense of "balance and rightness" that is typical of the style?
- Can you imagine the dress of the audience who might have heard this in Mozart's time?

Although you could listen to this work in an abstract manner, knowledge of the lifestyle and composing practices of the time provides for a fuller understanding of the work.

Music may play a more active role than simply reflecting the societal norms of the time. Consider, for example, the evolution of rock and roll that from its inception was a rebellion against the conventions of post-World War II society. The involvement of the United States in the Viet Nam war concentrated this rebellious attitude into a full-scale social protest against the war and "the establishment" in general. This movement, which changed certain aspects of

American society, used music as a primary vehicle to achieve its goals. In many instances the message was direct, as in "Blowin' in the Wind" by Bob Dylan.

How many roads must a man walk down before you call him a man?
Yes'n how many seas must a white dove sail before she sleeps in the sand?
Yes'n how many times must the cannon balls fly before they're forever banned?
The answer my friend is blowin' in the wind,
The answer is blowing in the wind.

LEVELS OF INTERACTION

Much of the music in your daily life receives less than your full attention or, in some cases, none at all. Background music in offices and restaurants, for example is designed to create a "sound environment" of which you are only occasionally aware. It is likely that you have music playing in your room much of the day and perhaps even when you are studying. In these instances, depending on what you are doing at the time, music may be in the foreground or the background of your consciousness. However, when listening to your favorite type of music in a concert setting, you probably focus your attention entirely on the music. These listening activities show that you routinely control your level of interaction with music according to circumstances.

Active Listening
CD 1:7

***Appalachian Spring,* "Variations on a Shaker Melody," Aaron Copland**

Listen to this example twice and follow the directions exactly to get the most out of this activity.

- First hearing

   Do everything you can to avoid listening to the selection. Daydream, talk to a friend, read, or do homework from another class.

- Second hearing

   Describe this example as specifically as possible.
   Can you identify specific instruments?
   How loud or soft is the music?
   How high or low are the sounds?
   Does it suggest a mental image of some kind?

   The purpose of this experiment is to have you experience a single piece of music first with little interaction and then with the total concentration that is characteristic of focused listening. The goal of our future exercises is to better equip you to understand music during focused listening.

LIVE PERFORMANCE

Until the use of musical recordings became widespread, early in the twentieth century, all music was heard only in live performance. Even after the recording industry became well established, listening to and, in many cases, dancing to live music were preferred social activities. The dance music of the swing era in the years preceding World War II and early rock music of the fifties and sixties are good examples of this trend. However, in the last few years, listening, often combined with viewing, has become a much more passive activity.

For a time, a key difference between recorded music and live performance was the quality of the sound. From the early Edison phonographs with their distant, thin sound, we moved to 78 rpm records, then to long-playing records and later cassettes, videos, CDs, and the Internet. Although it may never be possible for a recording medium to recreate the sense of space found in concert halls, it is clear that sound quality alone is no longer a major reason to attend live performances.

In spite of these technological advances that allow us to enjoy both the sight and sound of live music in the comfort of our homes, large numbers of people continue to attend concerts of a variety of musical styles. A primary explanation for this seemingly contradictory behavior is that music has always been, to a large extent, a means of communication. At some point, you probably have heard the cliché, "music is the international language." You may have also realized that communications are clearest when they are carried out in person. No technology will ever duplicate the energy and excitement of the live music setting.

People go to live performances not only for the immediacy of communication but also for the spontaneity of live music. For some styles of music (jazz, for example), spontaneity is crucial and each performance is unique. Even for music that is written down, variety is expected and the number of variables is nearly limitless. For any given piece of music, each conductor develops his or her own distinct version within some accepted parameters for the style of the music. Moreover, each performance of the work by the same conductor will differ as a result of changes in his or her emotional outlook and ideas about the work. These same factors will also influence each performer's interpretation of the piece. Concerts are like athletic events in that one reason to attend them is to experience the variety of each performance. In a way, we attend concerts to discover the outcome.

ATTENDING CONCERTS

Concert settings differ dramatically, and so does concert etiquette. The formal, subdued nature of a symphony orchestra concert is dramatically different from the casual atmosphere of a rock concert. To be sure, the appreciation of the music and the "performance" by the audience are essential elements of both settings. However, in an unfamiliar concert setting you may feel unsure about when to applaud. These conventions can be complicated, as a few examples illustrate. The rock concert audience often recognizes the beginning of a familiar tune by applauding, while the symphony concert audience never applauds at the beginning of a work. Applause at the completion of important solos is usual in opera, jazz, and rock performances but not in solo recitals. If you are in doubt, a good rule of thumb is that applause or other signs of appreciation should not detract from the performance, and the safest plan is to wait until the entire selection is completed. In fact, in formal symphony, chamber music, and recital settings, the accepted practice is to hold applause until all movements of a work by one composer are finished.

The first work shown after intermission on the concert program will serve as our model for discussion. On the left, this particular sonata by Prokofiev is identified by the key (D major) and the opus number (94). Whether assigned by the composer or by a scholar at a later date, the opus, or work, number is the most accurate way to identify a particular work. For example, if Prokofiev wrote more than one sonata in D major, each has a different opus number. At the center of the page the performers' names are listed (this sonata was composed for flute and piano), and the composer's name and dates appear on the right. Under the sonata heading, the four movements are listed. Although there are pauses between the movements, applause is proper only when the fourth movement is completed. Arrows mark the appropriate places for applause in this sample program. As you can imagine, your own "solo" applause at other times would be quite embarrassing.

It is also important to know that if you are late for a performance, you should enter only at the end of a work (in some formal concert halls you will be asked to wait until intermission). As a closing note on attending live concerts, attire for symphony and chamber music concerts is usually semiformal, but on special occasions formal dress may be appropriate. Practices vary from place to place, so if you are in doubt, it is best to ask someone connected to the event.

From this general discussion, you probably realize that the next step in enhancing your understanding of music is to add to your musical vocabulary. More importantly, some "hands-on" experimentation with these elements will open a new world of understanding for you in all of your interactions with music.

PROGRAM

Trio, Op. 8   Dmitry Shostakovich
   Andante—Allegro—Moderato—   (1906–1975)
     Allegro

       Sarah Gentry, *Violin*   Ko Iwasaki, *Cello*
             Julian Dawson, *Piano*

Four Russian Songs   Igor Stravinsky
   Selezen   (1882–1971)
   Sektantskaya
   Gusi, levedi
   Tilim'—bom'

      Bonnie Pomfret, *Soprano*   Jill Rubio, *Flute*
      Martha Burwell, *Harp*   Douglas Rubio, *Guitar*

In memoriam Dylan Thomas (1954)   Igor Stravinsky
   Dirge—Canons and Song

       Michael Schwartzkopf, *Tenor*
   Charles Stokes, *Trombone*   John Rehm, *Trombone*
   Arved Larsen, *Trombone*   John Eustace, *Trombone*
   Sarah Gentry, *Violin*   Nicholas Currie, *Violin*
    Arthur Lewis, *Viola*   Ko Iwasaki, *Cello*

Intermission

Sonata in D Major, Op. 94   Sergey Prokofiev
   Andantino   (1891–1953)
   Allegretto scherzando
   Andante
   Allegro con brio

    Max Schoenfeld, *Flute*   Paul Borg, *Piano*

Trio in G Minor (1932)   Aram Khachaturian
   Andante con dolore, con molto espressione   (1903–1978)
   Allegro
   Moderato

    Aris Chavez, *Clarinet*   Sarah Gentry, *Violin*
          Julian Dawson, *Piano*

Understanding concert etiquette, including how to read the program,
will increase your enjoyment of the experience.

CHAPTER

3

Rhythm: Music Moving Through Time

Rhythm is the most basic element of music. Rhythm existed in nature before music was even "invented"—in our heartbeats, our breathing, our walking and running, and the sound of waves washing the shore. Other, much slower rhythms are perhaps felt rather than heard—the phases of the moon, the rotation of the earth around the sun, the tides of the sea, and other phenomena in nature that occur with predictable regularity.

Rhythm can be broadly defined as the *temporal organization of sounds in music.* Music differs from the visual arts in that we are not able to experience the entire musical work all at once, in the same way that we can take in a painting. To look at a painting in the same way we listen to music, we would have to slide a piece of paper with a narrow vertical opening across the painting's surface. The organization of music is perceived in just this way, and rhythm plays an important role in creating musical direction or movement through time.

Active Listening
CD 1:8

"Der Erlkönig," Franz Schubert

The rhythmic energy of this song's fast piano accompaniment depicts the rapid galloping of a horse through the night, while the vocal soloist sings different roles depicting the narrator and the three characters in the Goethe poem of the same title. When we return to this piece later in the text you will learn that the dramatic decrease in rhythmic energy at counter number 1:31 signals the entrance of the evil Erlkönig (the elf king).

RHYTHMIC ORGANIZATION IN WESTERN MUSIC

Most of the music you hear is based on traditions that evolved in Western European cultures, which prescribe that time is divided into *regularly spaced rhythmic pulses* called **beats.** If you were to feel your pulse on your wrist, a graphic representation might look like this:

• • • • • • • • • • • • • • •

© Bettmann/CORBIS

The Persistence of Memory, Salvador Dali

Notice that each beat is evenly spaced. In music the *speed of the beats* is called **tempo.** After vigorous exercise you find that your pulse has a faster "tempo" than it did when you checked it earlier while you were relaxed.

"Stars and Stripes Forever," John Philip Sousa

Active Listening
CD 1:9

"We Three Kings of Orient Are," Traditional

CD 1:10

- To find the beat, react naturally to the music by tapping your foot on the floor or your finger on your desk.
- Find the beat in each of the two examples. Remember that the beat will be evenly spaced. Do not be confused by the more complex rhythmic patterns superimposed on the basic beat.
- Which of the two examples has the faster tempo?

METER

In many musical works *beats are grouped into regularly recurring patterns,* normally with a stronger accent on the first note of each pattern, creating what is called

meter. A meter signature, which looks like a mathematical fraction, is used to inform performers of a particular grouping of beats, which is generally a pattern that is divisible by two or three.

• •|• •|• •|• •|• •|• •|• •|• •|• •
1 2 **1** 2 **1** 2 **1** 2 **1** 2 **1** 2 **1** 2 **1** 2

• • •|• • •|• • •|• • •|• • •|• • •
1 2 3 **1** 2 3 **1** 2 3 **1** 2 3 **1** 2 3 **1** 2 3

Each of these *groupings of beats that make up the recurring pattern* is called a **measure.** By placing emphasis on the first beat of each group, or measure, meter becomes an important tool for enabling the listener to hear rhythmic organization.

Active Listening
CD 1:8

"Stars and Stripes Forever," John Philip Sousa

CD 1:10

"We Three Kings of Orient Are," Traditional

- While listening to each of the two examples heard above, first establish the beat as you did before.
- Identify the stressed beat of each measure to determine whether beats are grouped in twos (duple meter) or three (triple meter).

Tempo can affect how we hear and understand meter. Listen to "We Three Kings" at a faster tempo. You should gradually begin to hear the rhythms joining into two slower beats, each made up of three faster pulses. This *simultaneous perception of two different levels of beat* is called **compound meter.** A graphic representation of this phenomenon would look like this:

1 2 3 **4** 5 6 **1** 2 3 **4** 5 6 **1** 2 3 **4** 5 6

Sometimes composers create an **irregular** or **asymmetric meter** by *grouping twos and threes in an irregular fashion.*

Active Listening
CD 1:11

String Quartet in F, Fourth Movement, *Vif et agité,* Maurice Ravel

The quartet copes with the excitement of a fast five-beat measure—here in various combinations of two and three beats per measure.

CROSSROADS

Although there isn't a literal relationship between terms in music and those in the visual arts, a comparison of the meanings in each discipline can help you understand some of the general principles that apply to both. Rhythm in the visual arts describes the repetition of shapes or images that helps create unity in an artwork much as repetition of musical materials creates structure in a musical composition.

Impressionist painter Claude Monet created a series of paintings of poplars, this one at twilight. The visual rhythm is apparent in foreground and background trees and their reflections in the water. With a little imagination you should be able to relate the tall trees (strong beat) and short trees (weak beat) patterns to the musical concept of meter. This is perhaps easier to see in the reflection of the trees in the water in the foreground.

Tate Gallery, London/Art Resource, NY

Poplars on the Epte,
Claude Monet

OTHER RHYTHMIC PRACTICES

Not all music has meter. The examples that follow demonstrate the diverse ways in which rhythm can be organized.

Active Listening
CD 1:12

Silver Apples of the Moon, Part II (excerpt), Morton Subotnick

An electronic work by American composer Morton Subotnick is an example of a contemporary rhythmic practice. Not only is meter omitted, but a beat or pulse is only occasionally felt. Listen at counter number 1:22 for an example of this vague sense of beat.

Other possibilities of rhythmic organization include **flexible** or **unmetered rhythm** that is dictated by the stress patterns of words or by dance movements or by the complex rhythmic practices of non-Western cultures.

Active Listening
CD 1:13

Kyrie XI (Kyrie Orbis Factor), Gregorian chant

Gregorian chant derives its rhythm from the accents of the syllables in the Latin text. This respect for the natural rhythm of the words reflected the intent of the medieval church to have the text understood. At the time this music was created, our current concepts of meter did not exist.

Active Listening
CD 1:14

"Chemutengure," *mbira* music from Zimbabwe

Polyrhythm is *the simultaneous sounding of more than one rhythm or meter.* It is frequently encountered in African music and European and American classical music of the twentieth century. This recording contains the pattern of two played simultaneously against three.

The *mbira* is an instrument constructed with metal strips of different lengths fastened to a wooden resonator. The player produces sound by plucking the strips with the thumbs which is why it's known as the "thumb piano" in this country. It is widely used throughout sub-Saharan Africa as a solo instrument, in ensembles, and as an accompaniment to singing.

- For the first 22 seconds (12 measures), two *mbiras* play a repeated two-part pattern in two-four meter with two fractional pulses to the beat (and two beats to the measure).
- For the remainder of the example, the two parts divide, with the first *mbira* shifting to six-eight meter (three fractional pulses to the beat, but still two beats per measure) while the second instrument stays in two-four.
- Try tapping these two patterns simultaneously with your hands, one hand tapping two pulses and the other tapping three.

You likely hear that the second instrument slightly anticipates the beats by a fraction of a section. This rhythmic conflict between two meters is an instance of another rhythmic practice, called syncopation. **Syncopation** is the result of *rhythms contradicting the underlying metric pulse, often by not lining up with the "strong" pulses that create meter.* We will elaborate on this concept when we discuss some musical styles that feature syncopation prominently.

Kebjar Taruna, **Bali**

Active Listening
CD 1:15

In this example you will hear another rhythmic idea, called **colotomic structure.** This means that the entrances of certain instruments in the Balinese ensemble, called the gamelan, mark off the progress of the piece. Although the sense of a beat can be discerned, the larger time markers (mostly gongs) help make the listeners and the ensemble players aware of their locations in time and their musical responsibilities at that moment. Listen for these changes at counter numbers 00:05, 00:13, and 00:34.

In the course of studying with this text you will learn more about the various types of rhythmic usage introduced here. You can build upon these concepts and develop a fairly sophisticated rhythmic sense with little difficulty.

CHAPTER

4

Melody:
The Horizontal Dimension

We have seen and heard how rhythm guides our attention and organizes our experience of music. Equally important to our understanding of what makes music is **melody:** *a succession of musical tones organized in a meaningful fashion* (they could be visualized as a horizontal arrangement, as if they were a "train" of tones). Melody is very often associated with singing, which is an almost irreducible, basic human musical impulse. Since the notes in a melody typically occur one after the other, most melodies can be sung by a single person. Good melodies are also memorable—simple enough to remember but individual enough to be distinct. Many simple, singable melodies are widely known. Think, for example, of "Three Blind Mice," "Twinkle, Twinkle, Little Star," "America," "My Country 'Tis of Thee" ("God Save the Queen"), "Amazing Grace," "Here Comes the Bride" (the "Wedding March" from Wagner's *Lohengrin*), "Happy Birthday," or "We Shall Overcome."

MELODIC BUILDING MATERIALS

THE PITCH DIMENSION

Studying the components that make up melody will give you a fuller understanding of how it functions. The most basic component is **pitch,** which can be defined as *the highness or lowness of sound.* This term can be used in a relative sense of high and low—"a high-pitched instrument" or "how low was that sound?"—or in a specific sense: "the pitch c." Relating pitch to a keyboard should help you understand these concepts.

The white (or *natural*) keys on the piano are identified by the letters A, B, C, D, E, F, G. This sequence of letters is repeated for each subsequent *octave* (eight notes, c to c, for example) on the keyboard. The black notes on the keyboard are designated by a letter name and a sharp or flat. For example, the black note immediately above D is called D-sharp while the one just below is D-flat. The keyboard below should clarify these relationships for you.

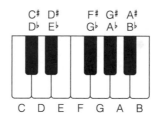

You may have noticed that D-sharp may also be called E-flat. The choice of which to use is based on the direction of the melody (sharps for ascending and flats for descending).

SCALES

Certain *sequences of pitches* called **scales** have become standard building materials for the melodies of music. Probably the most common is the **major scale** (one example is C major—*all the white notes on the keyboard from one C to the next*).

Active Listening CD 1:16	**"Joy to the World"**
CD 1:17	**"Twinkle, Twinkle, Little Star"**
CD 1:10	**"We Three Kings of Orient Are"**
CD 1:18	**"Here Comes the Bride" ("Wedding March"),** *Lohengrin,* Richard Wagner

Listen to the melody of the Christmas carol "Joy to the World." It begins by stating a major scale, first downward, then a portion of the scale is stated back up. The rest of the melody traces segments of the scale in different directions and ends by descending to *the main note of the melody* (the **tonic**). The melody for "Twinkle, Twinkle, Little Star" is also formed from a series of descending major scales (after an initial leap up from the *tonic* note). Listen.

Major and minor scales are the most common scales in Western music. One type of **minor scale,** the so-called "natural" or "pure" minor, may be visualized and heard by playing the *white keys of the piano from a to a.* Another Christmas carol, "We Three Kings of Orient Are," is an example of a melody that begins with a descending minor scale. Listen.

A wide range of other scales can be found in music, and these greatly enhance the potential for variety in melodic construction.

MELODIC CONTOUR, MOTION, AND RANGE

Of course, most melodies are not simply scales or scale segments repeated over and over. In the three melodies above, we have also heard notes *repeated,* notes *skipped to and from,* and notes quickly *changing direction* from up to down or down to up. This variety in how notes are put together allows a great flexibility of melodic construction. Every melody has its own *characteristic linear pattern or shape* called **melodic contour.** This shape or contour may be diagrammed graphically or it may be described in words. For example, "We Three Kings" can be represented by a descending line (repeated) followed by an arch as you can see in the transcription below.

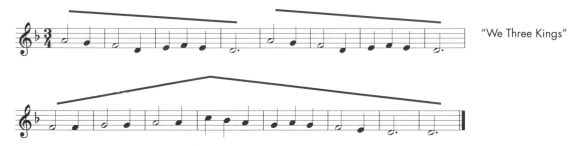

"We Three Kings"

Think through (or listen to) the tunes listed above and describe the melodic contour of each segment of the melodies. In all instances, keep in mind that we can only approximate the musical impact through words or illustrations. There is always something more than these explanations and images can capture!

We can broaden our discussion of melody by becoming more detailed in our consideration of the pitches and rhythms that make up melodies and how they are put together. The **range** of a melody is the *distance from the highest note to the lowest note*. For example, "Joy to the World" uses eight notes (the tonic appears both at the bottom and at the top), while "Twinkle, Twinkle Little Star" uses only six (beginning on the tonic, skipping to the sixth note, but omitting the seventh). We can conclude that "Joy to the World" has a wider *range* than "Twinkle, Twinkle Little Star," although neither has an especially extensive one.

Melodies move by **step** *(to an adjacent note in the scale)* or by **skip** *(movement that omits one or more notes in the scale)*. "Twinkle, Twinkle Little Star" and "Joy to the World" exhibit a mostly *stepwise* melodic movement. "Here Comes the Bride," on the other hand, is built mostly from *skips*. Listen. Musicians use the words *conjunct* to describe stepwise movement and *disjunct* to describe melodic motion by skips.

The **musical notation** in the transcriptions below can be viewed as graphs: Every line and every space between the lines represents a note of the scale. Notice how the notation for "Joy to the World" represents consecutive notes while the notation for "Here Comes the Bride" shows the skips between notes.

"Joy to the World"

"Here Comes the Bride"

Active Listening
CD 1:19
"The Star Spangled Banner"

Listen next to "The Star Spangled Banner." This melody contains both stepwise and skipwise movement. The opening segment consists of a series of skips that move quickly through a wide range of the major scale. When you consider the third segment too, the range is much wider than that of the first segment. In fact, the *wide range* of this melody is one of the reasons it is so notoriously difficult to sing well (and so often performed poorly on the many occasions when it is heard!).

Active Listening
CD 1:20
"Amazing Grace"

Listen to "Amazing Grace." When we consider all the pitches used in the melody, and the range, we find one interesting feature: Only five of the seven lettered pitches are present. These are arranged so that both skips and steps are present. The range is easily singable, and the final note (the tonic) is in the middle rather than at the bottom.

Limiting this *scale* to *five pitches* from the named seven yields what is called a **pentatonic scale.** Such a scale is found in many types of music—notably in folk musics and Asian (especially Chinese) traditions.

Pentatonic Scale

"Amazing Grace"

Other scales can be made from the pitches represented on our piano keyboard. For example, a **chromatic scale** is *made up of every pitch (black and white)* in succession, while a **whole-tone scale** *uses every other pitch (black and white).*

RHYTHMIC ASPECTS OF MELODY

So far, we have talked about the pitch aspect of melody. All of the melodies that we have considered have rhythmic elements, too. The metric organization in "Twinkle, Twinkle Little Star," "Joy to the World," and "Here Comes the Bride" is duple; in "We Three Kings" and "Amazing Grace" it is triple. Yet each melody has some characteristic rhythmic patterns that help us recognize its unique identity. Note the sturdy long-short "dotted" pattern at the beginning of "Joy to the World" and "Here Comes the Bride." Compare this with the lilting long-short pattern that begins "We Three Kings" and "Amazing Grace." And contrast these patterns with the steady, even rhythm that begins "Twinkle, Twinkle Little Star." Careful matching of the words of a song with pitches and rhythms is a key to creating a memorable melody.

But not all melodies have especially distinctive rhythms or pitches. Some tunes consist of a single pitch that is used for a sort of rhythmic recitation. Many ritual chants operate this way so the words may more easily be understood. Rap music even eliminates pitch as a consciously constructed melodic element. The rise and fall of its *melodic contour* reflects the momentary emotion or emphasis of the performer rather than a predetermined, composed sequence of pitches.

Some music has pitch contour but no metric arrangement of rhythms. Various forms of chant consist of beautiful sequences of pitches that are performed with no special rhythmic arrangement. Of course, the natural accents of the words or the grouping of more than one note to a single syllable create subtle rhythmic emphases. But we don't experience the "foot-tapping" impulse that a metric melody can create.

CROSSROADS

Can you see aspects of melody such as linear movement and shape in this painting? In a landscape, the viewer's eye is often drawn from left to right by the visual motion in the painting. In *Stone City*, by early twentieth-century American artist Grant Wood, it is the road that draws your eye from left to right and then to the center background. This final direction is reinforced by rows of plants and trees in the foreground and the background. In a very similar way, melody is often the thread that leads our ears through a musical composition. Like the road in the painting, melody is supported by harmony and rhythmic repetition.

Joslyn Museum, Omaha, Nebraska/SuperStock

In *Stone City*, by Grant Wood, the road serves a function similar to that of the melody

USES OF MELODY

MELODY AS A STRUCTURAL ELEMENT

When *a melody serves as the primary horizontal building material for a piece of music,* we usually call it a **theme.** The following melody (the "Ode to Joy") is the primary theme in the last movement of Beethoven's Ninth Symphony. This symphony is unusual in that a chorus and vocal soloists are used in the finale. Using a text by the eighteenth-century German poet Friedrich Schiller, Beethoven is commenting on the triumph of humankind over adversity. When the Berlin wall was dismantled, this work was performed at a concert conducted by Leonard Bernstein and carried with it the same positive message.

You may have noticed that the melodies covered this far consist of various segments that follow each other like phrases or sentences in speech and writing. Like a sentence, a melody has shape (listen to the rise and fall of your voice as you speak a sentence) and direction. In addition, we tend to speak in phrases that we can complete using a single breath. The physical limit on how long a human can continue making a single verbal or musical statement influences both the structure of our language and the structure of much of our music. Although music that does not use the human voice can extend this limit somewhat, our perception of what music says is tempered by this very human limitation of our breathing.

This human aspect of melodic design is reinforced by other musical elements like rhythm, harmony, or dynamics. As such, it will be covered later as **form,** or *how all elements of music contribute to an overall musical shape or structure.* The analogy with language, however, is appropriate to reflect on in our discussion of melody. This analogy may help you understand that, like sentences, melodies are complete musical thoughts and may be punctuated by pauses.

Active Listening
CD 1:21

Ninth Symphony, Finale, "Ode to Joy," Ludwig van Beethoven

- While listening to the "Ode to Joy" theme from the finale of Beethoven's Ninth Symphony, identify places where the musical sentence should be punctuated.
- Write down the counter numbers where you think a comma should be used (incomplete musical thought).
- Write down the counter numbers where you think a period should appear (complete musical thought).

Another interesting perspective on melody is what goes along with it. Many types of music consist of melody alone. Think of a mother singing a lullaby to put her baby to sleep. Traditional religious chants are also typical examples. Whether sung by one or many persons, chant is normally a single melodic line. Folk songs, too, are conceived as a melody. However, they often are provided with some sort of instrumental accompaniment—perhaps strummed chords to provide a "background" to the melody. Such accompaniment may be more or less complex and sometimes competes with the primary melody for our attention.

Other musical examples are made up exclusively of melodies. These combinations require composers and performers to produce musical thoughts that coordinate well together while still being distinguishable from one another.

Fitting melodies together is not just a process of providing an accompaniment or "background"; it is one musical reflection of life's complexities—many things going on at the same time. Some complicated musical works make effective use of the idea of combined melodies. Genres such as the fugue (see Chapter 24) or dramatic situations in an opera where several characters all sing at the same time (Chapter 23) exemplify some potential uses of simultaneous melodies. Simpler versions include the effective combination of the trombone melody in the final strain of Sousa's "Stars and Stripes Forever" with a **countermelody** *(a melody that is of secondary importance to the primary melody)* in the piccolo (Chapter 11).

Certain melodies have come to evoke some of our shared cultural associations. Part of this association is due to the words that go with the melodies. Think of "Joy to the World," or "We Three Kings" again. We associate these tunes with the season of Christmas. Of course, a particular melody does not always "mean" the same thing. Consider "My Country 'Tis of Thee." The patriotic associations that this tune has are based on completely different words in Great Britain ("God Save the Queen"), and are quite nonexistent in many other countries of the world. Still, we do think of commonly heard melodies as having a quality of sound. There are religious melodies ("Amazing Grace") or patriotic melodies ("The Star Spangled Banner") or protest melodies ("We Shall Overcome"). Even without the words, the tunes recall the purpose to us. Some melodies create these associations without having texts. Think of the theme from *Jaws* and how it has been used to evoke a sense of terror (mock or real) in television advertising. Cartoons have contributed many examples to our fund of musical associations.

But before we explore some of these cultural associations, we need to consider several other characteristics of music. Now that you have some understanding of the horizontal aspect of music, you can move on to the vertical realm: harmony.

Harmony:
The Vertical Dimension

Harmony, the vertical dimension of music, is a Western concept that came into being in Europe during the ninth century. In the broadest sense, **harmony** *is produced whenever two or more pitches sound at the same time.* The earliest example of harmony of which we have written record is called organum, sacred vocal music composed for use in the Catholic Church. **Organum** consists of a *melody accompanied by a second part or second melody that moves parallel to it at a specified interval.* An **interval** is *the distance in pitch between two notes sounded together or one after the other.* Intervals are named by counting the number of letter names between and including the two notes. For instance, the interval from A moving up to F is a sixth because it involves six letter names (A-B-C-D-E-F). From A moving down to F is a third (A-G-F).

The intervals characteristic of *organum* were the fourth and fifth, the second voice part (or second voice melody) being an interval of a fourth or fifth below the first. When men and women sang together, the result was four parts: the melody and the parallel part a fourth or fifth below, plus the octave duplication of these parts.

"King of Heaven, Lord of the Wave-Sounding Sea,"
Organum with parallel fourths

Active Listening
CD 1:22

From this very simple and primitive beginning, our concept of harmony developed. The next step in the practice of two or more parts sounding together is called polyphony, the technique of combining melodies in such a way that they complement and harmonize each other.

"King of Heaven,
Lord of the Wave-
Sounding Sea"

Giovanni Gabrieli (ca.1555–1612) was the greatest Venetian composer of the late Renaissance. He was among the first composers to indicate on the score which instruments should perform. Gabrieli wrote compositions for string and brass instruments and for voices. This piece represents the beginning of a transition to a type of harmony that still functions in much of the music we hear today. In this piece, Gabrieli alternates homophonic sections, in which chords are used to harmonize the melodies, with pure polyphonic sections, in which the harmony is produced by combining melodies. The homophonic sections are examples of the evolving system of harmony.

LISTENING GUIDE

Canzona in echo duodecimi toni à 10, Giovanni Gabrieli

CD 1:23

00:00   Homophonic texture, melodies added

00:17   Imitative polyphonic texture, faster tempo

00:29   Begins homophonic to imitative using ornamental lines

00:46   Imitative texture, organ and cornets

1:06   Homophonic, ornamental lines added

COMPONENTS OF HARMONY

CHORDS AND PROGRESSIONS

When the concept of harmony became increasingly important, terms evolved to describe this vertical aspect of music. *Three or more notes sounded together* are called a **chord.** The most common type of chord is one that consists *of three different notes;* it is called a **triad.** Triads typically are constructed with notes separated by the interval of a third or, to put it another way, are built using every other letter name of a scale. For example, A-C-E and F-A-C are each triads, but C-D-E is not.

The second most common chord in Western harmony contains *four different notes* and is called a **seventh chord.** Once again, the four notes of a seventh chord are structured in thirds, which results in using every other letter name. C-E-G-B is a seventh chord, but C-D-E-F is not.

The triad is the basis of Western harmony. The seventh chord (essentially an extension of a triad) has become characteristic of much of today's jazz and commercial music.

When *different chords systematically follow each other in a piece of music,* we describe the musical result as a **chord progression.** A familiar example of a simple chord progression is the twelve-bar blues. The blues, a form that is basic to much jazz and popular music, originated sometime in the late 1800s. In its most common form, the blues utilizes only triads and seventh chords; its distinctive twelve-measure structure is easily recognized, and musicians are quick to identify it by the sound of a characteristic pattern of chords—the harmony that underlies the form. Working musicians learn this pattern: Pianists and guitarists learn to play the chords; bassists learn to "walk" a bass line so the important notes of each chord are evident; trumpet, saxophone, and other melody players learn to "run the chords"—that is, *play the pitches of the chords up and down in a sequence* known as an **arpeggio.** The blues chord pattern is an important part of the "universal language" of the jazz or popular musician.

C	F7	C	C	F7	F7	C	C	G7	F7	C	C	Blues Structure

```
 C    F7   C    C    F7   F7   C    C    G7   F7   C    C          Blues Structure
|1...|2...|3...|4...|5...|6...|7...|8...|9...|10..|11..|12..|
 ••••  ••••  ••••  ••••  ••••  ••••  ••••  ••••  ••••  ••••  ••••  ••••
C: I    IV(♭)7 I    I    IV(♭)7 IV(♭)7 I    I    V7   IV(♭)7 I    I
```

Follow the structure of the blues in the above diagram. Each dot in the diagram indicates a beat (or tap of the foot); the vertical lines divide those beats into measures (four beats per measure); the chords are indicated at the top of the diagram. By looking at the chord symbols, you can tell that one chord is a triad and the other two are seventh chords.

Active Listening
CD 1:24

Twelve-Bar Blues

- How many repetitions of the twelve-measure pattern do you hear? These patterns get progressively more complex.
- Name what is added with each statement of the pattern, or
- Identify how each new statement differs from the previous one.
- Listen very carefully to hear how the chords are always the same in each repetition of the pattern.

TONALITY

The term **key** implies *a series of notes that have certain functions in relation to one another.* The example of the blues you just listened to is in the key of C, which means that it is based on the notes of the C scale: consecutive white notes on the piano beginning and ending on C (the notes C, D, E, F, G, A, B, and a repetition of C at the top). C is the most important note in the scale, and the chord built on the note C is the most important chord in this key. It feels like "home" and provides a sense of satisfaction and completion when you reach it at the end of a piece. People who make a serious study of harmony would call this chord in the key of C the "one" [I] chord, because it is built on the most important note—the first note of the scale. This is also called the "tonic" chord. In the key of C, this chord consists of the notes C-E-G. Roman numerals are used to designate these harmonic implications of the scale notes.

Two other important chords in every key are the chords built on the fourth and fifth scale notes: F and G in the key of C. These "four" [IV] and "five" [V] chords are called "subdominant" and "dominant" respectively. They also serve very specific functions in harmony, functions that are more active or produce more tension than the feeling of rest produced by the tonic (I) chord. The five (V) chord is the chord most likely to have a seventh added: in the key of C, G-B-D-F. The four (IV) chord is usually a triad: F-A-C in the key of C. However, in the blues, the characteristic "blue note" is added to the four (IV) chord, making it also a seventh chord: F-A-C-E flat.

This may seem like a lot of technical jabber, but it is really very helpful for the musician. If you glance at the blues diagram above, you will notice that the three different chords are C, F, and G or, in harmonic terms, I, IV, and V. Knowing that, you could play the blues in any key; for instance, in the key of G, I would be G, IV would be C, and V would be D. In every key, you will have the same sense of arriving "home" when you reach the final tonic (I) chord.

The sensation of a particular chord being "home" and other chords functioning in relation to that chord is known as **tonality.** The majority of songs begin with the tonic chord and move away from that chord; the harmonic "story" of the song is the tale of how the harmony progresses back to the tonic chord. Each of the other chords has a function in assisting us to find our way back "home."

The basic blues is not a very complicated structure, only twelve measures long and made up of three different chords. But the sequence of chords (the harmony) is very important. One of the characteristics of all harmony is that it is continually evolving, moving from simple to complex. There are many variations of this blues harmony; a few of them are simpler and some of them are more complex. The simple ones come from early blues styles that are a century old; the more complex come from contemporary jazz performance. Even now, blues harmony continues to evolve.

Although we have used the blues to illustrate this system of harmony called tonality, it actually developed during the sixteenth and seventeenth centuries. It was described in a text by Jean-Philippe Rameau (1683–1764) in 1722 and brought to its definitive application in the music of Johann Sebastian Bach (1685–1750).

Bach was a humble church musician who composed music primarily for use in religious services. His output of *chorales* (well over 300) has served as the basis for the study of harmony for more than two hundred years. Although he used only triads and seventh chords, his harmonic vocabulary is never boring.

The composition we will hear is an interesting combination of a worshipful chorale in a homophonic style, with a lilting dancelike accompaniment in a polyphonic style. That dancelike melody begins and ends the composition and provides an interlude between the chorale sections. There are four chorale sections; each section is divided in half by a short break. The third and fourth chorale sections are very close together so it would be possible for you to mistake them as being a single statement, but the third section is in a different key. Similar to the chord changes in the blues progression but lasting longer, the *process of key change,* or **modulation,** generally involves a group of chords (a progression) that creates the sense of a new key.

"Jesu, Joy of Man's Desiring," Johann Sebastian Bach

Active Listening
CD 1:25

- Listen to the composition, noting that the third statement (CN 1:25) sounds different because of the change of key. Notice how satisfying the return to the original key is for the ending of the piece.
- Play it a second time, stopping the recording after the third chorale statement (CN 1:38).
- Does it feel satisfying or complete without the final return to the original key? This is the power of tonality.
- Identify the counter number at the beginning of each statement of the chorale.

HARMONIC TENSION

As was stated earlier, the harmonic flow within a key moves away from the initial tonic chord, producing tension, and then progresses back to the tonic chord to find rest. Moving to a different key and then returning to the original one can produce an even stronger feeling of tension followed by relaxation.

Another way to produce musical tension and relaxation is by using musical elements called dissonance and consonance. **Dissonance** is often thought of simply as *sounds (intervals or chords) that are "unpleasing" to our ears,* while **consonance** is thought of as *"pleasing" sounds.* Actually, dissonance serves a very useful purpose in that it implies musical activity (tension), and moving from dissonance to consonance provides resolution (rest): the ebb and flow of music. This is much like the old gag, "Why do you enjoy having an elephant stand on your foot?" "Because it feels so good when he gets off." Music is an art of motion, and the resolution of dissonance is one way of producing that motion.

You probably weren't aware of any dissonances, or harmonic clashes, as you listened to "Jesu, Joy of Man's Desiring." This is partly because Bach treated dissonances very gently and smoothly; it is also because we are accustomed to hearing this style of harmonic setting. Today, we easily accept sounds that might have been shocking to listeners in Bach's day.

The music of Wolfgang Amadeus Mozart (1756–1791) will probably also sound consonant to you. Mozart's harmonic style was different from Bach's, but his treatment of dissonance was equally gentle. During the baroque period (Bach) and the classical period (Mozart) composers tried to maintain a balance between consonance and dissonance in which consonance predominated and dissonance was used carefully, even discreetly. Rarely do our ears find a shocking harmonic clash in the music of either of these composers.

Active Listening
CD 1:6

Eine kleine Nachtmusik, First Movement, *Allegro*, Wolfgang Amadeus Mozart

- As you listen again to this movement, make note (using the counter numbers as reference) of any places that seem to you to be dissonant. You may find two or three, or you may find none.
- Compare your results with those of others in the class (you are likely to find differences of opinion). This activity illustrates the fact the consonance and dissonance are relative terms that are subject to personal interpretation.

Chronologically, the distance from Mozart's lifetime to that of Anton Webern (1883–1945) is a century and a half. Harmonically, the distance is light years. Webern was one of a group of twentieth-century composers who wrote music described as "atonal" (meaning that no one note or chord felt like "home") and "dodecaphonic" (literally twelve-tone: meaning that all twelve notes, black notes and white notes on the piano, were employed equally). The harmony of this music was based on a predetermined ordering of the twelve notes of the *chromatic scale* rather than on triads and seventh chords.

Contrast this short work by Webern with the Mozart example. Remember that dissonance is relative. What one person hears as dissonant may not bother another person at all. What one person finds terribly annoying may be musically rewarding to someone else.

Active Listening
CD 1:26

Six Pieces for Orchestra, No. 2 Bewegt, Anton Webern

- How far do you get into the composition (use counter numbers for reference) before you notice or are disturbed by the first dissonance?
- How would you describe the consonance-dissonance balance in this piece?
- Is there a feeling of resolution and completion when you hear the final chord?

When the world makes reference to a group of people or to a situation as being "in harmony," the reference is really to being "in consonance," as we have been defining these terms. We hear in this example that harmony can really be quite dissonant.

A lot happened to harmony during the century and a half between Mozart and Webern. Specifically, many composers experimented with the concepts of dissonance and tonality, stretching musical boundaries and possibilities. Mozart's music led to that of Ludwig van Beethoven (1770–1827), who expanded the harmonic vocabulary he inherited by using dissonance more liberally.

In the music of Bach and his contemporaries, certain patterns of chords were established as the basis of composition. By virtue of their being used over and over again, these chord patterns established the feeling of tonality that characterizes church hymns and popular music today. With these chord patterns and the resulting tonality came certain harmonic expectations regarding the movement of chords. For instance, compositions end with a I chord and the next-to-last chord is V. These patterns and expectations were the building blocks of composition for centuries.

Harmonic structures can be built using intervals other than thirds. Remember that the earliest manifestations of harmony used fourths and fifths. A number of twentieth-century composers employed harmonies built in fourths. Two famous examples were Alban Berg, who was a close friend of Anton Webern, and Paul Hindemith.

Today, musicians in the fields of electronic music, rap music, and some other musical styles do not employ harmony in a traditional sense. They rely on the intensity of sound, lyrics, or rhythmic drive to give meaning to their musical statements, which often come as isolated sounds rather than as part of a harmonic context. Recently, however, the importance of tonality has been reemphasized in the music written for the concert hall, and tonality remains the central feature of popular music. And the I, IV, and V chords remain the basis not only of the blues but of most country/Western tunes, contemporary Christian music, and virtually all "easy listening" music.

Strength and Color in Music

STRENGTH IN MUSIC

Dynamics is the musical term that refers to *how loud or soft sounds are*. You can demonstrate dynamics by adjusting the volume control on your sound system. For a live acoustic (nonamplified) performance, dynamic markings usually appear on the music—*piano* (soft), *forte* (loud), and so on—as instructions to the performers. These markings sometimes have as much to do with the number of people taking part (strength) as with how loud each person is playing or singing (volume).

If you participated in a music ensemble in high school, you may understand strength in numbers from personal experience. If you participated in an inexperienced choir with only twenty members, you know not only about the pressure put on each performer but also how anemic a *forte* you were able to produce. On the other hand, a select group comprised of the same number of the best singers in the school could produce a substantial, confident *forte*. Yet, if you measured the decibels produced by the small, select group and compared it to a 150-voice choir singing softly, the larger ensemble is likely to be louder. It goes without saying that these terms such as *piano* and *forte* are relative.

Composers ask for changes in dynamics through markings in the music. Again, if you have participated in an ensemble you have some idea how dynamic markings operate. Hearing these changes is up to the listener.

Active Listening
CD 1:27

**Fifth Symphony, First Movement, *Allegro con brio*,
Ludwig van Beethoven**

- Listen to the opening of this example and decide whether each of the following counter numbers is *forte* (loud) or *piano* (soft):

  CN 00:00
  CN 00:05
  CN 00:13

- Listen again to confirm your choices. Is there any counter number where you think the dynamic level is somewhere in between *forte* and *piano*?

COLOR IN MUSIC

Have you ever wondered why you are able to distinguish one person's voice from another or identify an instrument as a trombone and not a trumpet? The answer lies in the fact that natural sounds are actually a composite made up of a primary pitch and a series of other pitches called overtones or partials. Variations in the amount each partial is emphasized in a given sound are what enable us to perceive distinctive and identifiable sound "colors." Thus, for example, the specific set of partials emphasized by the trumpet allows us to distinguish it from the trombone even when pitch and volume are the same. This distinctive quality or *color of sound* is known as **timbre**.

Georgia O'Keeffe created a series of pictures that were inspired by music. She came to believe that abstract form in visual art could create mental images of music. In *Blue and Green Music* she creates a variety similar to the kind that composers achieve through various combinations of instruments (timbre) by varying value (light and dark) and hue (shades of color).

Blue and Green Music, Georgia O'Keeffe

BLENDING COLORS IN MUSIC

Although it is useful to understand timbre in the case of an individual instrument, realizing how timbres are combined in music is perhaps more valuable. Composers not only make choices about how many instruments or voices to use, but also they are particularly concerned with how the timbres are combined. That is, they are particularly concerned with **orchestration:** *the process of choosing instrumental combinations for a band or orchestral work.*

Symphonie Fantastique, **Fifth Movement, Conclusion,**
Hector Berlioz

- As you listen to this short excerpt, identify the counter number each time you hear changes in orchestration.
- Pay special attention to the tone colors (timbres) and how they change.
- Listen a second time to determine if changes are made in dynamics, timbre, or both.

TIMBRE IN SYNTHESIZED SOUNDS

Timbral variety in sounds that are created electronically is almost limitless. Synthesizers can emulate natural sounds and conventional musical instruments or create sounds that are unlike any natural sounds.

The Lion's Tale, **Pauline Oliveros**

- At each of the counter numbers indicated below decide whether you think the sounds are natural or synthetic.

  CN 00:00   CN 00:49
  CN 00:14   CN 01:09
  CN 00:19

We have seen how various elements that make up the raw materials of music can be identified and have learned some of the vocabulary that is used to describe them. In most music we listen to, however, we seldom encounter these elements alone. Music is made up of various combinations of these elements and differing emphases upon them.

CHAPTER

7 Thickness in Music: Texture and Density

TEXTURE

Another term that describes how music is constructed is texture. **Texture** results from *the balance between the vertical* (harmonic) *and horizontal* (melodic) *realms in a given musical work.* The texture of a piece of music can be **mono-**

phonic *(a single melody)*, **polyphonic** *(made up exclusively of interwoven melodies)*, or **homophonic** *(a prominent melody supported by chords)*.

When a single melody is heard without any accompaniment (as when you are singing in the shower), the texture of the piece is *monophonic* (literally meaning *one sound*). Most folk musics of the world, whether Western or Eastern, were created as monophony. Chant is another type of music that is typically monophonic. Think back to the chant that we listened to in Chapter 3. Recall that the texture remained a single melody regardless of whether it was sung by one singer or by the entire choir.

In present-day concert arrangements, many monophonic pieces are performed with added vocal or instrumental parts, making the new texture either homophonic or polyphonic. Examples of homophonic arrangements are hymns, many of which started as monophonic melodies. The hymn type of homophonic texture usually consists of four voice parts (soprano, alto, tenor, bass); the lower three voices sing chord tones more or less in the same rhythm as the soprano part, which has the melody.

CROSSROADS

The watercolor *In a Levantine Port* by American artist John Singer Sargent provides an opportunity to relate vertical and horizontal lines with the melodic and harmonic aspects of texture in music. Density of lines also varies, with the right background having the most and the left background the least.

Brooklyn Museum of Art/Central Photo Archive

In a Levantine Port,
John Singer Sargent

A more common type of homophonic texture consists of a predominant melody with an accompaniment that is rhythmically more independent of the tune than the lower voices in a hymn.

"Mean Old Bed Bug Blues," Bessie Smith

In this example two guitars accompany the singer in a homophonic texture of the second type: predominant melody with accompaniment. The tune opens with a short introduction followed by three 12-bar blues choruses. Each time the voice enters, the accompaniment is reduced to simple strummed chords. However, between vocal statements the instrumental parts are more complex.

LISTENING GUIDE

"Mean Old Bed Bug Blues," Bessie Smith

CD 1:2

Introduction

00:00   Instruments set the stage for the vocal entrance and introduce the arpeggiated guitar pattern that will appear in each instrumental fill.

Chorus 1

00:11   Instrumental fills include emphasized bass notes and arpeggiated guitar pattern.

Chorus 2

00:49   Second guitar embellishment added to instrumental fills.

Chorus 3

1:26   Accompaniment becomes louder, more complex second guitar embellishment.

Composers of Western church music have often employed polyphonic texture because it has traditionally been regarded as an appropriate manner in which to represent its serious subject. This Mass was composed for six voice parts, and its opening is a clear example of a polyphonic texture. One voice enters first and other voices follow at two-beat intervals. All of these initial entrances use the same melody.

Active Listening
CD 2:1

Missa Papae Marcelli, Kyrie, Giovanni Pierluigi da Palestrina

Just as serious kinds of music sometimes find places for lighter textures, so popular kinds of music, such as the Broadway musical, will occasionally find a place for polyphony.

WEST SIDE STORY, "TONIGHT" QUINTET, LEONARD BERNSTEIN

In this excerpt the composer has chosen to bring into superposition two themes that had earlier been heard separately, the gang theme and the love theme. The plot of *West Side Story* centers on Tony and Maria, a couple in love who come from rival street gangs. **Counterpoint** is a specific type of polyphony in which *melodies are pitted against each other* rather than simply combined. Bernstein uses these two themes in counterpoint to represent the central dramatic tension in his musical: Will Tony and Maria be allowed to stay together or will gang warfare win out?

West Side Story, "Tonight" Quintet, Leonard Bernstein

CD 2:2

LISTENING GUIDE

00:00   Selection opens with the gang theme

1:27   The familiar "Tonight" love theme becomes the predominant melody

2:43   Both themes appear in counterpoint

DENSITY

To describe the texture of music as being largely homophonic, monophonic, or contrapuntal (or some combination of these) is only to begin our exploration into a composer's use of sound. Also of importance is a broader view that includes description of the music's **tonal density** *(the number and kinds of voices and instruments being employed)* as well as its **rhythmic density** *(the amount of rhythmic activity).* An overall sense of musical density also takes into account volume and tone color as well as texture.

In the previous chapter this piece was used to demonstrate the variety of timbres that can be created through computer manipulation. Now focus on the level of rhythmic activity. You will notice that it is quite beyond the reach of ordinary human musical performance capabilities. This example creates variety by varying rhythmic density.

Active Listening
CD 1:4

The Lion's Tale, Pauline Oliveros

- Begins with rhythmically dense vertical texture.
- Rhythmic activity subsides, speed slows.
- One part remains slow, accompanying part is faster than either of the other sections, creating more horizontal density.

An example of variety in tonal density can be heard in Berlioz' *Symphonie Fantastique,* a piece you heard in the earlier discussion of orchestration.

Symphonie Fantastique, **Fifth Movement, Hector Berlioz**

- Begins moderately dense.
- Diminishes in tonal density.
- Gradually increases in density.
- Decreases again.
- Increases one final time.

Determining how all the elements of music work together allows us to describe what is going on at any particular musical moment. We can also compare moments over the course of a piece of music and discover the overall organization of the work. Such descriptions of a work's structure, or form, are covered in the next chapter.

CHAPTER

8   Musical Structure

FORM: THE ARCHITECTURE OF MUSIC

We have already discovered that melody and harmony work together to create a sense of tonality in many musical compositions. In fact, all aspects of most pieces of music are part of a balanced, carefully thought out plan that is audible to you as listener. Thus, **form** *is the overall design of a musical work that can be heard by the listener.*

It might surprise you to realize that obscure academicians do not decide whether a musical work is "good" or "lasting." The arts are popular in the sense that such decisions are a composite of the opinions of all interested people over a period of time. It follows, then, that it is in a musician's (or composer's) best interest to create a form that is clear and obvious to all sorts of listeners, including those with little musical training. A composer must achieve a balance between loud and soft, repetition and contrast, high and low, and all other aspects of musical composition in order to keep your attention.

CONVENTIONS OF IDENTIFYING FORM

The keys to your recognition of form are repetition, variation, and contrast. As in geometry, we use letters to identify the parts of a musical form. We label the first formal section with the letter A, the second section with B, and so on for

The composition of Raphael's *School of Athens* (1508) is similar to the kind of formal balance and clarity that is found in the music of Mozart. The relationship between symmetry and asymmetry in the painting is more or less parallel to the one that exists between repetition and variation in classical music. A series of four arches beginning in the foreground focus your attention on the two figures in the center. The hues of their clothing are repeated on some figures in the painting and yet contrasting colors are found on others. The figures are more or less symmetrically placed with the obvious exceptions of a man lying on the steps and another leaning on a block in the foreground. The variety of poses in which the figures are set is significant.

Vatican Museums and Galleries, Rome/Fratelli Alinari/Superstock

Notice the symmetry and formal balance in Raphael's *School of Athens*.

each subsequent contrasting section, and we identify repeated sections by repeating the same letter. A section that is a variation—recognizably a repetition but not identical to the original—is given the same letter with a prime attached; for example A′ (A prime).

"The Star Spangled Banner," Francis Scott Key

Active Listening
CD 1:19

Musical memory is an important tool in developing critical listening skills. The following exercise should convince you that you have a certain amount of natural ability in this area.

Listen in your mind to "The Star Spangled Banner" (see lyrics). The first line of text begins with "Oh, say can you see" and ends with "twilight's last gleaming?" Notice that the second section ("Whose broad stripes . . .") begins with the same melodic idea as the first line of text. In fact, the entire second section is musically identical to the first. Accordingly, the first two sections could be labeled AA.

Oh, say can you see by the dawn's early light
What so proudly we hailed at the twilight's last gleaming?

Whose broad stripes and bright stars through the perilous fight,
O'er the ramparts we watched, were so gallantly streaming?

And the rocket's red glare, the bombs bursting in air,
Gave proof through the night that our flag was still there.

Oh, say does that star spangled banner yet wave
O'er the land of the free and the home of the brave?

A continuation of your mental listening should reveal that the third section ("And the rocket's red glare . . .") differs from A, so it should be labeled B. The final section ("Oh say does that star spangled banner . . .") is not similar to either A or B, so it can be called C. The overall form then, can be diagrammed AABC.

When words are present (as in "The Star Spangled Banner"), text repetition (or lack thereof) can be represented in the formal diagram. The repeat of a capital letter indicates both the same music and the same words, while a small letter shows that the music is the same but the text is different. Because the first section of music in "The Star Spangled Banner" is repeated with a different text, our formal diagram should read AaBC.

SECTIONAL FORMS

A short piece like "The Star Spangled Banner" balances repetition and variation so the listener hears it as organized. In fact, this fundamental concept of musical structure is present in very-large-scale musical works. One very common way of creating this balance is returning to opening thematic material at the end of a work.

TERNARY FORM

The simplest of these balanced formal patterns is the ternary form, which can be represented by the letters ABA. In such large-scale works as operas, can-

The Washerwomen, by Vincent Van Gogh, is made up of several large sections created with repeated pen strokes and some contrasting areas of detail. A large area in the right foreground is made up of long lines; shorter lines make up a section to the center left. In the center, between these two, is a smaller cross-hatch area. Another section composed of dots begins in the left foreground and curves around to the right background. The buildings in the background are created by a combination of vertical and horizontal lines. The area in the right center, where the washerwomen are, is made up of a variety of pen strokes and is set off by the bridge.

Like "The Star Spangled Banner," this artwork is made up of sections, and the balance between repetition and variation is of critical importance.

Otterlo, Rijksmuseum Kröller-Müller/Art Resource, NY

The Washerwomen,
Vincent Van Gogh

tatas, and oratorios, featured solos for singers often use this form and are typically called *da capo* arias. If you played in band in high school, you are likely to have obeyed a "D.C." sign in one piece or another. This abbreviation for the

Italian *da capo* (literally *from the head*) instructed you to return to the beginning of the piece to a repeat of the opening section. Unknowingly, you were performing a piece in the ternary form. The *da capo* designation was used in operas as early as the beginning of the seventeenth century to save the composer the labor of writing out the A section yet again.

A much larger version of the ternary idea that is used in instrumental concert music from Western Europe is *sonata form*. Later, we will investigate the details of this form and its variants. Here, the goal is for you to get a sense of its overall structure. As with "The Star Spangled Banner," your ability to remember the opening melody is of great importance. Mozart makes this task relatively easy by repeating the A section and by making the B section very brief.

Active Listening
CD 1:6

Eine kleine Nachtmusik, First Movement, Wolfgang Amadeus Mozart

- The A section opens.
- The entire opening section is repeated, giving you a second chance to remember the themes.
- The middle section opens with material related to the A section but immediately wanders off in other directions.
- Identify the counter number when the A theme returns again.

We will return to this work later and learn the details of this formal pattern.

THE REFRAIN IDEA: RONDO FORM

Another formal concept that involves the return of opening musical material is the *refrain* idea. If you have heard the familiar Christmas carol "Deck the Halls with Boughs of Holly," you already know an example of this technique. In this carol, each line of poetry is followed by what is known in the English madrigal tradition as a "fa-la" refrain: fa la la la la, la la, la, la. If you know this carol very well you will be able to figure out that the first two refrains are the same, the third is quite different in pitch, and the last brings the form to a close. The overall form is AaBa with "fa-la" refrains ending each section.

In a general sense, *rondo* form is like the refrain in reverse: The original A returns after each new section of music. A rondo typically has a minimum of five sections represented by the letters ABACA.

One fact that may not have been clear above is for there to be a "return" of A first, there must be a contrasting section (B). This contrast may involve variation of the original thematic material as in Mozart's *Eine kleine Nachtmusik,* or, as in this example, it may consist of dramatically different musical ideas.

Piano Sonata in C Major, Third Movement, Rondo,   **LISTENING**
Wolfgang Amadeus Mozart   **GUIDE**

CD 2:3

00:00   A section

00:18   B—first contrasting section

00:33   Return of A

00:52   C—second contrasting section

1:13   Final return of A

VARIATION TECHNIQUE

Another important way of structuring music involves **variation technique:** *An original idea is stated and then repeated a number of times,* but *each repetition is in some way a variation of the original material.* Typically, *the original material is returned to toward the end of the variations* to bring closure to the work. Variation technique may employ a theme, a chord progression, or even merely a bass line as its basis. In jazz, the variation principle is used frequently, and the variations themselves are usually improvised rather than composed. Jazz performers often work from a "fake book," which contains the "theme" and chord progression for a large number of jazz tunes. The rest is up to the imagination of the performer. A significant amount of jazz is based on a blues progression, other aspects of blues style, or both. When we heard this example in Chapter 5 our attention was focused on the chord progression. This hearing is centered on variation technique.

Active Listening
CD 1:24

Twelve-Bar Blues

- Opening 12 bars (theme)
- First variation
- Second variation
- Closing 12 bars
- Identify the changes you hear in each of the variations:

  First variation
  Second variation

- Does the original material return for the closing 12 bars?

TEXT AS DETERMINANT

All of the formal patterns described above (except for "The Star Spangled Banner") employ some sort of abstract formal design to create order. However, in many instances (like "The Star Spangled Banner"), a text imposes its order on the music. Some of the most basic examples of this text-generated form occur in the chant of various religions from around the world. To one degree or another, the natural rhythms and inflections of words create the rhythms and pitches in these chants. In some other instances, words are organized into formalized rhythmic patterns, which create the rhythmic organization of the music. Rap music has a great deal in common with both of these approaches, although for the most part pitch is not a significant factor in rap. In the next listening example, a muezzin (an Islamic official) calls worshipers to prayer by chanting texts from the Koran, originally from the top of minarets on mosques.

LISTENING GUIDE	*Adhan*, The *Muezzin*'s Call to Prayer
	CD 2:4
	00:00 Phrase 1: descending then ascending shape
	00:10 Phrase 2: similar to the contour of phrase 1
	00:20 Phrase 3: ascending melodic contour
	00:30 Phrase 4: descending contour, similar to phrase 1

STROPHIC FORM

From a musical perspective, far more interesting examples occur when the music is somewhat less dependent on the text. Many songs use a structure called **strophic** in which *each stanza of text is sung to the same music.* Instances of strophic text setting include the hymns of the Catholic liturgy, the chorales and hymns of the Protestant faiths, and many patriotic songs.

Perhaps the easiest way to understand this formal pattern is to visualize a page in a church hymnbook. In most instances one version of the music is set with four or even six verses of text. It is important to remember that while there may be an introduction to a piece in strophic form, there should not be any contrasting sections between verses. The strophic technique works best with simple lyrical texts and can be found in works ranging from popular and folk songs to Schubert lieder. In the following song by William Billings, five stanzas of poetry are set to the same melodic and harmonic treatment.

"Chester," William Billings

Active Listening
CD 2:5

- Write down the first three words of each stanza of poetry.
- Is the music exactly the same each time or are there differences in interpretation?

NEW WAYS OF ORDERING MUSIC

CHANCE MUSIC

For much of the twentieth century composers were preoccupied with finding new, original ways of organizing music, as well as creating new sources of sound. Among these many experiments, chance music, minimalism, and the use of electronic sound sources have had the greatest impact on musical form. At the beginning of the twenty-first century, it is clear that none of these new methods has completely replaced traditional methods of composing. However, new types of formal organization and sound sources have added greatly to the list of choices available to the composer and in some cases have changed the way we react to music.

Chance has always been a part of nearly all musics. That is, live performances of a given symphony differ each time it is performed by a different orchestra or conductor. Even with the same orchestra and conductor, the moods of the performers, their health on a given day, or the condition of their instruments cause each performance to be slightly different. Improvised music and music from the many oral traditions of the world are by design even more likely to vary from performance to performance. Chance music or indeterminacy dramatically increases the role of these unpredictable elements. **Indeterminacy** involves *instructions or actions taken by the composer or performer that result in an unpredictable musical outcome*. This is not an entirely new idea, for as early as 1751 a composer named John Hayes proposed composing by spattering ink on a staff. John Cage, a major proponent of indeterminacy offered the following description:

> I think perhaps my own best piece, at least the one I like the most, is the silence piece [*4' 33"*, 1952]. It has three movements and in all of the movements there are no sounds. I wanted my work to be free of my own likes and dislikes, because I think music should be free of the feelings and ideas of the composer. I have felt and hoped to have led other people to feel that the sounds of their environment constitute a music which is more interesting than the music which they would hear if they went into a concert hall.

The composition Cage is referring to, *4' 33"* will help you understand his intended process.

Active Listening

4' 33", **John Cage**

- This piece is in three parts with specific durations: 30", 2' 23", and 1' 40".
- These durations were arrived at by chance.
- The performer makes no sounds at all during this piece.
- The composition, which is devoid of a rhythmic structure, consists of the random sounds that occur in the environment you happen to be in during that specific time.
- To approximate the performance of this work, select one of the durations given above, emulate the usual attentive state of a concert setting, and listen intently for the specified length of time.

The questions raised by this example extend far beyond the realm of form. In fact, our basic definition of music as *sound organized in time* is challenged by this piece. At the very least the idea of form created by chance suggests that composers can explore options other than sectional forms in organizing their music.

MINIMALISM

Another compositional technique that creates a new approach to form is minimalism. **Minimalism** involves using *limited musical materials in a texture that features few (minimal) changes in rhythm, melody, and harmony.* In practice this typically involves repeating musical ideas with an occasional change of a single feature, and it often results in a kind of hypnotic effect. Unlike most traditional music, "minimal" music does not seem to be rushing forward through a series of themes or creating harmonic and rhythmic intensity, but rather presents a uniform tapestry that features occasional subtle changes. Minimalism creates new expectations not only for form but also for melody, harmony, and rhythm. This approach to composition is prevalent in a number of contemporary styles, including popular musics such as techno.

Active Listening
CD 1:3

Satyagraha, **Act III, "Martin Luther King, Jr.," Part 3, Philip Glass**

- Focus your attention on the vocal soloist.
- While the text does change, does the melodic line vary from its original form?
- In what ways does the accompaniment change?
- Is there any sense of a traditional chord progression?

FORM IN ELECTRONIC MUSIC

The creation of electronic sound manipulation, the invention of synthetic sounds, and the advent of computer control of sound have added to the ways in which musical form can be created. Technology provides the means to produce limitless timbres and rhythms that can be performed at unimaginable speeds. This has enabled composers to create soundscapes in which timbre, rhythm, and simultaneous sounds are explored in entirely new ways. While we have listened to the excerpt below in other contexts, it is useful to pay attention to how the features of timbre, rhythm, and simultaneous sounds create a sense of musical form.

Silver Apples of the Moon, **Part II (excerpt), Morton Subotnick**

Active Listening
CD 1:12

• How do the various musical elements coincide to allow you to distinguish sections in the music?

The various kinds of musical structure we have investigated can serve as a checklist for many of the kinds of music to which you may listen. As useful practice, check CD liner notes or program notes for live performances for hints about how the music is structured. More than anything, listen carefully for repetition, variation, and contrast, and let your ear be the guide.

CHAPTER

The Sources of Music: Voices and Instruments

9

VOICE

The voice is perhaps the most universal of all musical instruments. It is the only instrument that everyone owns, and vocal music has been part of nearly every culture in almost every epoch. There have been times when the voice was the only instrument accepted in certain settings (the early Catholic Church, for example).

It is thought that the larynx, or voice box, evolved from a simple mechanism that was intended to protect the airway and provide added abdominal pressure for activities such as heavy lifting. The ability to make sounds seems to have been an added bonus. The act of singing involves the delicate coordination of the breath and the small muscles of the larynx. As you may have noticed after cheering for your favorite sports team, your voice is fairly susceptible to injury or even permanent damage. This relative frailty of the vocal mechanism makes the diverse timbres and dynamics the voice is capable of even more amazing.

Even in any given decade or country, the human voice is called upon to produce very divergent sounds. The following examples, all composed in the United States during the twentieth century, illustrate this fact.

Active Listening
CD 2:6

Porgy and Bess, "There's a Boat Dat's Leavin' Soon for New York," George Gershwin

CD 2:7

"I Heard It Through the Grapevine," Whitfield-Strong (Marvin Gaye)

CD 2:8

Pierrot Lunaire, "Der Mondfleck," Arnold Schoenberg

- How do these examples differ in timbre?
- What vocal "special effects" help identify the style?
- Would any one of these singers be likely to cross over to one of the other styles?

Throughout history, voices have been combined in a variety of ensembles, the most common in Western music being the mixed chorus. Music for this group is written in four parts, with women singing the two higher parts (soprano and alto) and men singing the lower parts (tenor and bass). This ensemble can be found in a wide variety of churches, concert halls, high schools, and universities and provides the composer with great flexibility in timbre, dynamics, and range. Other common ensembles include women's choir, men's chorus, boy's choir, barbershop quartet, as well as small combinations of soloists found in operas and popular music. These examples give you some idea of the diversity of timbres and styles found in vocal ensembles.

Active Listening
CD 2:5

"Chester," William Billings

CD 2:9

"I Want to be Ready," Traditional

- Could singers from one group move to another and still have an appropriate vocal sound?
- Which century might each piece come from?

INSTRUMENTS

WIND INSTRUMENTS

Wind instruments are those in which the *sound is produced by a vibrating column of air.* These instruments are classified according to how the vibration is initiated: flutes, reeds, cup mouthpieces, and free wind instruments. The instruments in this broad category range from simple to complex and, in some form or another, are part of almost every musical tradition. The illustration on page 50 shows several examples of each classification.

The wind instruments that are used in Western music (page 52) are commonly divided into two subgroups: woodwinds and brasses.

Gustav Holst's First Suite in E-flat was originally written for the military (concert) band. As you probably already know, the band idiom is centered on wind and percussion instruments with the occasional addition of a piano and/or string bass. This first movement of the suite is in theme and variation form based on the first eight measures. One way composers create variety in music is by using different instruments or instrumental combinations. Here is the instrumentation of the theme and the first six variations.

First Suite in E-flat for Military Band, First Movement, Chaconne, Gustav Holst

LISTENING GUIDE

CD 2:10

Theme

00:00   Tuba and euphonium play the theme.

Variation I

00:17   Low trombone plays the theme.
Cornets and first trombone play the countermelody.

Variation 2

00:33   Bass clarinet, tenor saxophone, and bassoon play the theme.
Oboe, clarinets, and saxophones (saxes) play the countermelody.

Variation 3

00:49   Tuba, euphonium, and low saxes play the theme.
Woodwinds, cornet, trombone play an answering figure.

Variation 4

1:03   Low brass and low saxes play the theme.
Other woodwinds/brasses, plus timpani, play an answering figure.

(continues on pg. 50)

Variation 5

1:18   Low saxes and brass play the theme in short note values.
        Woodwinds play legato sixteenth notes. Note the use of cymbals.

Variation 6

1:32   Cornets and trumpets play the theme.
        Trombone plays obbligato with low brasses and woodwinds.

Active Listening
CD 2:10

**First Suite in E-flat for Military Band, First Movement, Chaconne,
Gustav Holst**

- Listen to several more variations and identify the instruments you hear.
- Can you guess which instrument in the band plays parts that might be
  played by the violins in the orchestra?

STRING INSTRUMENTS

Instruments in which the *sound is generated by a vibrating string* are called **string
instruments**. The string may be bowed, plucked, or struck to begin the sound.
The illustration on page 53 shows some examples of string instruments: bows,
lyres, harps, lutes, and zithers. Western instruments of the string family
include the harp, some keyboard instruments, guitars, and the violin family.
String instruments have played a primary role in Western art music, as the
illustration on page 54 shows.

Active Listening
CD 2:11

Trio No. 2 in C Minor, Third Movement, Felix Mendelssohn

- This piece features violin and piano; the cello plays a supporting role.
- The work opens with violin and piano.
- Each time the featured instrument changes, identify the name of the new
  instrument.

PERCUSSION: DRUMS

Percussion instruments *are instruments that produce a sound when struck or shaken.*
Drums *are almost exclusively percussion instruments in which the sound is produced by
the vibration of a stretched piece of skin or plastic (a head).* While many cultures
around the world have used drums, no culture is more noted for these instruments than the people of Africa. In the example on page 54, we hear African
drums, including the *kalangu* or "talking drum." By changing tension on the
strings that connect the upper and lower heads, the player is able to change the
pitch of the instrument, making sounds that are somewhat like "talking." Obey
combines this and other African features with stylistic features of Western pop
music.

(text continues on pg. 54)

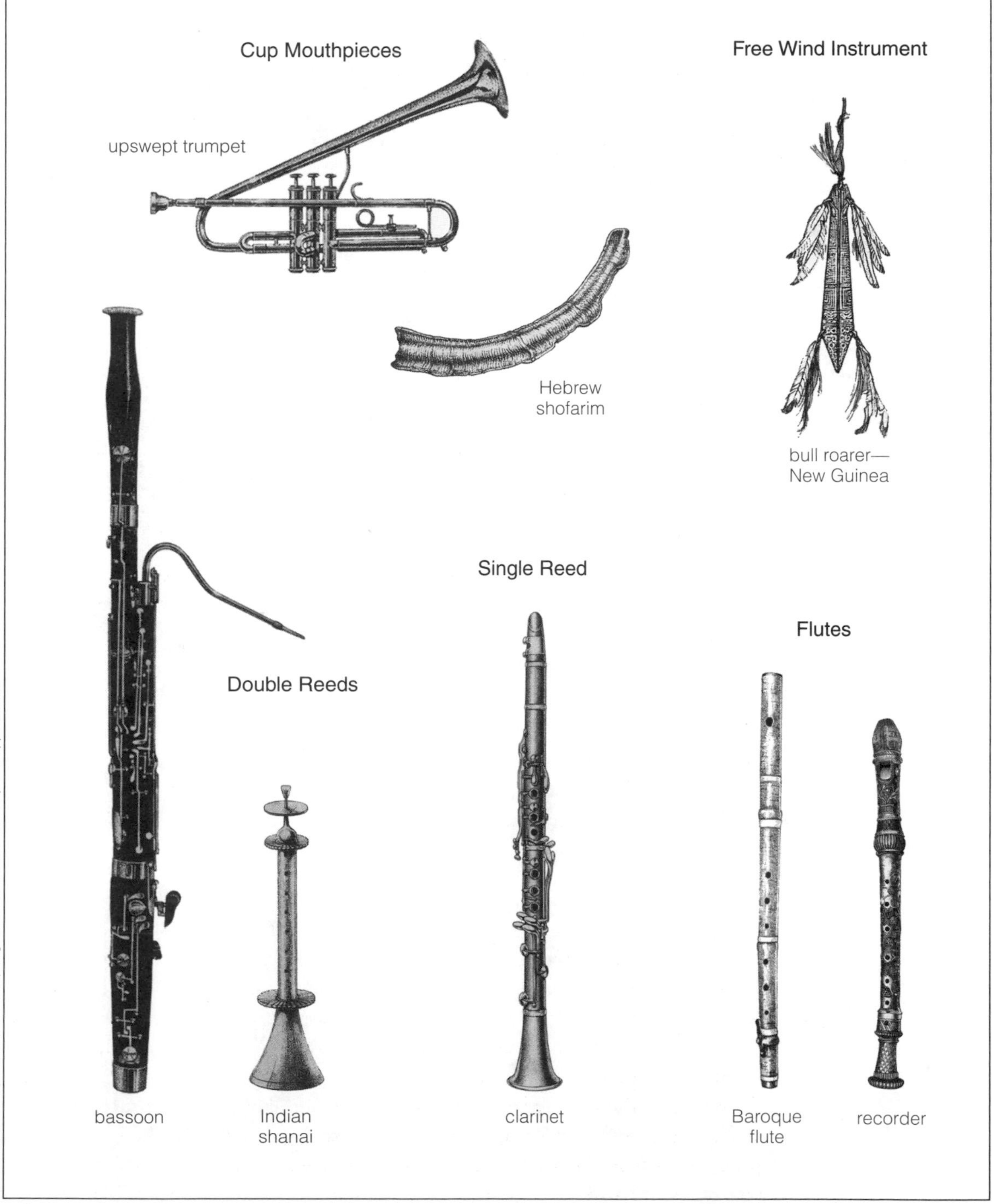

Cup Mouthpieces

Free Wind Instrument

upswept trumpet

Hebrew
shofarim

bull roarer—
New Guinea

Single Reed

Flutes

Double Reeds

bassoon   Indian   clarinet   Baroque   recorder
                 shanai   flute

Wind Instruments

52 PART II TERMINOLOGY

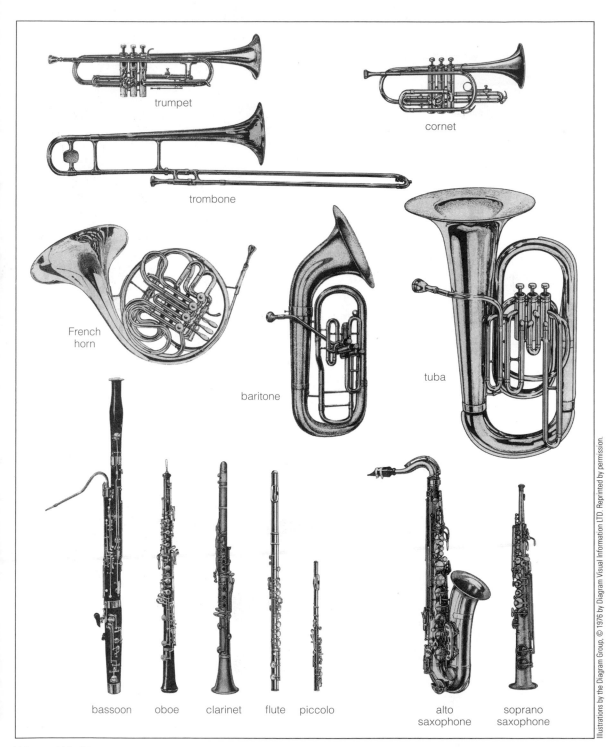

trumpet

cornet

trombone

French
horn

baritone

tuba

bassoon oboe clarinet flute piccolo

alto
saxophone

soprano
saxophone

Western Wind Instruments

Lyre

Zithers

Appalachian
dulcimer

musical bow

kerar—Ethiopia

Lutes

harp

lute

violin

17th Century
guitar

piano

harpsichord

String Instruments

violin

viola

cello

string bass

Illustrations by the Diagram Group. © 1976 by Diagram Visual Information LTD. Reprinted by permission.

Violin Family

Active Listening
CD 2:12

"Asiki Mi Ti To," Chief Commander Ebenezer Obey

- Introduction. Accompanying drummers play a steady repeated pattern over which the talking drum enters.
- Electric guitar and flute establish background vamp.
- Solo and ensemble voices join in.
- Drum interlude, again featuring the talking drum.
- Solo and ensemble voices.

Drums used in Western music came from a variety of cultures and were introduced at various points in history. Timpani or kettledrums were the first percussion instruments added to the Western orchestra, sometime during the seventeenth century. However, the drum set did not come about until the beginning of the twentieth century when marching musicians in New Orleans bolted their drums together for evening performances indoors. Most other

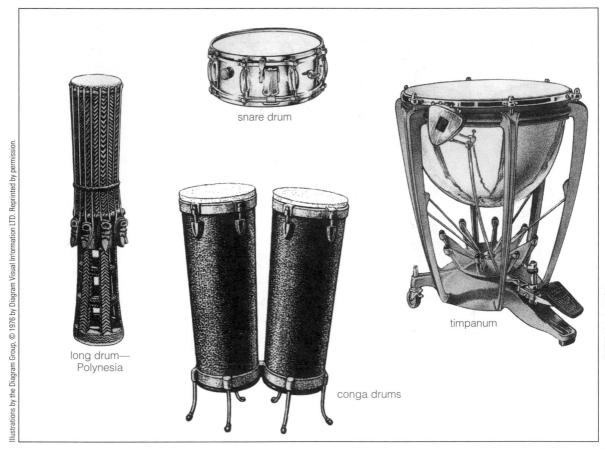

Illustrations by the Diagram Group. © 1976 by Diagram Visual Information LTD. Reprinted by permission.

snare drum

long drum—
Polynesia

conga drums

timpanum

Drums

hand drums come from around the world and were added to Western music later in the twentieth century.

OTHER PERCUSSION INSTRUMENTS

Drums are not the only percussion instruments; others made of a flexible material are played in a variety of ways including shaking, plucking, striking, and stamping. The illustration on page 56 shows some of these instruments. In *Segera Maдu*, from Bali, we hear the many metal gongs, xylophones, and bells of the *gamelan* along with the *angklung*, a folk instrument made of numerous bamboo tubes.

An extraordinary variety of these instruments has been used in modern band and orchestra music. Currently, orchestral percussionists are expected to be able to play all of the percussion instruments in both categories.

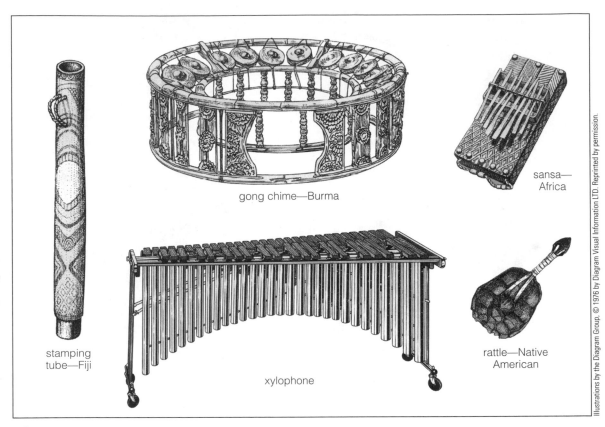

gong chime—Burma

sansa—
Africa

stamping
tube—Fiji

xylophone

rattle—Native
American

Illustrations by the Diagram Group. © 1976 by Diagram Visual Information LTD. Reprinted by permission.

Other Percussion Instruments

**LISTENING
GUIDE**

Segera Madu, Bali

CD 2:13

00:00   Higher pitched, fast xylophone pattern with low xylophone sound

00:35   Angklung enters, xylophone pattern and low xylophone continue

---

SYNTHETIC INSTRUMENTS

Synthetic instruments *are those in which the sound is produced electronically,* not by the vibration of some natural material. Instruments such as synthesizers use oscillators to produce sound electronically. Other instruments such as the electric guitar, in which a natural vibration is amplified and/or modified electronically, are not synthetic instruments.

The recent transition in sound production methods from analog (using coded voltages) to digital (using numbers) has allowed for the interaction of computers, musical instruments, and synthesizers. To enable these devices to interact effectively regardless of the manufacturer, an *industry standard system of communication* called **MIDI** (Musical Instrument Digital Interface) was created.

Instruments that do not create sound but trigger the actions of a computer/synthesizer are called **controllers.** These include guitar controllers, drum machines, keyboard controllers, wind controllers, and keyboard mallet controllers. Computers are also able to reproduce natural sounds through a process called sampling. A **sampler** is *a device that takes successive digital snapshots of a natural sound over time.* This digital information can then be used to recreate the sound synthetically. In another process called **sequencing,** *the digital data that is necessary to play back MIDI sequences and files is stored in a computer.* In many cases, a single instrument (a keyboard, for example) may contain preprogrammed, sampled sounds that can be sequenced into its computer memory and played back as desired.

ENSEMBLES

Instruments and/or voices that perform together are called **ensembles.** Such groupings provide for greater diversity in volume, pitch, and timbre than a solo voice or instrument can create. The possibilities of "color" variety that can be achieved through mixing instruments are as limitless as they are in painting, making timbre a significant factor in creating variety in music.

Ensembles can be made up of like instruments—string orchestra, men's choir, or synthesizer ensemble—as well as mixed instruments—gamelan, orchestra, jazz quartet, concert band, or opera. Different cultures, subcultures, and styles may have preferred instruments or ensembles. In Western art music, the symphony orchestra is a more or less standard combination of winds, strings, and percussion, as the illustration on page 58 shows.

Bands use a larger complement of brass and woodwind instruments than an orchestra but do not employ strings, with the possible exception of a string bass. In addition, the band typically uses euphoniums (baritones) and saxophones, instruments that are not regular members of the orchestra.

Early jazz instruments include the cornet, clarinet, banjo, trombone, tuba, and fiddle, and the modern drum set began to evolve in this setting. Contemporary small jazz groups often include a rhythm section made up of piano, bass, and drums along with one or more solo winds.

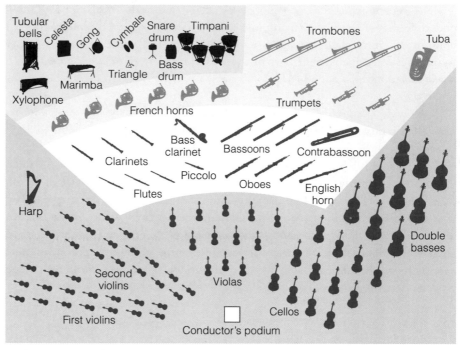

Orchestra Seating Plan

The "big band," which is still a part of many high school and university programs, usually consists of five saxes, four trombones, four or five trumpets, and rhythm. On the other hand, rock and commercial groups favor rhythm and percussion instruments over strings and winds. In fact, the usual instrumental rock group is derived from the rhythm section of the jazz band. The synthesizer continues to increase in importance in these styles. Ensembles in world music are much more difficult to generalize about and will be covered throughout the text.

CHAPTER

Learning About Music: Finding the Best Approach

10

THE TIME PERIODS OF WESTERN ART MUSIC

In the first chapter we talked about the great diversity of styles of music that are readily available for your enjoyment. Now that you have learned about musical terms and concepts, it should be clear that this diversity often depends on the date and place of composition, the setting for which the music was intended, and/or the cultural background of the composer. Since you have easy access to such a large and varied musical landscape, it is necessary to have an approach for the next five units that will allow us to cover these diverse musical topics in a comprehensive and unified manner.

Traditional study of music in the United States has normally emphasized the Western European historical tradition (*classical* music) with some discussion of its transplantation to the North American continent. This approach proves very useful for a historically conditioned view that concentrates on types of European music, its origins, influences on it, and important musicians (mostly composers). Through this approach you may gain an understanding of where terminology comes from, how people have taught and learned music, what some traditional functions of music are, how musical styles have changed over time, and what music we still listen to today.

The names and general time frames of the several historical periods reflect categorizations common to other arts. The *Middle Ages* span the longest period. Since so little music survives from classical antiquity (ancient Greece and Rome), the great religious and secular music spanning the five or six centuries before about 1400 represents the earliest significant body of European music we still have. There are difficulties in recreating some of this music, but in general, we know a good deal about it from about 800 on. The *Renaissance* in music evolved from those intellectual movements in literature, architecture, and painting that arose in Italy during the fourteenth century. Considerably more music remains from the Renaissance (the fifteenth and sixteenth centuries) than from the Middle Ages. The development of music printing at the turn of the sixteenth century contributed to the preservation of much of this music. The Reformation and its reaction, the Counter Reformation, offered many opportunities for the creation of important church music. Yet, the humanistic spirit inspired increasing amounts of secular vocal and instrumental music.

The beginning of the *baroque* era coincides with two important developments in European music: the invention of opera and the flourishing of independent instrumental music. Around the year 1600, drama with music was developed, especially in some Italian court circles. Its eventual move to the public sphere sparked a popularity that some might consider unexpected. Distinctions (sometimes artificial ones) between opera, church music, and instrumental music are characteristic of the music written between 1600 and around 1740. So are differences in so-called national styles, particularly Italian, French, and German. Nonetheless, a good deal of similarity in the musical results meant that when the Enlightenment encouraged a pursuit of "naturalness" in the mid-eighteenth century, a recognizable change in musical style was evident. The *classical* era (1750–1825) ushered in a type of music that has been a staple of concert music ever since. Narrowly defined as high-quality or "model" music represented by the works of Haydn, Mozart, and Beethoven, classical music comes closest to being a truly unified, recognizable style.

A reaction to musical classicism occurred in the nineteenth century when the *romantic* spirit pervaded the arts. Music was viewed as the most romantic of

CROSSROADS   What is "classic?" If you ask a chef, you might get the answer, French cuisine. If you are a car buff, you might get the answer, a '57 Chevy. These provide examples of one meaning of the word, classic: something recognized broadly as being of high quality, a model in its category. In the arts, however, there are a couple of related meanings for the words classic or classical. One meaning has to do with the civilizations of ancient Greece and Rome, "classical antiquity." During the Renaissance, examples of classical literature, architecture, and sculpture began to provide inspiration for the writers, architects, and artists of the time. (The word "renaissance" refers to a "rebirth" of the arts of antiquity.) During the eighteenth century, after discoveries at Pompeii revealed much about Roman art and life, an overt modeling of Roman characteristics became fashionable. This was apparent especially in the visual arts, architecture, and furniture design. In music, however, there was essentially nothing to model after. Even now, we know little of the music of ancient Greece or Rome aside from its theoretical basis. Yet, by extension, the music of the late-eighteenth century has become known as "classical" partly because of the outstanding quality of the works of Haydn, Mozart, and Beethoven and partly in imitation of the designation of those other art forms.

all the arts, and it was cultivated for its very descriptive yet indefinable qualities. Romantic music explored extremes—musical miniatures alongside grand opera. By the beginning of the twentieth century, the notion of extreme size (number of musicians and length of musical works) had been stretched to its aesthetic limits. Much twentieth-century music, quite indefinable as a single style, has been characterized by a diversity of musical idiom, performance opportunities, and audiences. Terms like *modern music* somehow seem inadequate now. Musicians and listeners alike have come to recognize and appreciate the inherent qualities of a variety of music, including much that is not European in origin. This means, of course, that the historical study we have just described becomes problematic to our current task of learning about many different musics. (The table below gives a brief survey of the major historical periods in Western music.)

Period	Approximate Dates	Key Words	Musical Style
Middle Ages	c. 600–1450	Christianity	monophony
Renaissance	c. 1450–1600	humanism	polyphony
Baroque	c. 1600–1750	absolutism	functional harmony
Classical	c. 1750–1825	enlightenment	instrumental genres
Romantic	c. 1825–1900	self-expression	chromatic harmony
Twentieth Century	c. 1901–2000	diversity of style	expansion of tonality

THE GEOGRAPHICAL PERSPECTIVE

Another way of studying music is to consider the cultural differences that reflect its ethnic or geographical distribution. This method of study encompasses not only our historical view of European music but also the independently developed musical traditions of other cultures. With it we can describe the range of musical experiences exemplified by folksongs and dances from various ethnic heritages or the highly sophisticated court musical cultures of places like Japan or China. A bewildering array of musical expression presents itself in the many recordings that have been made of music from diverse tribes, villages, and regions throughout the world. A historical record is present in the writings from literate societies such as those in China, India, or the Near East. Yet, aside from the many cross-cultural connections that can be traced by using this perspective, we are not usually any closer to a meaningful understanding of these many musics, nor are we really helped in making our own listening choices.

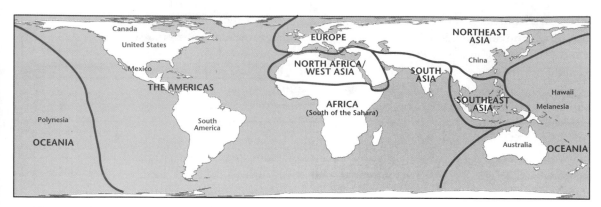

World Music Cultures

There are so many manifestations of musical culture to deal with that we are often left merely with descriptions of instrument types and a rough comparison of their timbres, or with descriptions of the texts of songs and plays and the stories they tell. Any concise discussion of the music itself tends to be so technical in its vocabulary and arcane in its nuance that we are easily overwhelmed by it all.

Besides, the very nature of these so-called *world* musics has changed dramatically in the last fifty years. At the beginning of the last century a number of these musical cultures were more or less isolated, neither having an impact on outside cultures nor being influenced by contact with the outside world. An increase in research in world musical cultures (ethnomusicology) and in communication among cultures has created an international interchange of musical styles and instruments. In our current world culture, not only are compact discs of world music readily available in most music stores, but world styles and instruments are routinely integrated into everything from popular songs to art music. Clearly our approach must reflect this current circumstance.

FUNCTION AS AN APPROACH TO MUSIC

In recent years, music scholars have paid greater attention to the place and function of music in society. Consideration of musical differences in light of similar functions provides a useful framework for a discussion of musical style and substance. The functional perspective can also suggest connections between differing musical cultures, their technical vocabulary, and musical structures. The present-day student is indeed fortunate to live at a time when he or she can enjoy the fruits of all these approaches.

We will be looking at and listening to music from four general perspectives related to the function or use of music. Of course, these overlap, sometimes to a considerable degree. Nevertheless, the usefulness of drawing comparisons in spite of vast differences in sound offers an interesting view of our musical universe. The four categories are ritual music, folk music, concert music, and commercial music.

RITUAL MUSIC

A specific, observable kind of behavior based on established or traditional rules is called ritual. By extension, *music used in carrying out these traditional behaviors* is **ritual music.** Rituals depend on some belief system for their complete meaning. Since none of us can possibly take part in all of the many rituals that humans have devised, we would need to imagine some original context to understand what some specific ritual is actually about. However, we can make some interesting observations by dealing with music apart from its strictly ritualistic function. Indeed, many interesting manifestations of musical expression stem from some ritual music no longer used directly for a ritualistic function.

Music that functions as ritual is very often sacred music, music that enhances religious observances. In a formal way, such music is an integral part of **liturgy,** the *official words, actions, music, and other behavior that constitute a religious ceremony.* However, not all sacred music is ritual, and not all ritual is necessarily religious or sacred. Dramatic music portraying religious or sacred topics is not exactly ritual and certainly not liturgical. Rituals and their attendant music lie hidden in many everyday human experiences.

FOLK MUSIC

Often called "the music of the people," **folk music** *communicates on a direct personal level and is readily accepted by a large percentage of a population.* An important defining feature of folk music is the *anonymity of its creators.* In addition, it is *usually performed by amateurs* and—at least until recent years—has been *most often transmitted by oral tradition,* meaning that it has been passed along by imitation and repetition rather than by musical notation. This fact explains why sometimes several versions of a tune sound alike even though the words (and even the language) may vary considerably from one version to another and from one geographic location to another.

Folk songs may deal with a wide range of subjects including love, work, war, parental responsibilities, political convictions, folk legends, secular expressions of religious beliefs, or nationalism. Folk music has always had an influence on more sophisticated musical styles. Classical music composers such as Brahms, Stravinsky, Copland, Still, Dvořák, or Bartók have all used folk elements in their compositions. In the last century, however, the ease of distribution of all sorts of music has made this transfer of styles much more complex. Modern recording technology and other forms of communication have made available to the composer professional performances of folk and folklike music from around the world.

The gradual redefinition of folk that took place in the twentieth century often makes it difficult to categorize specific pieces that carry familiar labels. Take the blues, for example. At the beginning of the twentieth century, blues were rather neatly described by the definition of folk music given above: It was not notated, it communicated directly, it was accepted by large segments of the African-American population, and it was more or less anonymous. As the century progressed, the blues experienced a rebirth with a postmodern mixture of folk, commercial, and art music elements. Similar things have happened to country, bluegrass, jazz, and rock, all of which began as folk music. All have experienced some sort of commercialization. Jazz and some sorts of rock are now even referred to as art (or concert) music.

CONCERT MUSIC

Concert music is *intended primarily for the focused attention of the listener*. It most familiarly includes Western European art music ("classical"), a refined music, often requiring technically advanced musicians for performance. Great classical traditions also exist in other areas of the world, such as Japan, India, or the Middle East. In earlier times concert music was developed for and maintained by a cultural and economic elite. Music from our other three categories can be included in this category if it is presented in a concert setting. Consider for example the Mass or the sacred cantata, both pieces composed for a religious context but now typically taken out of their "ritual" setting and performed in a concert setting. In a similar fashion, many types of traditional folk music are transformed into concert music, often for a commercial purpose. And finally, to complete these connections, a concert setting is just one of several ways promoters can sell commercial music.

COMMERCIAL MUSIC

Music created for the primary purpose of generating revenue for the writers and performers can be considered **commercial**. Often the same individuals perform dual roles of composer and performer. This week's "top forty" will provide you with more than three dozen examples! Commercial music is primarily the product of twentieth-century technology and economics. However, connections with the other functions of music are obvious from a twenty-first century perspective. For example, the recordings of Gregorian chant that topped the charts in England in the 1990s reflect a commercialization of music created originally for ritual purposes. The commercialization of folk and concert music has already been mentioned.

Some might regret this blurring of categories. It does make it difficult or even impossible to make classifications absolutely clear. But we should remember that this is a part of *our* cultural environment. The availability of so many diverse varieties of cultural expression—art, literature, music, film, cuisine, clothing—surrounds us constantly. Perhaps a musical example from the world of American politics can demonstrate this. Forty years ago President Kennedy presented Pablo Casals, the great Spanish cellist, in concert at the White House. Also, during his short term in office, he sponsored American high school students who were classical musicians in performance there, too. The most recent ex-president played the saxophone. News sources reported four U.S. Senators singing barbershop quartet music in semipolitical public. What these reflect is the increasing recognition and celebration of a multiplicity of valid musical tastes.

We Americans, at the beginning of the twenty-first century, are able to capitalize on this diversity. Music, in its commercial aspect at least, embodies the concept of so-called "niche" markets that typifies commerce in our country today. There are so many discoveries in store for the curious listener.

Defining Ritual Music: What, When, and Where

Every morning you wake up, get out of bed, and get yourself ready for the day. Most of us do this with a certain pattern or sequence of events that has become comfortable (and effective) for us. This is our "routine" or our "ritual." Music can be a part of that ritual, whether it is turning on a CD or the radio or singing in the shower. Many other ordinary events involve such habits and repeated actions, even though we sometimes might want to reserve the word "ritual" for more significant activities.

The *Britannica Macropedia* states that "Ritual is a specific, observable kind of behavior based upon established or traditional rules." Music is often an important part of observable behavior that is a part of a ritual. However, "All rituals are dependent upon some belief system for their complete meaning." Music is easily divorced from its ritual context, and that separation potentially changes its "meaning." For example, in the early twenty-first century, "concert" or "secular" performances of "sacred" music reflect this change from an original ritual intent to some other context. Therefore, in considering ritual music, we often need to imagine its original context to understand what is "ritual" about it. On the other hand, we can draw some interesting parallels by considering this music independent of its strictly ritualistic functions. Many musical experiences stem from the use of ritual music no longer directly used in a ritual.

Music that functions as "ritual" is very often "sacred" music, music that enhances religious observances. In its formal uses, such music is an integral part of "liturgy," the official words, actions, music, and other behavior that constitute a specific religious ceremony. However, not all sacred music is ritual, and not all ritual music is sacred. Dramatic music portraying religious or sacred topics is not invariably ritual and certainly not liturgical. For example, consider Saint-Saëns' opera based on the story of Samson and Delilah or a Javanese shadow play illustrating an episode from the *Ramayana*. More familiar to you may be the musicals *Jesus Christ, Super Star* or *Joseph and the Amazing Technicolor Dreamcoat*. In a secular ritual, the U.S. presidential inauguration in Washington, D.C., is not aligned with any specific religion, under the provisions of the Constitution.

SMALL GROUP RITUALS

Some types of ritual are individual or concern only a relatively small group of people. In many instances, matters of daily life or survival are insured by the use of ritual. For example, the !Kung Bushmen (known as the *San* in their language) of the Nyae Nyae area of the Kalahari Desert in southwest Africa live an elemental life. The seminomadic Bushmen are hunters and gatherers and have no crops or herds. Although their music shares many characteristics with that of the Pygmies (whom they resemble physically and from whom they are probably an offshoot that migrated southward), there are noticeable differences. One is that the Pygmies have hunting dances while the Bushmen have none, devoting the largest part of their dancing to curing ceremonies. The Bushmen believe that two gods who live in the sky give them medicine songs, which have curative powers and can ward off evil spirits. These songs have titles taken from powerful images—of animals such as the eland and giraffe and of entities such as rain and sun. The songs are sung with dancing accompaniment at night around a fire. Women dance around the medicine men, singing while they dance.

The following listening example is characteristic. Like much African vocal music, this Giraffe Curing Ceremony consists of repeated melodic patterns supported by clapping and held notes in secondary voices. You will hear women singing and clapping while medicine men, who are in a trance, grunt and produce various other utterances that are thought to have a healing effect.

Giraffe Curing Ceremony, Bushmen, Africa

Active Listening
CD 2:14

- Sound fades in—three elements to begin:

   Rhythmic clicking and clapping
   Shouts or cheering
   Melody: four descending notes repeated throughout, often sounding like background.

- Rhythmic grunting sounds
- Three or four high shouts
- Rhythmic "heavy breathing"
- Five high shouts
- Melody becomes louder, more foregrounded.
- Sound fades quickly at the end.

   As you listen to the recording:

   Try singing the constant note that the inner voices are singing.
   Clap your hands with the rhythm.
   Imitate the grunting and the "heavy breathing" that goes on.

Other contexts for musical rituals include sporting events, where the playing of the national anthem is part of the beginning ritual. Later on, fans shout out rhythmic cheers. Specific musicians or groups, like the pep band at a basketball game or the marching band at a football game, are likewise part of the musical rituals at a sporting event. One well-known example of a musical sports ritual was the late Harry Carey singing "Take Me out to the Ball Game" during the seventh-inning stretch at Chicago Cubs baseball games.

Fraternal organizations, although not as common as they once were, usually have elaborate rituals that are kept secret. The feeling of belonging that these groups engender involves shared experiences—including musical ones—that are exclusive to the group. Examples can be hard to come by, owing to the customary secrecy that such groups maintain, especially about their rituals. Historically, however, we can demonstrate the musical connection. The eighteenth-century composers Wolfgang Amadeus Mozart and Franz Joseph Haydn both belonged to a Masonic lodge in Vienna during the 1780s. Mozart composed music for their rituals, which has come to be known outside the lodge due to his fame and importance.

When large groups of people gather for special events, activities can become even more recognizably ritualistic. For example, academic graduations are important milestones in most of our lives. And the association of those events with the march "Pomp and Circumstance" by the British composer Edward Elgar has become very well known. Weddings, particularly in the United States, are associated with two processional marches (by German composers Richard Wagner and Felix Mendelssohn) that were originally parts of stage works but have become nearly obligatory in the traditional ritual of the marriage ceremony. Other traditional musical components of a wedding include the singing of a love song and the dance music performed after the ceremony at a reception.

Funerals and memorial services involve ritual mourning music. A notable example is the slow movement of the second Piano Sonata by Polish composer Frédéric Chopin, a funeral march. Played by a band, it is used in actual funeral processions. Formal political or military funeral processions include muffled drumming that conducts the mourners along the route to the interment. The bugle call "taps" is so much a symbol of a funeral that it has become the representative sound piece used on American news programs for any important death announcement. The biblical description of the Last Judgment heralded by trumpets has inspired numerous artworks and musical compositions incorporating the instrument because of the written association.

CEREMONIES FOR PUBLIC OFFICIALS AND THE NOBILITY

Happier events include celebration of heroes or inauguration of public officials. Announcement of such events and the entry of the person to be honored have long been associated with trumpet fanfares. Think of the pomp of an English coronation or the various royal weddings that have been televised over the past 20 years. Even historically, the use of "herald trumpets" is well documented. Trumpets and trumpetlike instruments are a cross-cultural phenomenon. Archaeological sites provide evidence that trumpets were valued enough to be interred with important persons.

Active Listening
CD 2:15

Fanfare Welcoming the Sultan of Zinder, Niger

This selection is from the country of Niger, bordering the southern Sahara. Niger has been strongly influenced by Arab traders from the north, who converted most of the population (about 80%) to the Islamic faith and influenced many other aspects of their culture, including their music.

In this recording a fanfare is played by the sultan's orchestra welcoming and honoring him at public appearances. It features, in addition to African per-

Robert Washburn

African transverse
trumpet player

cussion of drums and metallic instruments, two *kakakis*, long straight-out copper or brass trombones (without slides), which play two notes each, and a double reed instrument, the *algaita*, which is like our oboe but without keys and
with open holes to be fingered to change the pitches as on a fife.

The music is very repetitive, and it should be remembered that its function is to enhance a ceremony and not to be heard as concert music. The
kakakis play the same figure over and over, as do the drums, while the oboe
part is also repetitive but varies its pattern slightly from time to time. The
oboist uses a technique called "circular breathing," which involves inhaling
through the nostrils while retaining a closed-off pocket of air in the mouth
which is blown into the instrument, maintaining a continuous sound. Try
this—without the instrument, of course.

Even when a large audience is not present, noble or royal courts can have
elaborate rituals that accompany day-to-day activities or function as entertainment. As an example, consider Japanese court music. Chinese musical instruments were adapted for use in Japanese court music rituals. The principal
musical style is called *gagaku*, "elegant music"; it was traditionally administered
through an official music bureau. It exists in several categories: *bugaku* is dance
music that has two principal forms, *komagaku* and *togaku*. *Komagaku* derives
from Korean and Manchurian sources, and the dancers wear primarily green
costumes. *Togaku* contains elements of Indian and Chinese music, and the

dancers wear red costumes. Gagaku is called *kangen* when it is performed instrumentally without dancing. When used for dancing, *gagaku* employs several wind instruments: the *sho,* sounding like our harmonica; the *hichiriki,* a double reed instrument sounding like our oboe; and the *ryutiki,* a type of flute. Various drums of differing sizes are also used. When *gagaku* is performed as concert music, two string instruments, the *koto* (a zither) and the *biwa* (a plucked lute), are added. The following musical example includes some of the instruments of the *gagaku* tradition. You will notice how sparse the music is, just right for ritual contemplation. The slow pace and minimal melodic notes are gracefully enhanced by the bending of pitches.

LISTENING GUIDE

Hyojo Netori, Japan

CD 2:16

00:00   *sho* (organlike sound; chords)

00:06   *hichiriki* (oboelike sound; slow melody with very few notes; bending of pitches)

00:25   *kakko* (drum; strokes begin slow and get faster)

00:38   *ryutiki* (flute; continues melody; *sho* and *hichiriki* drop out)

Koto players

Robert Washburn

MILITARY RITUALS

Military organizations have evolved many distinctive rituals and ceremonies. Turkey evolved an interesting variety of music: Janizary or Mehter music, military band music played by horse-mounted musicians who accompanied troops into battle. In the late-seventeenth century, Turkish armies reached the gates of Vienna before the Austrians drove them back. Their music, played by wind instruments and percussion, was intended to stir the soldiers' feelings of patriotism and build their courage to fight their adversaries. Patriotic texts were sometimes sung.

"Ceddin Deden," Turkish Military Band Music
of the Ottoman Empire

**LISTENING
GUIDE**

CD 2:17

00:00   *zurnas* (oboelike instruments), *nakkare* and *davul* (drums), and *zil* (cymbals)

Verse 1—Phrase pattern a a b c c. Vocal with *nakkare* and *davul*

00:20   a phrase

00:25   a phrase

00:29   b phrase

00:34   c phrase

00:42   c phrase

00:51   *zurnas*, *nakkare*, *davul*, and *zil*

Verse 2—Same phrase pattern as first verse

1:10   vocal with *nakkare* and *davul*

1:40   *zurnas*, *nakkare*, *davul*, and *zil* return and end

---

You might notice the march meter and rhythmic patterns. Another interesting feature is the repetition of the last phrase in a section (c c in the verses and f f in the interlude). Viennese imitations of this music became popular in the eighteenth century and later influenced Haydn, Mozart, and Beethoven, who wrote some "Turkish" styled pieces. The inclusion of the triangle and cymbals in the percussion section of symphony orchestras and symphonic bands resulted from this Turkish influence. Several of these style characteristics were regular features of the military march.

CROSSROADS

"THE STARS AND STRIPES FOREVER," JOHN PHILIP SOUSA

In the United States, much military music has become known beyond the contexts and constraints of military ritual. Our most famous march, "The Stars and Stripes Forever," is the product of the mind and pen of a Marine Corps bandleader, John Philip Sousa. Sousa (1854–1932) was famous as a band director and composer of marches. He served as leader of the United States Marine Band from 1880 to 1892, setting the standard of excellence for which it continues to be known today. In 1892, Sousa formed his own band with which he toured the world, giving over ten thousand concerts — the most popular elements of which were always marches he had written. His band introduced ragtime to European audiences, adding an international dimension to this American craze. At the turn of the twentieth century, a music historian wrote, "There is probably no composer in the world with a popularity equal to that of Sousa." Band music had been a part of our tradition since the Revolutionary War. Sousa reinvented its central feature, the military march, making it a uniquely American musical statement.

The musical design of marches is often an alternation of clearly marked march sections with trio sections. The term "trio" comes from the fact that originally these sections were played by only three performers. Reflecting its past, the trio is usually played softly — at least when it first appears.

LISTENING GUIDE	"Stars and Stripes Forever," John Philip Sousa

CD 1:9

00:00		Introduction
00:03	A	march theme
00:17	A	repeat
00:30	B	contrasting style, more lyrical woodwind melody
00:44	B	repeat
00:58	C	trio legato melody, much softer
1:25	D	break strain, boisterous descending passages
1:47	C'	trio theme combined with piccolo solo
2:14	D	break strain repeat
2:36	C"	trio theme in trumpets, piccolo solo with trombone countermelody added

Now that we have covered some of the ways that ritual music intersects with your life and is integral to rituals around the world, we can move on to some specific views of this type of music. The first of these is music that was created specifically for use in religious services.

CHAPTER

12

Ritual Music as Part of a Religious Service

CHANT

The association of music with sacred rituals is very old. References in the Bible and other ancient texts highlight the importance of music to the formal religious experience. *Music that plays a prescribed role in religious ritual* is called **liturgical music.** The beginning of a ritual can be announced by music—the ringing of bells, a fanfare by loud instruments, or a simple call to prayer or worship.

The Muslim call to prayer, the *adhan*, is sung five times a day from the top of minarets on mosques by a *muezzin* (although, regrettably, in recent years, a real person has been frequently replaced by a loudspeaker and a recording). Since he sings the call in the open air, he places his flattened palms facing forward on either side of his mouth to project the sound and sings in a rather high pitch range for increased audibility. He praises the greatness of Allah and chants texts from the Koran, the holy book of Islam.

Recitation of sacred texts is part of most ritual ceremony or liturgy. These texts may simply be read aloud, but more often they are chanted according to some musical formula.

Adhan, The *Muezzin's* Call to Prayer	LISTENING GUIDE

CD 2:4

00:00	a	begins with a pitch rise to a high sustained note ("Allah"); continues descending to final word: ("akbar") (Allah is Great)
00:10	a′	varied repetition of the same
00:20	b	begins lower; ends with high sustained note
00:30	c	continuous pitch variation until fade out

CROSSROADS   Bells are associated with ritual in many different cultures and for several purposes. At a Buddhist temple, for example, ringing certain bells three times brings good luck or wish fulfillment. The ringing of a bell has for centuries signaled the highpoint of the Roman Catholic Mass, the Elevation of the Host. In this instance, it serves the practical purpose of letting people who are not actually in attendance know that the special moment has arrived. The peal of a carillon celebrates the presentation outside the cathedral of a newly married royal couple in England. In other, less religious, contexts, bells accompany the rituals of military ship boarding and the changing of the watch. A school bell signals both the beginning and the end of a class period. A bell signals the beginning and the ending of a boxing round. It seems somehow fitting that even Pavlov's dogs ended up with bells signaling their ritual of eating!

Gregorian chant plays an important role in much Western European art music. It is so named because of the medieval tradition that God dictated the text and music of the Church's liturgy to Pope Gregory the Great (ca. 600). Actually, the music and texts developed over many centuries and only gradually came to be viewed as the unified collection of sacred songs that constitutes the liturgy of the Church. Its appeal is evident in the simplicity of its musical elements and in the strong religious association with such sounds. **Chant** is *monophonic music performed by singers,* often a soloist and choir in alternation. It uses a *limited range of pitches* and *free rhythms* often reflecting the rhythms of the words. The text is usually Latin and is determined by the function of the Church's ceremonies. A highly elaborate set of appropriate texts underlies the individual daily services (the *Mass* and the *Offices*) arranged in the church year (Advent or Lent, for example). Some texts, called *Proper,* are appropriate only to a specific day (for example, Easter Sunday) or to a season (for example, Lent). Others, called *Ordinary,* are appropriate on many occasions, some even called for every time a particular type of service is performed. The Greek invocation *Kyrie eleison* is the first Ordinary text of the Mass.

Active Listening
CD 1:13

Kyrie XI (Kyrie Orbis Factor), Gregorian chant

a	two singers	*Kyrie eleison*	Lord have mercy
a	entire chorus	*Kyrie eleison*	
b	two singers	*Christe eleison*	Christ have mercy
b	entire chorus	*Christe eleison*	
a	two singers	*Kyrie eleison*	Lord have mercy
a'	entire chorus	*Kyrie eleison*	

- Notice the subtle difference in sound you hear between the pair of singers and the group.
- The letters a and b point out where the beginnings of the phrases are alike, but you also might hear that the endings of both a and b are also alike.
- A liturgically complete rendering of this chant would include three statements of all three units. Did you hear that in this example the statements *Kyrie eleison* and *Christe eleison* are sung only twice, not three times?

Among the influential characteristics of Gregorian chant is formal repetition. In a Kyrie, for example, you most often hear each of the musical phrases sung three times. These threefold statements have some religious significance, reflecting as they do the Christian idea of the Trinity (father, son, holy ghost). They also fulfill a musical need. Statement and immediate repetition *(Kyrie eleison)* provide familiarity with the musical material. After a new musical idea provides contrast *(Christe eleison)*, a return to the original idea *(Kyrie eleison)* provides coherence. The musical pattern is one that has persisted in Western European music for centuries: *A B A,* or *ternary.* Other formal designs involve repetition of entire musical/textual units called stanzas or strophes. Hymns provide the best example of this formal type. *Each stanza of text is sung to the same music.* This is called **strophic form.** More freely composed chant melodies conform to the phrases of the text and do not necessarily show such symmetry. There may be internal repetition, but not the predictable nature of strophic or ABA forms.

Staatiche Museum; Berlin

Monk by the Seashore,
Casper D. Friedrich

"Dies irae"

Further developments in chant used other, original formal organizational patterns. The chant type known as sequence is an example. **Sequences** are composed of *paired verses of text sung to single musical phrases*. A famous sequence, the "Dies irae" (attributed to the thirteenth-century Thomas of Celano), is well known for its melody and its association with death. It forms part of the Requiem Mass, or the Mass for the Dead. Because of this association, composers have borrowed it over the centuries to relate to death in their compositions; the first eight notes especially have come to suggest some association with death or the afterlife.

In this excerpt, *most syllables are sung to a single note*. This type of **syllabic** text setting is different from the *Kyrie* in the example above. There, *many notes are sung for each text syllable*, a text setting called **melismatic.** An interesting formal feature in the Dies irae is the complicated repetition of the phrases. The segment *abc* repeats immediately (the paired verses mentioned above). It also returns near the end of the excerpt in another pair. The segment b returns alone in the third and fourth strophes without a or c.

Active Listening
CD 2:18

"Dies irae," Gregorian chant (excerpt)

a	*Dies irae, dies ille*	Day of anger, that day
b	*Solvet saeclum in favilla*	will dissolve the world in ashes
c	*Teste David cum Sibylla.*	as witness David and Sibyl.
a	*Quantus tremor est futurus,*	What trembling there will be
b	*Quando judex est venturus,*	when the judge shall come,
c	*Cuncta stricte discussurus!*	all shall thoroughly be shattered!
d	*Tuba mirum spargens sonum*	The wondrous trumpet, spreading its sound
b	*Per sepulcra regionum,*	throughout the tombs of all regions,
e	*Coget omnes ante thronum.*	will gather all before the throne.
d	*Mors stupebit et natura,*	Death will be stupefied, also nature,
b	*Cum resurget creatura,*	when all creation arises
e	*Judicanti responsura.*	to answer to the judge.
f	*Liber scriptus proferetur,*	A written book will be brought forth
g	*In quo totum continetur,*	in which everything is contained,
h	*Unde mundus judicetur.*	by which the world will be judged.
f	*Judex ergo cum sedebit,*	When the judge is seated,
g	*Quidquid latet apparebit*	whatever is hidden will be exposed;
h	*Nil inultum remanebit.*	nothing will remain unavenged.

a	*Quid sum miser tunc dicturus?*	What am I, miserable one!, then to say?
b	*Quem patronum rogaturus*	What patron shall I request,
c	*Cum vix justus sit securus?*	when the righteous are scarcely secure?
a	*Rex tremendae majestatis,*	King of dreadful majesty!
b	*Qui salvandos salvas gratis,*	who freely saves the redeemed,
c	*Salva me, fons pietatis.*	save me, fount of mercy.

Much sacred ritual music is chant. It seems appropriate for the human voice to sing in unison so the words may be understood. Indeed, most of us think of religious events or something sacred when we hear chant. It is interesting that so much variety of sound and effect is possible with such limited musical means. Even so, the human impulse to elaborate or ornament is strong. This can be accomplished by such simple means as including instruments with the chanting or by developing special musical devices that supplement the original chant, occasionally to the detriment of an easy understanding of the text.

TSHETRO JINEB, BUDDHIST RITUAL

Buddhist ritual music can be exceptionally colorful. Various instruments may accompany the chant, including a single hand bell, a pair of small cymbals, a long copper natural (no valves) trumpet called the *dung-chen,* and a double-reed wind instrument, the *surna.* The long trumpets (six to nine feet) are used to accompany the chant when it is sung outdoors; while indoors, shorter trumpets are used. In earlier times, and sometimes in the present, these were fashioned from a human thighbone. This use is thought to symbolize the transitory nature of human life ("Here today, gone tomorrow"), while it is the spiritual life that endures. The double-reed instruments supply preludes and interludes to the singing.

Tshetro Jineb is an invocation to the Buddha of Boundless Life, an example of ritual music. "By ceasing to think of my body and its senses I become merged in the void." In this example we hear a chorus of monks, two *surnas,* two *dung-chen,* two large drums, cymbals, and a smaller drum.

Tshetro Jineb, Buddhist Ritual

LISTENING GUIDE

CD 2:19

00:00   rhythmic chanting, low-pitched voices, gradually becoming louder

00:08   *surna* melody, ornamented, bending pitches followed by long held note, punctuated by drum beat

00:09   low-pitched *dung-chen* drone connects sections

00:37   voices chant in time to drums, seven-note groups

Buddhist monks, pilgrims, and tourists at the temple of Swayambhunath

Lhasa Tokulhmandu; NGS

CHANT IN POLYPHONIC SETTINGS

The conception of music consisting of more than one strand of sound going on at once is a part of many musical traditions. However, the elaboration of this process and its systematization in Western European art music is especially significant. The conscious manipulation of melodic strands to weave a musical fabric is so deeply ingrained in our music that it is difficult to imagine it not happening. We can see the origins of the process among the earliest preserved examples of European music. Gregorian chant was sometimes embellished to enhance the musical effect, and not incidentally to honor important events or occasions. This elaboration occurred in a number of ways. Important in the process, however, was the preservation of the "God-given" melody, the original chant. Combining new melodic strands with the original chant seems to be the origin of *polyphony* and our polyphonic tradition. The cultivation of independent melodies led to an integration of them in "harmonious" patterns, combinations of pitches that "sound" good. As described in Chapter 5, this effect is what we know as *harmony*. But the earliest efforts in polyphony were not concerned with chords, but rather with agreeable combinations of melodies.

Conductus are *vocal compositions used during processions*. Conductus are either monophonic or polyphonic, filling a middle ground between monophonic chant and polyphonic chant elaboration, though not actually based upon chant. Composers writing polyphony faced the problem of coordinating melodies rhythmically. Conductus solve this problem by having the various melodies move roughly in the same time with the same words. This means that the independence of the various melodies involves pitches rather than rhythms. The result sounds as much like a succession of chords as a super-position of melodies.

Active Listening
CD 2:20

Ave Virgo Virginum à 3, **Anonymous**

- Listen for three voice parts, moving mostly by step over phrases of two or three lines of text
- Notice how the highest- or the lowest-sounding voices sometimes have motion when the two other voices don't. This gives considerable variety to the basic long-short rhythmic pattern that dominates the piece in triple meter.

Verse 1

a	*Ave, virgo virginum*	Hail, virgin of virgins,
	verbi carnis cella,	shrine of the word made flesh,
a	*in salutem hominum*	who for man's salvation
	stillans lac et mella.	does distill milk and honey.
b	*Peperisti dominum,*	You did bear the Lord,
	Moysi fiscella,	and were a basket of rushes to Moses;
c	*et radio*	from your rays
	sol exit, et luminum	the sun shines forth, and the star
	fontem parit stella.	brings forth the source of light.

Verse 2

a	*Ave, plena gratia,*	Hail, you who are full of grace;
	caput Zabulonis	on Satan's head
a	*contrivisti spolia*	you have trampled, the spoil
	reparans predonis.	of robbers have you restored.
b	*Celi rorans pluvia*	O you who shed rain from heaven,
	vellus Gedeonis,	fleece of Gideon,
c	*o filio*	intercede for us
	tu nos reconcilia,	with your son,
	mater Salomonis.	mother of Solomon!

Verse 3

a	*Virgo tu mosayce*	Virgin who did see
	rubus visionis,	Moses' thornbush,
a	*de te fluxit sylice*	from your rock flows
	fons redemptionis.	the fount of redemption.

b	*Quos redemit calice*	Those whom Christ has redeemed
	Christus passionis,	through the chalice of His Passion,
c	*o gaudio*	O, with joy
	induat glorifice	He clothes in the glory
	resurrectionis.	of His resurrection.

"VIDERUNT OMNES," *ORGANUM QUADRUPLUM*, PEROTIN

Another technique of creating polyphony evolved from efforts to make the melodic lines independent not only in pitches but also in rhythmic activity. Organum was at first a general term for any music with several melodies but later became an elaboration of chant that differentiated the rhythmic activity among the two or more musical voices. The chant, sung by the lowest of the voices, was sustained in long notes, leaving little to recognize of the original melody. Over this *tenor* ("held out") voice, one or more additional melodies were spun out, chantlike in their conception. The rhythmic coordination was eventually achieved by having the upper melodies sing in rhythmic patterns (rhythmic modes) that created the pulsating of a beat, very much like *conductus*. Perotin was a Parisian musician who lived at the turn of the thirteenth century. He seems to have been associated with the church of Notre Dame, where he possibly succeeded the composer Leonin. The organum *Viderunt omnes* is an elaboration of an *Introit*, the first part of the Mass Proper that is sung on Christmas Day. As was the custom, Perotin elaborated only certain words with polyphony, leaving much of the Introit performed monophonically. The excerpt here consists of only the first two words. In the rest of the work you would hear chant sung in alternation with the vibrant sounds of the organum sections. Notice that sections occur when the long-held note either articulates another syllable of the text or changes pitch. Woven around that "tenor" voice are the remaining three voices, singing a long-short pattern that creates groupings usually of four pulses. The effect is quite hypnotic. The full text reads as follows.

Viderunt omnes fines terrae salutare	All the ends of the earth shall see the
Dei nostri:	salvation of our God:
Jubilate Deo omnis terra.	All the earth shall rejoice in God.
Notum fecit Dominus salutare suum	The Lord has made known His salvation
ante conspectum gentium.	before the face of all the peoples.
Revelavit iustitiam suam.	He has revealed His righteousness.

Although much chant is religious, there are other associations with chanting. A crowd chanting in unison at a sporting event or at a political demonstration comes to mind. Yet, the seven examples we have studied in this chapter are unmistakably religious. This comes in part from particular words that are easily understood (invoking the deity, Allah or Kyrie, for example). The sound itself, usually intimate and quietly expressive, has become a part of our collective musical experience and expectation of things sacred.

"Viderunt Omnes," *Organum quadruplum* (excerpt), Perotin

CD 2:21

00:00	*Vi-*	long note sustained by all voices
00:12		rhythmic motion begins, repetition of four-pulse groups, tenor sustained
00:58	*de-*	new syllable, continuation of patterns, tenor sustains on same pitch
1:26	*runt*	different pitch for tenor, long note all voices
1:28		rhythmic activity begins
2:29	*om-*	rhythmic activity begins immediately
3:40	*nes*	long-held notes bring to close

LISTENING GUIDE

CHAPTER

Double Duty: Sacred Music In and Outside the Church

13

THE EVOLUTION OF NONLITURGICAL RELIGIOUS MUSIC

At several points in the history of religious music, long-standing style features were gradually phased out. In Western musical culture, one major change involved the disappearance of the melody (musical notes) of chant as part of the fabric of a polyphonic composition. What resulted were entirely "new" musical settings of religious texts. Such compositions were not always used in religious services but often performed in concert or settings other than the church.

Josquin Desprez (ca. 1440–1521) is generally considered the master composer of the Renaissance. Josquin came of age in the fifteenth century, and he followed some of the typical career steps for that time, possibly singing in Milan at the Cathedral and later at the Ducal court and the Papal Chapel, and having associations with the courts of Ferrara and the Collegiate Church at Condé. He had a reputation as an outstanding singer and composer, and as an individual was known as someone who was not especially willing to bow to an employer's every request.

The many **motets**, *polyphonic settings of sacred Latin texts*, that Josquin wrote display the individuality and skill in text setting for which he is most famous. Sometimes he followed the traditional pattern, using chant melodies to construct a composition. In other instances he led in the evolutionary process

LISTENING GUIDE	*Ave Maria, gratia plena à 4*, Josquin Desprez		
	CD 2:22		
	00:00	Four voices, beginning with the highest voice, enter at different times but sing same musical phrase—in imitation	1	*Ave Maria, gratia plena.* Hail Mary, full of grace.
	00:17	On *gratia*, new imitation, voices enter in the same order	1b	
	00:38	Variation of musical line 1, same order of imitation	2	*Dominum tecum, virgo serena.* The Lord is with you, gentle Virgin.
	1:00	Variation of musical line 1b, same order of imitation	2b	
	1:17	Two upper voices, followed by three lower voices	3	*Ave cujus conceptio,* Hail, whose conception,
	1:41	All voices sing lines 4–6 together in chords (homophonic), then in close imitation (polyphonic) melisma at the end of the section on *laetitia*	4	*Solemni plena gaudio,* Full of solemn joy,
			5	*Caelestia, terrestria,* Fills the heaven, the earth,
			6	*Nova replet laetitia.* With new rejoicing.
	2:18	Two upper voices in imitation	7	*Ave cujus nativitas* Hail, whose birth
	2:30	Two lower voices in imitation, repeating music of line 7	8	*Nostra fuit solemnitas,* Was our festival.
	2:44	All four voices in imitation	9	*Ut lucifer lux oriens* As the light-bringing rising light
	3:00	All four voices, in closer imitation, ending on a long note	10	*Verum solem praeveniens.* Coming before the true sun.

described above and composed entirely new music. His *Ave Maria, gratia plena* for four voices is an example of this latter practice. It combines several different musical textures. At the beginning *each voice enters, one after the other, singing the same musical line in an overlapping fashion.* This procedure is called **imitation.** Later, the voices appear two, three, or all four at a time. They combine in a fluent nonimitative polyphony, highlighting the successive repetitions of the text. Finally, all four voices come together in chords bringing the work to a conclusion.

3:18	Two upper voices	11	*Ave pia humilitas,* Hail pious humility,
3:25	Two lower voices, repeating 11	12	*Sine viro faecunditas,* Fertility without a man,
3:33	Two upper voices, variation of 11	13	*Cujus annunciatio* Whose annunciation
3:45	Two lower voices, ending on a long note	14	*Nostra fuit pergatio.* Was our salvation.
4:00	All voices sing text lines 15–18 in nearly chordal harmony	15	*Ave vera virginitas,* Hail true virginity.
	Change in triple meter	16	*Immaculata castitas,* Unspotted chastity
		17	*Cujus purificatio* Whose purification
		18	*Nostra fuit pergatio.* Was our cleansing.
4:38	Two upper voices, followed by three lower voices	19	*Ave praeclara omnibus* Hail, famous with all
5:00	Repetition of 19	20	*Angelicus virtutibus,* Angelic virtues,
5:21	Two upper voices, followed by three lower voices	21	*Cujus fuit assumptio* Whose assumption was
5:38	Two upper voices, followed by three lower voices	22	*Nostra glorificatio.* Our glorification.
6:02	All voices sing text lines 23–25 in chords	23	*O Mater Dei,* O Mother of God,
		24	*Memento mei.* Remember Me.
		25	*Amen.* Amen.

USING INSTRUMENTS IN SACRED MUSIC

The end of the Renaissance and the beginning of the baroque period in music history signal an important change in sacred vocal music. Chanting and chant elaboration continue their liturgical function. However, sacred compositions that are predominantly vocal begin to have instrumental components that are indispensable to the musical fabric. In performance, earlier compositions sometimes added instruments to the vocal lines or even replaced voices with instruments. Now, musical lines specifically for instruments are composed as integral parts of the musical composition. This feature of the music of the seventeenth, eighteenth, and nineteenth centuries becomes so prevalent that **a cappella** (unaccompanied choral) music becomes a less-important sub-species of vocal composition, recognized for its importance but not for its grand effect. Music *using voices and instruments together*, performed "in concert" (together), came to be known by the terms *concertato* or **concerto** (more on this in Chapter 22). It is no mere coincidence that the beginnings of independent instrumental music or the invention of opera, discussed in other chapters, occur at the same time as the development of a "concerted vocal music." With the increasing secularization of life in general and changes in venue for listening to music, sacred music comes more and more to resemble secular music in its musical content. The association with the texts, however, keeps the focus sacred no matter what the performing venue.

An example of this is the Bach cantata. Johann Sebastian Bach (1685–1750) stands at the peak of the development of a type of music associated with the German Evangelical (Lutheran) Church. Bach has attained an importance in Western European music equaled by few other composers. Yet, he remained a musician obligated to the conventions and employment opportunities of his time. As cantor of the Thomasschule in Leipzig from 1723 until his death, he was responsible not only for coordinating and composing the music for the four major churches of the city, but also for the education of the choirboys and for the maintenance of the musical instruments.

A **cantata** (the word in its initial literal meaning indicates something that is sung) was *a type of seventeenth-century secular music related to opera*. The German Lutheran cantata adapted some of the musical characteristics of the secular cantata to a religious context. Cantatas were composed to provide edifying music for the Lutheran service. Texts deal with the topic for the day, in the manner of the Proper texts in the Roman Catholic Church. The music makes use of all the potential musical forces, voices, and instruments that may be available in the church for which the work was written.

The cantatas of Bach are the finest examples of this musical form. Bach cantatas are 15- to 30-minute works consisting of texts that are taken from

Bach's cantatas were heard both in and outside the church. He wrote cantatas using both sacred and secular texts. While there were some musical differences, both types employed set numbers such as recitative and aria, used continuo, and included instrumental ensembles. All of these musical traits were characteristic of contemporary opera, a clearly secular style. Ironically, sacred cantatas are most often heard today in a secular concert setting.

CROSSROADS

© Dave Bartruff/CORBIS

A statue of Johann Sebastian Bach, Eisenach, Germany

chorales (see below), Biblical texts, or new poetry (often written in the poetic forms of opera—recitative and aria). The music that sets these texts is just as varied. Movements for chorus, either with or without independent instrumental parts, alternate with movements for solo singers. These movements employ the ever-present **continuo**, *a notated bass line* performed by a melodic instrument (cello, bassoon, or other bass instrument) *together with an improvised accompaniment* usually performed by a keyboard instrument. The arrangement of the various movements consists of alternations of the choral, solo, and instrumental sections. The use of so-called chorale texts and melodies marks these works as specifically appropriate to the German Lutheran tradition. **Chorales** are the melodies associated with *strophic religious texts* that came to be used in the Lutheran tradition. They came about because Martin Luther encouraged the musical participation of a church congregation, singing tunes with words in a language they understood (German). These chorales became an important part of many of the cantatas of the seventeenth and eighteenth centuries.

CANTATA 140, FIRST MOVEMENT, "WACHET AUF," JOHANN SEBASTIAN BACH

Bach's Cantata 140, "Wachet auf, ruft uns die Stimme," provides an outstanding example of the use of chorale. This cantata was written for performance in November (the twenty-seventh Sunday after the feast of Trinity). It consists of seven movements. Selected stanzas of the chorale text along with its associated

---

LISTENING GUIDE	Cantata 140, First Movement, "Wachet auf," Johann Sebastian Bach

CD 2:23

A Section

00:00	Instrumental introduction		
	Strings and oboes in alternation set up the triple meter with running notes emerging in the strings.		
	Continuo		
00:28	Voices enter. Soprano sings chorale in slow-moving tones. Other voices sing at a faster rhythmic pace.	1.	*Wachet auf, ruft uns die Stimme* "Awake," the voice of watchmen
00:44	Instrumental interlude		
00:49	Voices (as before)	2.	*Der Wächter sehr hoch auf der Zinne,* calls us from high on the tower,
1:06	Instrumental interlude		
1:14	Voices	3.	*Wach auf, du Stadt Jerusalem!* "Awake, you town Jerusalem!"

A Section Repeats with Lines 4, 5, and 6 of the Text

1:32	Instrumental introduction		
2:00	Voices	4.	*Mitternacht heisst diese Stunde;* Midnight is this hour;
2:15	Instrumental interlude		
2:21	Voices	5.	*Sie rufen uns mit hellem Munde:* they call to us with bright voices:

tune appear in the first, fourth, and seventh movements, all performed by the chorus or a part of it, accompanied by instruments. One can see that the text creates an "a a b" pattern among the groups of lines. The tune matches that form. It is heard in each of the three framing movements, surrounded by active moving lines or harmonized by additional three-voice parts. The other movements are based on new texts by an unknown poet forming two recitative-duet pairs (movements 2 and 3 and 5 and 6).

The first movement of Cantata 140 features the chorus accompanied by an orchestra contrasting the timbre of oboes with that of strings, all supported by a continuo group. The oboes and strings sometimes alternate motives, sometimes

2:38	Instrumental interlude		
2:46	Voices	6.	*Wo seid ihr klugen Jungfrauen?* "Where are you, wise virgins?
B Section			
3:04	Instrumental interlude		
3:24	Voices	7.	*Wohl auf, der Bräutgam kömmt,* Take cheer, the Bridegroom comes,
3:37	Instrumental interlude		
3:42	Voices	8.	*Steht auf, die Lampen nehmt!* arise, take up your lamps!
3:57	Voices in imitation Alto enters on long note.	9.	*Alleluja!* Alleluja!
4:33	Instrumental interlude		
4:42	Voices (as in lines 1–8)	10.	*Macht euch bereit* Prepare yourselves
4:52	Instrumental interlude		
4:58	Voices	11.	*Zu der Hochzeit,* for the wedding,
5:14	Voices	12.	*Ihr müsset ihm entgegengehn!* you must go forth to meet him."
5:32	Instrumental closing repeats introduction.		

share them. The orchestra provides a frame around the vocal parts—an introduction, conclusion, and interludes. The soprano part sings the chorale melody, while underneath it the alto, tenor, and bass voices sing it one after the other, overlapping, at a faster rhythmic pace. The whole movement represents the sort of rhythmic continuity typical of baroque music; once the meter and rhythmic patterns are established they don't pause until the very end.

GOSPEL MUSIC: A PART OF THE SERVICE AND THE CULTURE

Several types of contemporary religious ritual music are at home in both the service and in public performance. This is often the case for **gospel music,** *African-American singing enthusiastically affirmative of the singers' religious faith.* In a recording made in the Abyssinian Baptist Church in Newark, New Jersey, the singers number about 100. They give an accurate representation of the excitement of African-American gospel singing in congregations as well as choirs. Listen to the electronic organ providing background to the lead singer and the congregation who sing in a call and response pattern. Notice how clapping helps to articulate the beat of the song. The words are repetitive and vary only slightly over the several verses heard here. Variety occurs with the unpredictable return of the refrain and the "voices-only" section toward the end of the example.

Active Listening
CD 2:24

"Said I Wasn't Gonna Tell Nobody," Alex Bradford

- Introduction
- Verse 1 (repeat)
- Refrain
- Verse 2
- Verse 3
- Refrain (repeat)
- Voices only, instruments drop out
- Close with instruments

Out of this rich gospel music tradition came many innovative popular singers, such as Ray Charles, James Brown, Sam Cooke, Aretha Franklin, Wilson Pickett, and Whitney Houston. Houston's mother, Cissy Houston, is a gospel singer with a strong blues and rhythm and blues (R&B) orientation. Her recent recordings continue to draw rave reviews.

The religious origins of the musical examples in this chapter remain clear. Their musical styles, however, are subject to influences from nonsacred music.

Ritual Music with Added Dimensions

PALESTRINA AND THE COUNTER REFORMATION

Next to Josquin, the most famous Renaissance composer is Giovanni Pierluigi da Palestrina (ca. 1525–1594). Palestrina spent his entire career in Italy, most of it in Rome, employed by the religious organizations of the Catholic Church. He participated in the reforms of the Catholic liturgy and its music during the time when the Roman Church was feeling challenged by the ideas of the Protestant Reformation. Palestrina's compositions are intimately associated with the Counter Reformation and have come to represent most vividly the connection between a cappella vocal polyphony and church music. Well into the baroque era, Palestrina's music continued to be held up as the model for Catholic church music.

Palestrina's best-known composition embodying his concepts is the *Missa Papae Marcelli* (Pope Marcellus Mass). This Mass has become part of a legend

CORBIS

J. Hodgson Sculp.

Palestrina presents
Pope Marcellus with
his new Mass

LISTENING GUIDE

Missa Papae Marcelli, Kyrie, Giovanni Pierluigi da Palestrina

CD 2:1

Kyrie eleison

00:05	four quick entries in middle and upper voices, then chordal sound
00:08	lower voices emerge
00:17	repetition of short phrases
00:34	even sound, no obvious breaks
1:21	descending line to cadence

Christe eleison

1:26	upper voices, followed by lower voices in imitation
1:58	all voices share a descending motive in imitation
2:23	even sound, no obvious breaks
2:54	ends with incomplete cadence

Kyrie eleison

3:00	two high voices, followed quickly by two middle voices
	all voices combine to form:
3:07	regular succession of chords
3:39	stepwise lines
4:02	increasing rhythmic activity until end

in which Palestrina saved polyphony as a musical expression appropriate for church services in the face of reforms suggesting that Gregorian chant should be the only appropriate music. The six voices that comprise the musical texture sometimes sing independent melodies and sometimes create chords succeeding one on the other. The combination of textures is typical of the dense, many-voiced polyphony at the end of the Renaissance.

WAR AS A FOCUS

Religious music dominated the future United States' musical experience during the two centuries of its colonial history. This is not to say that the early colonists were without popular music, for this religious music was truly popular. It was spiritually uplifting, and equally important, it was enjoyable and filled homes as well as churches.

The early settlers of the New England colonies came with a rich musical heritage. They brought their voices but few musical instruments due to the limited cargo space available in their ships. This was not considered a serious loss by the Puritans, who prohibited the use of instruments in their worship service. However, singing was central to their everyday life, specifically singing prose and poetic translations of the Psalms of David, which were contained in books called "psalters." Here is a poetic translation of the opening of the Twenty-Third Psalm taken from a psalter known as the Bay Psalm Book:

> The Lord to mee a shepherd is,
> want therefore shall not I.
> He in the folds of tender grasse,
> doth cause me downe to lie.

One advantage of this translation is that it can be easily adapted (by simply lengthening the last word of the second and fourth lines) to fit into a four-beat-per-measure meter. This adaptability was important because many familiar songs were in this type of meter, and psalters often included only words, accompanied by lists of familiar melodies to which the words could be sung — melodies in the same meter as the text.

The Bay Psalm Book was such a psalter. The first book to be printed in the British colonies, it was published in 1640, went through twenty-six editions and was the dominant psalter well into the eighteenth century. Not until the ninth edition (1698) was notated music actually included. Even then, the music was found in a separate section at the back of the book, not immediately associated with the words.

This approach of relating text to familiar songs and another practice common in churches of that day called "lining-out" are indications of the growth of an aural tradition. Lining-out is a method of instruction in which the song leader speaks or sings a line or two of a song, which the congregation then repeats. These approaches rely on memory rather than on the ability to read music. Since people remember things differently, the result is usually inexactness in performance. The result was a deterioration in the quality of congregational singing.

Concern over this deterioration led to a very interesting phenomenon in the history of American music known as the "Singing School Movement." Singing schools began in New England during the first quarter of the eighteenth century, spread south into the Carolinas, and then followed the frontier westward. Singing schools were held in churches or schoolhouses and were led by itinerant musicians known as singing masters. Singing masters compiled songbooks, which they used to teach music skills; these books contained sacred and secular material, including their own compositions.

Many famous Americans such as Thomas Jefferson, Benjamin Franklin, and Francis Hopkinson were associated with music and music making during the last part of the eighteenth century. The most famous professional musician of the period was William Billings (1746–1800). Billings was a singing master in Boston churches and was the most popular composer of his generation. Billings' best known song is "Chester," a patriotic war song in strophic form for which he wrote the poem. Even though patriotism is the subject of the song, it is clearly imbued with religious fervor. Notice how each musical phrase begins with the same rhythm (long-short-short-long).

Active Listening
CD 2:5

"Chester," William Billings

Let tyrants shake their iron rod,
And Slav'ry clank her galling chains,
We fear them not, we trust in God,
New England's God for ever reigns.

Howe and Burgoyne and Clinton too,
With Prescot and Cornwallis join'd,
Together plot our Overthrow,
In one Infernal league combin'd,

When God inspir'd us for the fight,
Their ranks were broke, their lines were forc'd.
Their Ships were Shatter'd in our sight,
Or swiftly driven from our Coast.

The Foe comes on with haughty Stride;
Our troops advance with martial noise,
Their Vet'rans flee before our Youth,
And Gen'rals yield to beardless boys.

What grateful Off'ring shall we bring?
What shall we render to the Lord?
Loud Halleluiahs let us Sing,
And Praise his name on ev'ry Chord.

Sacred music in the twentieth century continues to serve either as ceremonial music for specific occasions or as church music. Providing an example of music composed for a specific occasion, the English composer, Benjamin Britten (1913–1976), was commissioned to write music for the consecration of St. Michael's Cathedral in Coventry, England, when it was rebuilt after being destroyed by bombing during the Second World War. A pacifist, he spent time in the United States during the war. His War Requiem, first performed in

1962, is a setting of the Latin requiem texts along with poetry by Wilfred Owen, a poet who was killed during the First World War. Britten's own pacifist feelings are evident in his juxtaposition of the traditional texts with Owen's verses describing the cruelty and futility of war. Britten's setting of the text "Dies irae" begins with brass fanfares alternating with the chorus almost chanting the text of the first four strophes of the sequence. A change in the orchestration and rhythmic patterns sets up the first statement of Owen's poetry sung by the baritone soloist.

War Requiem, "Dies irae" (excerpt), Benjamin Britten

Active Listening
CD 2:25

Dies irae, dies ille	Day of anger, that day
Solvet saeclum in favilla	will dissolve the world in ashes
Teste David cum Sibylla.	as witness David and Sibyl.
Quantus tremor est futurus,	What trembling there will be
Quando judex est venturus,	when the judge shall come,
Cuncta stricte discussurus!	all shall thoroughly be shattered!
Tuba mirum spargens sonum	The wondrous trumpet, spreading its sound
Per sepulcra regionum,	throughout the tombs of all regions,
Coget omnes ante thronum.	will gather all before the throne.
Mors stupebit et natura,	Death will be stupefied, also nature,
Cum resurget creatura,	when all creation arises
Judicanti responsura.	to answer to the judge.

Bugles sang, sadd'ning the evening air;
And bugles answer'd, sorrowful to hear.
Bugles sang, — Bugles sang.

CHURCH MUSIC WITH A COMMERCIAL SIDE

African-American churches at the turn of the twentieth century fostered gospel singing, following a decline in emphasis on spirituals, songs expressing deep religious faith, often based on African melodies brought to these shores by the slaves. Although African singing styles influenced the origins of gospel music, commercial interests continue to create variants of it. An important composer of early gospel music, Thomas A. Dorsey, wrote the following example. He began his musical career as a blues pianist, accompanying the famous blues singer "Ma" Rainey and writing some rather risqué songs for her. You can sense this blues background in his gospel music. The quality of his songs such as "Take My Hand Precious Lord" show him to be a cut above other

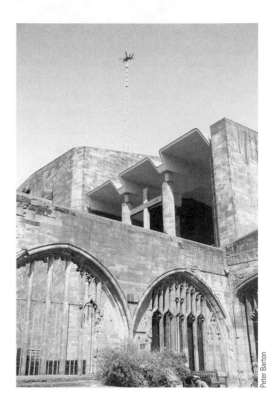

St. Michael's
Cathedral, Coventry,
England

gospel composers. This recording is performed by a "gospel quartet." In the gospel style of the first half of this century, a quartet could include four, five, or even six persons, as is the case here. One of them plays drums, one bass, and four sing close harmony.

Active Listening
CD 2:26

"Hide Me in Thy Bosom," Thomas A. Dorsey, The Dixie Hummingbirds

First Stanza

> Oh, Jesus hear me praying,
> Hear the words I'm saying,
> Watch my soul with eyes from on high.
> Oh, with the world I'm see'n around me
> No evil thoughts can bind me,
> Savior, if you leave me I will die.

Refrain

> Hide me in Thy bosom,
> Until the storm of life is o'er
> And rock me in the cradle of Thy love.
> Feed me, Jesus, feed me; Feed me, Jesus, feed me;

Feed me, Jesus, feed me; Feed me, Jesus, feed me;
Until I want no more,
And take me to Thy blessed home above.

Second Stanza
   Oh, make my journey brighter,
   Make my burden lighter,
   And help me to do good wherever I can.
   Oh, let Thy presence [build/fill] me
   Let the Holy Spirit fill me,
   And hold me in the hollow of Thy hand.

   Refrain

Often we hear Motown-influenced recordings of artificially "slick" gospel performances. These aren't the real thing, however. The emotion and enthusiasm of gospel music—with its foot stomping, wailing, and shrieking—excites the spirit and openly challenges the devil. In the words of *Time* magazine writer Christopher John Farley (April 8, 1996), "There's no salvation to be found in daintiness. If you want to baptize someone by the spirit, you've got to get your hands wet."

At this point in our survey of ritual music, there seems almost nothing left of "ritual." Folk elements, concert performances, and commercial profit all strongly compete for our consideration of this music's true function. It is time to move on.

CHAPTER

Ritual Music in the Concert Hall

15

ORATORIO: RELIGIOUS DRAMA WITHOUT ACTING

Another direction sacred music took was in part a result of the restrictions that religious authorities sometimes placed on other areas of society. Although never appropriate for performance during the liturgy, oratorios served at first as a religious substitute for secular entertainment. They were especially useful in the seventeenth century when popular opera houses were closed during the season of Lent. Composers have used the term "oratorio" in a variety of ways, but the word itself derives from the oratorio's place of performance (an Italian prayer hall or chapel). From their inception, oratorios told a religious or moral story through solo and choral singing with the accompaniment of an orchestra but without scenery, costumes, or action. Because of their complexity and social positioning, oratorios were influenced by popular or commercial interests instead of any ritual function.

Oratorio texts, although they may be based loosely on the Bible, were freely poetic plays. Often they drew on the lives of the saints or told an allegorical story. In Latin oratorios there was frequently a narrator. But soon the **oratorio** took on the *structure and dramatic character of a religious opera but without the customary sets, costumes, and acting.* Its composers and performers were, after all, drawn from the front ranks of those ordinarily engaged in operatic performances.

Oratorio, like opera, soon spread from Italy over the rest of Europe. Handel himself brought it to England. Although he succeeded in establishing himself as one of the finest composers of the time, as eminent for his suites and chamber music as for his Italian operas, Handel (1685–1759) eventually found it difficult to make a living in London producing operas. It was then that he turned to writing oratorios. Not only could he write them in the language of his public, he could also make use of the rich English tradition of choral singing. Among the various types of oratorios written by Handel, the best known is his popular *Messiah* (1742).

Another Handel oratorio dominated by choruses is *Israel in Egypt*, which was first performed in 1739. Fashioned from an anthem, "Moses' Song" (1738), it is based on the biblical story drawn, apparently by Handel himself, mainly from the books of Exodus and Psalms. In some cases, however, the words, so familiar and dear to the English people, derive directly from the *Book of Common Prayer* of the Church of England. The words call upon Handel to describe both the plagues of frogs, flies, and locusts that precede the exodus from Egypt and also, in Part Two, the thanksgiving of the Israelites for their deliverance. Rising to the challenge, the composer moves from strength to strength: He first depicts the plagues with amazing musical images, then brings the work to its highest point in the closing choruses, "The People Shall Hear" and (after an alto aria) "The Lord Shall Reign for Ever and Ever." Follow closely how aptly and expressively the composer sets the following words: "The people shall hear and be afraid. Sorrow shall take hold on them. All the inhabitants of Canaan shall melt away by the greatness of Thy arm. They shall be as still as a stone till Thy people pass over, O Lord."

Buoyed by an extraordinary technique forged over the years, Handel uses the orchestra to establish a mood and varied choral textures to express the words of this chorus. Observe especially the poignant sighing theme and harsh dissonances used to set the "melting away" of the inhabitants of Canaan, a musical device known as **word painting** *(using musical devices to illustrate the text)*. Choral textures range from imitative polyphony in four voices to passages of powerful block chords, and include as well simple unison singing (entirely unaccompanied) for "they shall be still as a stone."

Israel in Egypt, "The People Shall Hear," George Frideric Handel

Active Listening
CD 2:27

This section is set for double chorus (each consisting of sopranos, altos, tenors, and basses).

- It opens with a chromatically descending, then ascending accompaniment.
- The polyphonic setting of "the people shall hear" ascends and builds in density, leading to a homophonic setting of "and be afraid."
- "Sorrow shall take hold" is set polyphonically using chromaticism and a descending "sighing" motive to express the text. This is an example of word painting.
- "All the inhabitants of Canaan" is set homophonically, then polyphonically while "shall melt away" is introduced.
- "All the inhabitants" appears homophonically, followed by an extended polyphonic treatment of "shall melt away." The descending melodic ideas and chromaticism that illustrate "melt away" are additional examples of word painting.
- A return to the homophonic "All the inhabitants" and polyphonic "shall melt away" caps off this section.
- "By the greatness of Thy arm" is set homophonically in slower note values, and "they shall be still as a stone" is both monophonic and unaccompanied to again "paint" the text.
- An extended section on "till Thy people pass over" uses an arch-shaped melody set homophonically to illustrate the text. This section alternates with a homophonically set section on "which Thou has purchased."
- The chorus ends with "which Thou has purchased" set in longer note values to bring the work to a close.

St. Luke Passion, "Et surgens," Krzysztof Penderecki

To endure, any musical genre must appeal to major composers, and it must be adaptable to new styles. No recent oratorio can serve as a better example on both counts than the *St. Luke Passion* by the contemporary Polish composer Krzysztof Penderecki (1933–). Oratorios on the Passion (the suffering and crucifixion of Jesus) go back to the baroque period, and Penderecki pays homage to the great baroque master, Johann Sebastian Bach, by using the letters of his name as a musical motive. (In Germany the pitch "B" is B flat and "H" is B natural.) Far more striking to the ear is the composer's use of **tone clusters** *(a group of adjacent pitches sounded simultaneously)* and **quarter**

tones *(pitches smaller than the half steps of the piano)* in both the choir and the orchestra. Also there are passages half sung and half spoken and sometimes even whistled, and such devices as the **glissando** *(sliding between pitches)* in his large and colorful orchestra. Most of these style features can be heard in the excerpt.

LISTENING GUIDE	*St. Luke Passion*, "Et surgens," Krzysztof Penderecki

CD 3:1

00:00	Opens with bell-like sounds and tone clusters that lead to
00:30	Tone clusters in horns and woodwinds
00:34	Orchestra coalesces on unison which transforms to vocal unison
00:58	Vocal clusters and glissandos follow
1:11	Narrator (all text in free translation from the Latin): "Then the whole multitude arose and brought him before Pilate. They began to accuse him."
1:22	Orchestra clusters lead to chorus in what seems like random sounds: "We found this man perverting our people and forbidding us to give tribute to Caesar and saying that he is Christ the king."
1:40	Pilate: "Are you the King of Jews?" Narrator: "You say so."
1:45	Traditional choral sound on "Domine"—Lord
1:52	Pilate: "I find no crime in this man"; and he sent him back to Herod
2:13	Chorus in exclamatory and imitative styles: "Herod questions him but he did not answer."
2:35	Chorus in chant-like style: "Herod mocked him, dressed him in fine garments, and sent him back to Pilate."
2:54	Pilate: "Behold, nothing deserving death has he done. I will chastise and release him."
3:15	Random choral sounds: "Away with this man, release to us Barabbas."
3:24	Narrator: "Pilate addressed them again, wishing to release Jesus but they shouted."
3:34	Chorus: "Crucify him!"
3:40	Pilate: "What evil has he done? I have found in him no crime deserving death."
3:59	Chorus and orchestra: "Crucify him!"

Penderecki built part of his international reputation on the basis of these religious works, most notably the *St. Luke Passion* which received its premiere in London in 1967.

Krzysztof Penderecki,
St. Luke Passion
(1966), "Judas," score
50 × 35 cm

THE REQUIEM

Another departure of sacred music from ritual is its appearance on the concert stage. Historically, this first occurred when compositions written for ritual purpose were performed outside of the ritual context (typically outside of the church). An example of this would be an a cappella group performing a Mass Ordinary in a "secular" choir concert. In time the musical Mass was primarily composed for the concert setting. While both of the following masses were composed for the concert hall, each goes further in departing from the stereotypical Requiem Mass.

German romantic composer Johannes Brahms (1833–1897) wrote what he called *Ein Deutsches Requiem* (A German Requiem) to a text that he compiled out of Biblical verses rather than the traditional Latin requiem. Brahms

---

LISTENING GUIDE

A German Requiem, "Wie lieblich sind deine Wohnungen," Johannes Brahms

CD 3:2

00:00	orchestral introduction
	descending flute melody with string accompaniment
00:08	chorus with orchestral accompaniment
	choral homophony
	melodic line reverses the flute melody of the introduction

1. *Wie lieblich sind deine Wohnungen*	How lovely are thy dwelling places
2. *Herr Zabaoth!*	O Lord of hosts!

00:23	orchestra begins repetition of phrase, chorus continues
00:42	violins begin new idea, continued by tenors

1. *Wie lieblich sind deine Wohnungen*	How lovely are thy dwelling places
2. *Herr Zabaoth!*	O Lord of hosts!

1:00	repetition in all voices
	imitation among sections
1:15	homophonic close
1:20	short orchestral interlude
1:26	choral homophony, then imitation, lower to higher voices

3. *Meine Seele verlanget und sehnet sich*	My soul longeth, yea, even fainteth
4. *nach den Vorhöfen des Herrn*	for the courts of the Lord:

selected texts that emphasize the sadness yet inevitability of death, not the divine judgment of the *Dies irae*. He wrote and rewrote the work over a nearly fifteen-year period. Eventually, it became one of his greatest successes. The fourth of seven movements exemplifies his gentle yet effective setting of verses from Psalm 84. It begins with a descending instrumental line that is then mirrored in the ascending melody of the voices. The movement gradually becomes more complex, culminating in a forceful, imitative section that echoes the sentiment of the line of text, "my flesh crieth out." The movement ends as it began in peace and quiet reflection.

Brahms' individual selection of texts shows that the work was not intended for a liturgical situation. Texts that are liturgical, however, also can be given musical settings that are intended for concert setting rather than church service.

1:48	ending coalesces into choral homophony
2:02	homophonic chorus with accents in orchestra

5. *mein Leib und Seele freuen sich*	my heart and my soul crieth out
6. *in dem lebendigen Gott.*	for the living God.

2:10	continuation is smoother, orchestra supporting chorus
2:17	repetition with extended continuation
2:37	orchestral interlude similar to introduction
2:46	chorus like the beginning

1. *Wie lieblich sind deine Wohnungen*	How lovely are thy dwelling places
2. *Herr Zabaoth!*	O Lord of hosts!

3:21	music repeats as at 00:42, then extended

7. *Wohl denen, die in deinem Hause wohnen,*	Blessed are they that dwell in thy house:

3:50	imitative materials, aggressive emphasis on bass line

8. *die loben dich immerdar!*	they will be still praising thee.

4:15	increasing complexity and activity until . . .
4:36	sustained voices with pulsing sounds in orchestra
4:44	short orchestral interlude (like introduction)
4:48	voice sections in unison, then continue as homophony

1. *Wie lieblich sind deine Wohnungen*	How lovely are thy dwelling places
2. *Herr Zabaoth!*	O Lord of hosts!

5:24	orchestral closing

Sterling and Francine Clark Art Institute, Williamstown, Massachusetts

Rockets and Blue Lights (Close at Hand) to Warn Steamboats of Shoal Water, by J. M. W. Turner, is an example of romanticism in painting.

In the nineteenth century the great opera composer, Giuseppe Verdi (1813–1901), honored the memory of the great Italian writer, Alessandro Manzoni, by composing a requiem for the anniversary of his death (1874). Though not especially devout himself, Verdi created a powerful and very dramatic evocation of the requiem texts. Verdi does not use the actual medieval chant that is associated with the text.

Active Listening
CD 3:3

Requiem, "Dies irae" (excerpt), Giuseppe Verdi

- Verdi's dramatic setting of the "Dies irae" is announced by four loud chords.
- Strings in cascading scale passages.
- Chorus nearly shouts the first words of the sequence with a twisting, chromatic passage, dramatically depicting the anger and horror (*ira*) of the Last Judgment.

Dies irae, dies ille	Day of anger, that day
Solvet saeclum in favilla	will dissolve the world in ashes
Teste David cum Sibylla.	as witness David and Sibyl.

- Chords, reinforced by the bass drum, and the scale passages eventually dissipate into a hushed accounting of the second strophe of the poem.

Quantus tremor est futurus,	What trembling there will be
Quando judex est venturus,	when the judge shall come,
Cuncta stricte discussurus!	all shall thoroughly be shattered!

- After an inconclusive ending, the "Tuba mirum" is heard, this time with trumpets calling first from afar, then with ever increasing frequency and volume until the chorus enters to announce the terrible event.

Tuba mirum spargens sonum	The wondrous trumpet, spreading its sound
Per sepulcra regionum,	throughout the tombs of all regions,
Coget omnes ante thronum.	will gather all before the throne.

Each of the sections that follows in the sequence dramatically portrays the various moods of the sections of the text.

The pieces in this chapter are hybrids: intended for the concert hall but based on religious themes. They are "ritual related" works that function as concert music. Next we move on to folk music.

16   Folk Music in the United States

OUR FOLK MUSIC HERITAGE

THE SPIRITUAL

During the early 1800s our nation experienced an awakening of interest in religion known as the "Great Revival." This awakening was especially fervent in the South and West, which were predominantly rural areas with people and churches spread many miles apart. Because of these distances, the focus of the revival was the camp meeting, a gathering at a central location to which large groups of worshippers would bring tents, bedding, and food, planning to enjoy four or five days of sermons, prayer, and song. The singing was spirited, enthusiastic, and (most of all) loud. Masters and slaves attended together and sang the same music—revival hymns and spiritual songs.

The music they sang was usually of two types: the leader-chorus and the verse and refrain. The **leader-chorus** type closely resembles the **call and response** type so characteristic of African singing: in both, *lines of text sung by a soloist alternate with a sung group response.* Songs that tell a story are often in **verse and refrain,** the *action is told in a series of verses, and each verse is followed by a refrain.* Each verse is different, but the refrain is usually the same each time and often contains the point of the story, or the "punch line." Spirituals often combined the two types. Singers would raise and lower notes, slide from note to note, and add melodic embellishments to emphasize the emotional content of the words. These traits closely resembled the traditional elements of African singing. A synthesis was achieved that, when combined with the African affinity for rhythm, produced the black spiritual and laid the foundation for blues, jazz, country, gospel, and rock and roll. This West African-influenced rhythm is often referred to as "hot" rhythm; it is characterized by a driving pulse and syncopation that seems to demand bodily movement in response to the beat. It kept camp meetings lively.

The **spiritual** is the *first combining of African and European elements.* Texts filled with yearning for eternal peace and earthly freedom are set to melodies and harmonies learned in the shared religious experience of the African-American slaves and their white owners. These are given the urgency of the

Tuskegee University and Museums

The Tuskegee Choir

African rhythmic drive. There are spirituals for almost every state of emotion, from energetic songs such as "Ezekiel Saw de Wheel" to solemn statements like "Were You There."

The following spiritual exhibits many of the characteristics mentioned above. Although the harmonies are those of white church music, the rhythms are the syncopated "swinging" patterns of African-American music. This spiritual uses both the verse and refrain and call and response patterns that are typical of much African music, as are the phrasings and "bending" of pitches. The pentatonic scale is employed throughout.

"I Want to be Ready," Traditional Spiritual

Active Listening
CD 2:9

Refrain (full chorus)	I want to be ready, oh
	I want to be ready,
	I want to be ready, to walk in Jerusalem just like John.
Refrain (full chorus) repeat	
Call (female soloist)	John said the city was just for prayer
Response (chorus)	To walk in Jerusalem just like John.

Call (female soloist)	And he declared he'd meet me there.
Response (chorus)	To walk in Jerusalem just like John.
Call (male soloist)	I ain't been to heaven but I've been told
Response (chorus)	To walk in Jerusalem just like John.
Call (male soloist)	That the street's of pearl and the gate's of gold.
	To walk in Jerusalem just like John.

Refrain (full chorus)

Refrain (full chorus) repeat

Call (female soloist)	You said your Lord has set you free,
Response (chorus)	To walk in Jerusalem just like John.
Call (female soloist)	Why don't you let your neighbors be?
Response (chorus)	To walk in Jerusalem just like John.
Call (male soloist)	I never shall forget that day
Response (chorus)	To walk in Jerusalem just like John.
Call (male soloist)	When Jesus washed my sins away.
Response (chorus)	To walk in Jerusalem just like John.

Refrain (full chorus)

Refrain (full chorus) repeat

Refrain (full chorus) second repetition, loudly

Ending slows for emphasis of text

When studying the contributions of African Americans to the music of the United States, we need to understand a basic cultural difference. Traditional European culture is classified as "literate"; that is, it perceives, communicates, organizes, and stores information primarily through the medium of writing. By contrast, African culture is classified as "oral," perceiving, organizing, and communicating through rhythm and vocalized tone — relying on individual and communal memory to preserve its history. The oral culture "remembers" through song, dance, and intricate rhythmic tensions. Little distinction is made between the artist and the audience. Spontaneity and improvisation are valued above exact repetition. Many of these characteristics of African culture are typical of folk music, making African Americans important contributors to American folk music.

It is interesting to compare several types of religiously inspired choral music. In Chapters 14 and 15 several pieces that were from the European art music tradition were investigated. While these pack a considerable emotional impact, they are more impersonal than African-American music, with a Latin or German text and without the driving rhythms and pitch variations of gospel music. The singers are not as emotionally involved as the African-American performers we have heard, who sound as if they are expressing a direct personal and deeply felt conviction. The spiritual is sung in the colloquial English used by many African Americans of an earlier time. Many contemporary arrangements of spirituals represent a fusion of these African-American and European choral idioms.

The spiritual gained much popularity following the Civil War, and examples were gathered and published in collections. Editors of these collections complained about the difficulty of accurately writing down the music as it was performed. Notating the unusual musical effects and intricate rhythmic patterns was made even more complicated by the fact that spirituals were never performed twice in exactly the same way—typical of an oral culture, where a premium is placed on originality and spontaneity.

THE BLUES

The United States was a singing nation. All classes of people sang, including the slaves, who numbered more than three-quarters of a million by the year 1800. Harking to their African tradition, slaves had songs for every occasion and activity. While playing drums was forbidden (lest they be used as "talking drums" by which Africans sometimes communicated and therefore might incite an uprising), singing was encouraged, for work songs lightened the burden of enforced labor and increased productivity. These work songs were usually in the traditional call and response style. After the Civil War, African-American performers began to improvise a new type of song sometimes referred to as the "sorrow song," lamenting their many difficulties in a world still unfriendly in spite of emancipation. Shortly after the turn of the twentieth century the sorrow song acquired a relatively standardized structure and another name: the "blues."

At the beginning of that century the blues fit the traditional definition of folk music given above. They were not notated, communicated directly, were accepted by large segments of the African-American population, and were more or less anonymous, often the result of a collaboration by several individuals. Improvisation was an important part of them. There is a close relationship between blues and spirituals. It would appear that easy distinctions could be identified, such as that blues tend to express individual, worldly feelings while spirituals express the religious feelings of a group. However, the line dividing the two is not always easily drawn, as a classification of folk music called blues-spirituals demonstrates. One difference that appears to be consistent is that spirituals are unaccompanied while blues are accompanied.

First and foremost, **blues** is *an attitude*, a "down-in-the-chops," "plum-outta-luck," attitude. But musically the blues are also a *vehicle for improvisation* and as such must have a *structure* or *form* so musicians can play together. Even though there are many patterns and forms called blues, when musicians say "let's play the blues" they are referring to a certain set of chords and the structure shown below.

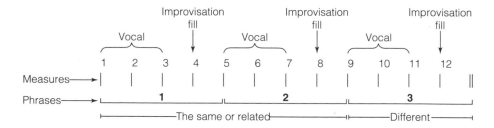

This diagram shows twelve measures with four beats in each measure. The twelve measures are divided into three complete musical ideas, or phrases, each containing four measures. When these were sung (as early blues almost always were), the singer would sing the first two measures of each phrase and the instrumentalist—who was often the singer—would improvise "fill" for the remaining two measures. This produces an effect of call and response—the singer providing the "call" and the instrumentalist the "response." The twelve-measure (or twelve "bar") pattern is the basic building block. A blues song would have many repetitions of this pattern.

Many of the great early blues singers were born in the Mississippi Delta region and migrated north to Chicago to escape the racial pressures present in the South. Bessie Smith (1894–1937) was born in Tennessee, sang the blues all over this country, and died in the Mississippi Delta. Smith, known as the "Empress of the Blues," began singing blues in a touring show in 1912, sharing

CROSSROADS

Although the blues style underwent many stylistic changes in its development over the years, beginning as a vocal idiom but early on becoming instrumental as well, certain qualities have remained almost a constant. The prevailing mood is one of sadness or depression, perhaps because of disappointment in love, loneliness, or longing for distant locations. The vocal style strives less for beauty of tone or precise intonation than for expressive communication of sentiments that are not serene or soothing. Even when the blues are played only on an instrument, the feeling comes through, as we will hear later in the example of Louis Armstrong (1901–1971), one of the greatest blues performers on the trumpet. And the standard twelve-measure basic blues chord pattern (sometimes more complex in more recent blues) is unmistakable.

the billing with "Ma" Rainey, who claimed to have named the blues and was the first blues singer to gain fame. Smith's singing style combined the coarseness of country blues with the more sensitive phrasing of classic blues. Her performances included "bending" pitches to produce "blue notes" and improvising melodic lines to convey her inner feelings. She made over two hundred recordings, many with famous jazz musicians, including Louis Armstrong.

When you heard this piece in Chapter 7 the emphasis was on texture. Recall that the accompanying instrument improvises a melodic line or rhythmic chord pattern to "fill" the rest of the phrase, bearing some resemblance to the "call and response" pattern. Here the focus is on the text.

The words and the melody of the blues generally followed an "AAB" form with each letter representing four measures of the twelve-measure form. The first two lines have the same text but a different chord progression, and the third line has a different text and chord progression. In this example the twelve-measure AAB form is heard three times. Each of these three verses takes one twelve-measure pattern. The accompanying instrument improvises a melodic line or rhythmic chord pattern to "fill" the rest of the phrase.

Active Listening
CD 1:2

"Mean Old Bed Bug Blues," Traditional Blues, Bessie Smith

Verse 1

A	Yeah, a bedbug sure is evil, they don't mean me no good.
A	Yeah, a bedbug sure is evil, they don't mean me no good.
B	Ain't he the woodpecker an' I'm-a-chunk-a wood.

Verse 2

A   When I lay down at night I wonder how kin a poor gal sleep
A   When I lay down at night I wonder how kin a poor gal sleep
B   When some is holdin' my hand others eatin' my feet

Verse 3

A   Bedbugs as big as a jackass will bite you an' stand an' grin.
A   Bedbugs as big as a jackass will bite you an' stand an' grin.
B   Will break all the bedbug laws an' turn around and bite you again.

Early blues performer Bunk Johnson claimed to have played the blues since his childhood in the 1890s. Well over a century has passed since then and the evolution of the blues has brought about a number of styles: country blues, classic blues, city blues, rhythm and blues, and soul. Muddy Waters, Howlin' Wolf, Bo Diddley, B. B. King, and many other performers are associated with the blues. As the century progressed, the blues influenced a variety of other musics including jazz, rock, gospel, and even classical. Maurice Ravel, George Gershwin, and Aaron Copland were several of the many "serious" composers influenced by the blues. Its presence is felt in many forms of popular music, in musical theater, and in concert halls.

Toward the end of the century the blues experienced a rebirth with a post-modern mixture of folk, commercial, and art music elements. At the same time, recordings of traditional folk musicians from early in the century have been reissued. Hence the blues are an example of how one type of folk music can function in a number of different roles in the music of today, depending on context and setting. Similar transformations have happened to country, bluegrass, jazz, and rock, all of which began as folk music. All have experienced commercialization and at one time or another have been presented in a concert setting.

ZYDECO

In the mid-1700s, a group of French-speaking Canadians, the "Acadians," moved from Nova Scotia to Louisiana. These "Cajuns," as they came to be called, brought with them a love for dancing and a body of music based on French folk songs. The typical *Cajun band* included fiddle, concertina (a small button accordion), guitar, rub-board, and triangle, as well as a vocalist. Cajun dances tended to be boisterous affairs, and performers developed a rather strident style of fiddle playing and singing to project the music above the sounds of clapping, thigh slapping, and boot stomping. This music soon absorbed elements of other local cultures—especially the blues. The rub-board (also called the *frottoir*) was adapted for use in the lively dance rhythms of Cajun music. It resembles a corrugated metal washboard and is worn like a baseball umpire's chest protector. When "rubbed" or scraped with metal picks it adds a novel and dominant rhythmic sound.

In the last fifty years, *Cajun music has combined with country, and rhythm and blues* to produce a style called **zydeco.** In this style, the piano accordion sometimes replaces the traditional button accordion for greater facility, and sax and drums are often added. The "king" of zydeco was Clifton Chenier (d.1987), whose rollicking piano accordion and singing in both English and French can be heard in such classic recordings as *Let the Good Times Roll.* Paul Simon's *Graceland* album includes a tribute to Chenier, and Mary Chapin Carpenter's *Down at the Twist and Shout* with its Cajun-Zydeco inflections won a Grammy in 1992.

JAZZ

Concert and marching bands were very popular during the second half of the 1800s. This was especially true in New Orleans, where military musicians returning from service in the Civil War revived a strong military band tradition established by the French founders of the city. By the late 1800s small bands of five or six players were found at almost every social activity, from dances to parades and funerals. They were also found as entertainment in the bars and brothels of New Orleans' famed red-light district, "Storyville." The music of these bands reflected many influences: French, Spanish, Creole, African, blues, and the banjolike rhythms of ragtime, which was just developing. The oral tradition was important in these bands as most of the music was played "by ear" and was open to each player's interpretation during every performance.

A style developed that became known as **jazz** and included three elements:

1. A lilting beat called "swing"
2. A characteristic rhythm called syncopation in which "offbeat" accents break up the regularity of beat that characterizes most classical music
3. Improvisation

Players would improvise individually in brief passages and also collectively. Instruments were chosen from among those used in the marching band, thus excluding "stationary" instruments such as the piano. Being the loudest, the cornet (or the trumpet) played the melody in an embellished or ornamented fashion. The clarinet added a secondary part, an *independent melodic accompaniment sometimes called an* **obbligato.** This was played above the melody of the cornet. Since the clarinet is a very flexible instrument capable of great technical facility, this obbligato was often highly elaborate. The trombone added a harmony part below the cornet, usually playing longer notes than those of the melody and adding melodic interest when the cornet was resting. In a marching band this harmonic element would be called a *countermelody*. These three instruments were called the *front line* because they stood out front, near the audience. The remaining three instruments were called the *rhythm section*: the tuba, which supplied the bass part; the banjo, which played chords in rhythm; and drums, which provided the beat.

In this so-called New Orleans jazz there is a contrapuntal texture in which the trumpet plays the *lead*, or melody, with embellishments and variations. The clarinet adds a countermelody, a more ornamented type of passage work, and the trombone supplies the lower portion of the ensemble. When used, the piano adds the background chords in a steady rhythm with some "filler" material in the right hand, supported by the string bass (often replacing the tuba) and drums.

Louis Armstrong was one of the most influential jazz musicians of the twentieth century. His scratchy singing style was a reflection of his improvisatory trumpet playing, and both were studied and imitated by jazz musicians for decades. Armstrong spent his early years in New Orleans, moved to Chicago as a member of "King" Oliver's Creole Jazz Band, and then became

Louis Armstrong (at microphone) and his "All Stars"

the leader of a large swing band. Thus he was involved in the development of three jazz styles. "Satchmo" popularized **scat singing** *(singing nonsense syllables and improvising with the voice as if it were an instrument).*

Our recording includes four of the finest Dixieland musicians of the period. While the piece is performed in the New Orleans rhythmic and melodic style, the inclusion of piano in the rhythm section and the substitution of the string bass for the tuba show the influence of the later "Chicago" Dixieland style. Elements resembling the "call and response" of vocal music can occasionally be heard in the instruments. Rhythmically, the piece features a **flat four**—*each beat of the measure (four beats per measure) receiving about the same amount of stress* or accent. In the repetitions, the style becomes more improvisatory—straying more from the original tune with more insertions on the part of the performers.

"Back O' Town Blues" (excerpt), Luis Russell and Louis Armstrong

Active Listening
CD 3:4

Louis Armstrong, trumpet; Barney Bigard, clarinet; Jack Teagarden, trombone; and Earl "Fatha" Hines, piano.

- Introduction features rhythm section; Louis Armstrong is heard speaking.
- Chorus 1 (based on blues progression) trumpet solo, trombone answers, clarinet plays obbligato.
- Chorus 2 more improvisatory in nature; instrument relationships remain the same.

The rich legacy of African Americans has been a major force in developing an American folk idiom. Music such as spirituals, jazz, and blues influenced many other musical styles and helped develop a unique identity for American music.

CHAPTER

Folk Music Around the World

17

Every part of the world's cultures has its own folk music tradition and we will now explore a few of them.

In Southeast Asia, the country of Indonesia includes two islands that have especially rich musical cultures—Bali and Java. While they share similar musical instruments, their music displays different expressive natures. A popular instrument in Bali is the *angklung*. This is a folk instrument made up of a set of numerous short bamboo tubes of graduated lengths loosely enclosed in small frames, a frame for each tube, or for a set of two tubes tuned in octaves. When the frames are shaken, the tubes rattle at definite pitches that are used to play melodies. Playing a melody requires as many players as there are different pitches in the melody, unless, as is sometimes the case, one player handles more than one frame.

CROSSROADS

The *angklung* technique is similar to that of handbell ringing or jug blowing practiced in some American amateur musical circles. In the case of handbell ringing, several players stand facing a long table on which are placed bells of varying sizes and pitches. Each player rings his or her bell when it is the melody or harmony note at the given moment. Usually the musical arrangement is quite simple and is often notated with numbers so that the bell ringers need not be able to read music. However, some groups become sufficiently proficient to perform pieces of considerable complexity in melody, harmony, and rhythm. This musical practice is often associated with Sweden, although it is common in many other European countries and the Americas. Handbell ringing is often associated with the Christmas holiday season. In jug blowing, the players blow across the tops of jugs that have been partially filled with varying amounts of water to enable the notes of the scale to be produced and each player produces a pitch at the proper time. All three of these practices in which *the melody notes are distributed among several players or singers* are called **hocket style.**

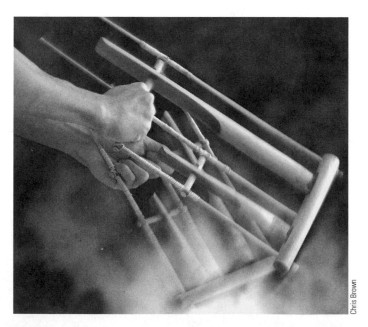

Angklung

Chris Brown

SEGERA MADU, BALI

In this example you will hear the *angklung* played as part of the **gamelan,** *a large ensemble consisting of a number of drums, gongs, xylophones, metallophones and sometimes a flute, a fiddle, and a hammered zither*. There are numerous gamelans in Java and Bali. They correspond in function to community bands and orchestras in the United States, staffed by amateurs with varying degrees of proficiency. There is wide latitude in the number of performers, anywhere from four or five to twenty or more. They perform to provide music for temple festivals, cremations, weddings, dance, and puppet theater performances—practically any event where music is needed. There are now many gamelans in the United States, with instruments imported from Indonesia. The purchase of one represents a considerable investment. The instruments are made by master craft workers who apply uniform colorful decorations to the instruments in each gamelan. The instruments cannot be interchanged between gamelans because of subtle differences in tuning between one group and another. When one visits the islands it is possible to hear numerous performances by going from village to village when festival days occur.

In this example, which was recorded in the village of Sajan in central Bali you will hear a five-tone (pentatonic) *slendro* scale, roughly corresponding to the black keys of the piano. If you listen carefully you will hear the angklung entering after several measures of the gamelan.

Active Listening
CD 2:13

Segera Madu, Bali

- Fast monophonic pattern of higher pitches.
- Low pitches begin at a moderate tempo and continue throughout, sometimes lining up with other parts, sometimes not.
- Complex, reiterated but evolving pattern begins.
- Softer version of the same pattern; angklungs enter, metallophones continue.
- Fade.

BHATIALI, INDIA

The folk music of India shows regional differences caused by many factors, including linguistic considerations, localization of instruments (since they are mostly handmade by local craft workers), subject matter of texts in vocal music, and the social function of the music. Many of the same practices found in Indian classical music are heard in the folk music, and the instruments employed are similar although less sophisticated and less challenging to play. Often vocal music and instrumental music are combined, and the instrumental portions are improvisations on the folk songs being sung.

Bansri and dotara
players

Hindu folk music has two principal sources of inspiration—religion and
nature. It usually deals with natural phenomena such as the changing seasons,
times of drought and monsoons, and sowing and harvesting. This example is
based on a song of a Bengal boatman. The rivers in the Bengal region are very
wide and sometimes can hardly be seen across. They represent both a threat
and a boon: a threat during the rainy season when it is difficult and dangerous
to cross them and a boon because they are a source of irrigation for the soil.
Hence rivers are a symbol of both life and the threat of death. In this example
you will hear prominently the *dotara,* a plucked four-string long-necked lute
whose body is carved from a single piece of wood; the *duggi,* a pair of drums
similar to the *tabla* but less exact in pitch; and bells. Although the tune is
played by instruments here, the melody is based on a song whose words warn
the boatman against crossing the river at a late hour, heading for the opposite
banks he cannot see, rowing against the raging current in his battered boat.
The music arouses loneliness and nostalgia in the boatman. The example was
recorded in western Bengal by a group of Pakistani refugees. It is in the
Khamaj mode, which is like our major scale with a lowered seventh scale
degree.

Active Listening
CD 3:5

Bhatiali, India

- *Dotara* enters in free rhythm.
- Bells enter followed shortly by *duggi.*

- More regular rhythm is established.
- Improvisation becomes more complex, *duggi* patterns faster.
- Example fades.

Although the words are not sung here, listeners in northern India are familiar with them and associate them with the melody. It is similar to the situation when a jazz trumpeter may improvise on a familiar popular song that is readily recognized even though the words are not sung.

CROSSROADS

El Baz Oichen, Morocco

In the Arab world of North Africa and the Middle East a number of indigenous folk styles can be heard. In Morocco the Berber people maintain a strong connection with their culture even though they have adopted many of the ways of the conquering Arabs who invaded their territory in the seventh century.

One of the favorite instruments in Morocco is the **amjad,** a bowed fiddle held vertically. It is not used as a solo or ensemble instrument, but as an accompaniment to a storyteller in the public marketplace who plays the instrument intermittently as a punctuation or interjection between episodes of his narrative. He holds the instrument by its neck and hits its single horsehair string with horizontal strokes with a short bow. He sings a semispoken melody in the familiar pentatonic scale. His story deals with a clever jackal who dupes various individuals through his craftiness and trickery.

Active Listening
CD 3:6

El Baz Oichen, Morocco

- *Amjad* enters with an almost "spoken" solo.
- Storyteller begins with long note values; *amjad* punctuates with short notes.
- *Amjad* solo.
- Storyteller in very rapid, often repeated notes; *amjad* interjects.
- *Amjad* solo, very fast with contrasting rhythmic shape.
- Storyteller, again very fast; *amjad* comments.
- *Amjad* solo, fade.

Sub-Saharan Africa is an area with such a wealth of folk music that it is difficult to select a representative example. In fact, most of the music of Africa could be considered folk music. It is essential in celebrating various rites of passage from birth through puberty, marriage, and death. In addition to these more momentous events, group singing accompanies everyday activities such as hunting, fishing, herding cattle, beer drinking, and other social activities as well as the agricultural high points of planting and harvesting. It is also used, as it has been through the ages, to soothe and lull children to sleep.

CROSSROADS

Except in large cities, street musicians seem to have become a vanishing breed in the United States. They are still to be heard in Paris, where they play on the streets and in Metro stations, expecting a donation; and in England "buskers" still can be found outside pubs and restaurants playing and dancing to folk and popular music.

Active Listening
CD 3:7

Festival Music of the Malinke, Mali

This music is performed on three *balafons* (similar to our xylophone), one of the players being a professional ***griot*** *(a musician who travels from town to town performing and carrying the news)* who plays the lead part while the other two players play simpler subsidiary parts. They wear copper bells on their wrists that rattle while they are playing. The women who sing intermittently scrape metal rods with a long nail when they are not singing. The song is in praise of their chieftain. The similarity of this music to early American jazz is noticeable, both in rhythmic characteristics and melody patterns. The lead *balafon* part is improvised and grows in intensity as the music proceeds.

These examples you have heard and the discussions accompanying them give testimony to the rich diversity of the world's folk music. It is an expression of many aspects of people's lives and feelings—what makes them happy, what makes them sad, their work, their play—their patriotism, their loves, their dislikes—running the entire range of human experience. Throughout the ages folk music has been an important factor in human activity. As we will discover in the next chapter, elements of folk music have also had an impact on concert music.

CHAPTER

18 Adapting Folk to Concert Music

We have seen how a "classical" style of instrumental music came about in the sixteenth century: Not long after instruments were first used to play along with sacred choral groups, filling in for missing voices or doubling voice parts, the instrumentalists soon realized they could perform without the voices, and a new idiom was born. As time went on composers such as Gabrieli and Monteverdi began writing pieces specifically for instruments. This eventually led to full-blown orchestral works—suites and concertos, by such baroque masters as Bach and Handel. But in the classical period that followed, Haydn and Mozart began occasionally to incorporate folk melodies in their serious works. Beethoven continued this practice to a degree, and by the mid-nineteenth century (the romantic period) the practice had become widespread at the hands of Liszt, Tchaikovsky, Brahms, Chopin, Smetana, Dvorák, and others. A group of composers called the "Russian Five," which included Borodin, Moussorgsky, and Rimsky-Korsakov, were avowed **nationalists** *(those who emphasized national elements in music)* and made extensive use of folk elements in their works. In the twentieth century the Hungarian Béla Bartók, the English Vaughan Williams, the French Darius Milhaud, the Spanish Manuel de Falla, and the American Aaron Copland continued the practice. These were only a few of the many composers who incorporated their native folk music into their major works.

IN THE UNITED STATES

As we learned in Chapter 14, during the Revolutionary War period religion was often closely associated with patriotism. William Billings' *Chester* became a rallying song of the Revolution. (Billings' fellow Bostonian, Paul Revere, did

Smithsonian American Art Museum, Washington, DC/Art Resource NY

Landscape with man on horse (untitled) by Edward Mitchell Bannister, nineteenth-century African-American artist

the original printing of this work.) A twentieth-century composer, William Schuman (1910–1992) wrote instrumental settings of *Chester* for both band and orchestra. Schuman, who also earned a reputation as president of the Juilliard School of Music in New York City and president of Lincoln Center, was awarded the Pulitzer Prize in Music in 1943. Many of his compositions can be classified as "Americana."

The three-movement *New England Triptych* is based on three of Billings' anthems, "Be Glad Then America," "When Jesus Wept," and "Chester."

Although Billings' *Chester* was originally a composed work, it became very familiar and went through various transformations that make it closely related to folk music. Billings' original text was marked by strong anti-British sentiments, and the song became a marching song for the Continental Army during the American Revolution. Several texts were adapted to the music, the following being the most familiar. Although we covered this piece in Chapter 14, it is worthwhile to reprint the text here to allow a comparison to Schuman's work. The text represents a narrative that progresses through the battle:

"Chester," William Billings

- Stanza 1, confidence before the battle

  Let tyrants shake their iron rod,
  And Slav'ry clank her galling chains,
  We fear them not, we trust in God,
  New England's God for ever reigns.

- Stanza 2, statement about allies

  Howe and Burgoyne and Clinton too,
  With Prescot and Cornwallis join'd,
  Together plot our Overthrow,
  In one Infernal league combin'd,

- Stanzas 3 and 4, the battle and its conclusion

  When God inspir'd us for the fight,
  Their ranks were broke, their lines were forc'd.
  their Ships were Shatter'd in our sight,
  Or swiftly driven from our Coast.

  The Foe comes on with haughty Stride;
  Our troops advance with martial noise,
  Their Vet'rans flee before our Youth,
  And Gen'rals yield to beardless boys.

- Stanza 5, thanksgiving after the battle

What grateful Off'ring shall we bring?
What shall we render to the Lord?
Loud Halleluiahs let us Sing,
And Praise his name on ev'ry Chord.

Schuman's music generally follows the outline of text narrative. Schuman said about his composition:

The works of this dynamic composer (Billings) capture the spirit of sinewy ruggedness, deep religiosity and patriotic fervor that we associate with the Revolutionary period. Despite the undeniable crudities and technical shortcomings of his music, its appeal, even today, is forceful and moving. I am not alone among American composers who feel an identity with Billings and it is this sense of identity which accounts for my use of his music as a point of departure.

Schuman's work for orchestra derives from both the spirit of the hymn and the marching song.

New England Triptych, "Chester," William Schuman	LISTENING GUIDE

CD 3:8

00:00	Statement of the original hymnlike piece scored lightly for woodwinds. The chorale theme is used as the basis for an extended piece built on varied statements derived from the theme.
00:49	The lower instruments play a pattern suggesting a drumbeat over which the piccolo plays the theme—suggesting the fife and drum musical combination that often accompanied marching troops in earlier times when a full military band was not available.
1:53	The mood becomes more agitated, sound of the snare drum is prominent, perhaps suggesting battle.
2:12	Original tune keeps threading through the texture and predominates in the rousing ending measures, suggesting victory.

IN EUROPE

European composers of classical music have used folk tunes as themes since the eighteenth century. The twentieth-century composer Béla Bartók (1881–1945) systematically collected folk songs from his native Hungary and used

Béla Bartók
recording songs
in Transylvania

© Archivo Iconografico, S.A./CORBIS

either them or new melodies he composed in the folk style in his compositions. By combining Hungarian elements with his own unique compositional style he introduced the flavor of the native music of his country to much of the world. Bartok said, "For my own part, all my life, in every sphere, always in every way, I shall have one objective: the good of Hungary and the Hungarian nation."

Although Bartók was widely recognized in Europe as a piano virtuoso, he had not been similarly recognized as a composer. When during World War II Hungary became allied with the Nazi Germany-Italy axis, German cultural officials published a list of composers whose works were *verboten* (forbidden) because the composers were Jewish or were too dissonant for Hitler's conservative musical tastes.

When Bartók learned that he was not on the forbidden list, he wrote requesting that he be placed there, so strongly did he oppose the Nazi ideals. Later he was able to escape from Hungary after becoming aware that his safety was in jeopardy because of his public anti-Nazi statements. Bartók arrived in New York City in 1940, little known and suffering from leukemia. He was given a modestly paying job at Columbia University doing folklore research from which he was later dismissed. He was provided funds from

CROSSROADS

Portions of the Concerto for Orchestra were written in a cottage overlooking Saranac Lake, in the Adirondack Mountains in northern New York State. Bartók had been advised to spend some time in the Adirondack village that has been noted for its therapeutic environment. The cottage was later allowed to deteriorate, but has been restored and is now open to visitors and is known as the "Bartók Cottage."

ASCAP (American Society of Composers, Authors and Publishers) to provide for proper care in nursing homes. In 1943 Serge Koussevitsky, conductor of the Boston Symphony Orchestra, commissioned Bartók to compose an orchestral piece of his own choosing. Bartók, who was very ill at the time, made a remarkable short-term recovery that enabled him to complete this composition, and it was first performed in 1944, the year before he died. It became widely performed after his death and was his first work to become established with the general public.

The title Concerto for Orchestra may seem a bit confusing. Normally one thinks of a concerto as being a showcase in several movements for a solo instrument, such as violin or piano, with orchestral accompaniment. Occasionally composers wrote concertos for several instruments in the same work, as did Bach, Beethoven, and Brahms. Bartók chose to highlight numerous orchestral instruments as soloists as well as the four sections of the orchestra (strings, woodwinds, brass, and percussion) each playing featured passages to utilize their ensemble sounds.

Bartók's compositions are particularly interesting because of his use of Hungarian folk elements in them. He was a dedicated collector of Hungarian folk tunes, traveling throughout rural Hungary to record and notate more than six thousand authentic folk songs sung by native singers, thus becoming one of the earliest **ethnomusicologists** (*individuals who specialize in the study of the music of specific cultures*). This material motivated his use of folk melodies and folklike elements in his compositions. He wrote many original themes using rhythmic and melodic styles in this idiom, which he harmonized in a more dissonant contemporary style than listeners were accustomed to.

The fifth and last movement of Bartók's Concerto for Orchestra is a good example of his fusion of these elements. Of interest too is a fugal passage. A **fugue** is *a musical procedure in which successive entrances of the same theme are heard in different instruments while the earlier entrants play free melodic material*. The movement gains in intensity and ends in a triumphant mood. Many feel that Bartók, being aware of his terminal illness and impending death, was stating his "life assertion" in this work.

LISTENING GUIDE

Concerto for Orchestra, Fifth Movement, Béla Bartók

CD 3:9

00:00   In a brief introduction the horns present a theme (marked *pesante*, meaning "heavily") which will be heard throughout the movement.

00:08   Strings are off on a fast-moving section (marked *perpetuum mobile*, perpetual motion) that suggests the whirlwind pace of a folk dance. This mood goes on for some length at various dynamic levels.

1:50   Various instrumental forces reach a climactic *fortissimo*.

1:53   The excitement subsides and there is a brief fugal passage using the theme heard at the beginning of the movement, but much faster. It is first heard in the bassoons and is soon imitated by clarinets and oboes.

2:03   A tranquil section characterized by solo flute and bassoon passages.

New Theme Enters

2:33   Tempo accelerates, the very fast tempo returns with an aggressive new theme first heard in the trumpets.

Development

2:45   This new theme is developed in various ways by using techniques associated with composers of the baroque and classical periods and generally exploring every conceivable exploitation of the theme as the musical excitement grows.

2:53   **Inversion,** playing the theme upside down

3:10   **Modulation,** playing theme in new keys

3:31   Tempo changes

3:41   Changing the instrumentation

4:29   **Augmentation,** lengthening the note values of the theme

4:34   **Fragmentation,** playing only small bits of the theme

4:52   **Stretto,** overlapping entrances of the theme

7:58   The movement comes to an end with a very exciting acceleration to a *fortissimo* closing. The folklike melodic elements are harmonized with dissonant chords and the rhythms have a primitive strength.

A composer may choose a culture other than his own to represent, as Bohemian composer Antonin Dvořák (1841–1904) did in his Ninth Symphony, *From the New World*, which he composed during a visit to the United States. Dvořák, who was known for his symphonies and chamber music, had already represented his own culture in operas and instrumental works.

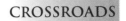

CROSSROADS

During his summer vacations in the United States Dvořák spent some time in Spillville, Iowa, a small town settled mostly by Czech immigrants and their families. Thus he maintained his familiarity with his own culture and its people while learning more about American culture. His upstairs lodgings over a shop in the town are identified by a historical marker and may be visited.

Bettmann Archive

Antonin Dvořák

    While in the United States (1892 to 1895), Dvořák became interested in the music of African Americans and American Indians. He was teaching composition at the National Conservatory of Music in New York City, which he headed. While there he urged his students to investigate their native wellsprings of music rather than imitating current European models, the prevalent practice at the time. Perhaps as an example of this concept he composed his symphony, *From the New World*, which was first performed by the Philharmonic Society of New York on December 15, 1893. In this work he did not employ authentic American folk songs but used musical ideas that suggest their style. The second movement of this four-movement work is cast in an overall ABA form, and its A theme is thought to have been strongly influenced by African-American spirituals.

In addition to providing an opportunity to listen to the folk nature of this melody, this Listening Guide will give us a chance to revisit musical phrase structure, something we covered in Chapter 4 with Beethoven's *Ode to Joy* theme. This example is made of four-measure phrases, but it is atypical in that there is an extension (like a coda on a small scale) before coming to the cadence.

LISTENING GUIDE	Symphony No. 9, *From the New World*, Second Movement (excerpt), Antonin Dvorák	
	CD 3:10	
	00:00 Introduction	
	00:38 A phrase	English horn enters with strings accompanying in block chords.
	00:44 A′ phrase	Phrase is complete this time with a slight crescendo at the end
	1:01 B phrase	Contrasting but related phrase at a higher pitch level
	1:11 B phrase	Repeated
	1:24 A	As in the beginning
	1:35 A″ phrase	Bassoon added, more crescendo and a greater sense of finality
	1:48	Extension, final fragment repeated twice, stretched out the second time
	2:01	Ascending arpeggio
	2:07	Repeated motive leading to cadence
	2:21	Final cadence, strings first then full orchestra

Folk music has been important and enjoyable in its own right since music began. In fact, the earliest music *was* folk music. And it has been a rich source of inspiration for many works in both the classical and popular idioms for many years. By focusing on how folk music was integrated into concert music, this chapter serves as an ideal transition to the concert music unit that follows.

CHAPTER

Diversity in Concert Music

19

INTRODUCTION

In the second chapter we listened to Copland's *Appalachian Spring* under two very different fictitious circumstances. In the second of these hearings, even the thought of having to address the class probably prompted you to listen more intently. When you choose to listen that intently the function of the music, regardless of style, is concert. **Concert music,** then, is *music for focused listening.* Concert music differs from ritual music in that it does not perform a supportive role for some other activity. In a similar fashion, it differs from commercial music in that it exists primarily for the enjoyment of the listener, not for financial gain. Concert music is often written down and may or may not have the kind of direct cultural connection to a particular group of people that is found in folk music. Finally, concert music may be art music—complex and with a serious intent—although that is not always the case.

Settings for concert music vary dramatically from one style to another. Symphony concerts often require formal attire, and recognition of the performance tends to be somewhat subdued. Opera is a bit more relaxed, with cries of *bravo* or *brava* accepted forms of recognition for a leading man or lady. Jazz performances can approach rock concerts in the enthusiasm of the audience. Performances of concert music from other parts of the world are different again, with Indian classical concerts lasting all night while the audience sips tea and appreciates the music. In all cases the setting and audience participation tend to follow a stereotype for the particular style and culture.

Parts V and VI use the ensemble as a primary organizational feature, with Part V focusing on large concert groups and Part VI on small concert groups.

As you probably remember, the three Requiem Masses were all intended for concert performance although they were based either on church liturgy or church teachings. Similarly, the works of Schuman, Dvořák, and Bartók were clearly concert music that used folk music as a basis. The goal of this apparent duplication is to help you learn to appreciate a single musical work from several perspectives.

CROSSROADS

Imbedded in both units is a survey of form and genre in music from the Western classical tradition. First, however, the remainder of this chapter will demonstrate the diversity of concert music through three musical examples.

Large concert groups that may first come to your mind include chorus, band, and orchestra and combinations of these ensembles that are used to perform works like operas and masses. In the previous chapter you were able to hear how folk elements could be used as the basis of concert music for orchestra. Also, in exploring ritual music we covered a variety of choral works (by Palestrina, Josquin, and Billings) as well as the combination of chorus and orchestra found in the Requiems of Brahms, Britten, and Verdi. A parallel example is the gamelan, a large ensemble we heard in Chapter 17.

GAMELAN

Non-Western ensembles tend to be smaller in size than Western, with the exception of the gamelan of Indonesia. ("Gamelan," remember, is comparable to the word "orchestra" or "band" in English-speaking countries, although, strictly speaking, it refers to the group of instruments rather than the performers.) It may vary in size from three or four instruments to more than twenty. There are family, community, and professional gamelans.

Given the flexibility in size of the gamelan and the variety of gamelan memberships, it stands to reason that this ensemble performs a variety of functions.

Balinese *gamelan*

Robert Washburn

Small gamelans are often used for background purposes while others perform purely for entertainment. Increasingly, there are gamelans staffed by skilled amateurs, in Bali, Java, and other places in the world, who most often perform in a concert setting. In fact, if you hear a gamelan in the United States, the performance is likely to be in a concert setting, where one or more players offer descriptive comments. The example that follows is included with that function in mind.

Several instruments are heard in this example, in which a dancer expresses the sudden changes of mood expressed by the gamelan. Musically, the composition is a series of repeated patterns that differ in length, mood, and character, allowing the dancer to express a wide range of emotions.

Kebjar Taruna, **Bali**

Active Listening
CD 1:15

- Try establishing the beat in this example. Is it more or less regular?
- Listen for patterns that are repeated. As the example proceeds, they become easier to hear.
- A pattern is repeated in an almost circular fashion.
- Does the regular pulse you found earlier seem to have anything to do with the patterns and their repetition?
- Do aspects of this example remind you of minimalism (purposeful use of minimal musical materials)?

Although performances by a gamelan may sound like random improvisation to the casual listener, they are actually very carefully structured, with each of the various instruments having a particular function in relation to the whole. Some play the basic theme; others paraphrase the theme, improvise on the theme, and provide accents at various points in the cycle. This assignment of different functions to different instruments is called colotomic structure. As you may recall from Chapter 3, colotomic structure means that the entrance of certain instruments in the gamelan marks off the progress of the piece.

LARGE JAZZ GROUPS

Another important large concert ensemble that is outside the parameters of "band, chorus, orchestra" is the jazz "big band." The most popular jazz style of the twentieth century was **swing,** named after the lilting yet driving rhythm associated with jazz. This *style is based on large ensembles of ten or more musicians who played written arrangements that incorporated improvised solos.* With the repeal of prohibition (1932) came large dance halls, and these larger venues demanded larger bands. In addition to a vocalist or two, these bands included three sections of instruments: brass (trumpets and trombones), woodwinds (saxophones), and rhythm (piano, bass, drums, and sometimes guitar). Their repertoire included popular ballads as well as *songs usually associated with jazz* that are called **jazz standards.** This was the first jazz style to enjoy nationwide exposure through live radio broadcasts and to be extensively recorded. Recording increased its popularity but forced bands into a pattern of three-minute-long arrangements, the time limit of one side of a 78 rpm record. While swing was both popular and intended for dancing, the following is truly a concert performance, one that sets the stage for jazz to eventually be called art music.

Benny Goodman grew up in Chicago during the 1920s, the heyday of Chicago Dixieland. Fine jazz clarinetists such as Barney Bigard influenced him. Goodman's band included fifteen instrumentalists in addition to himself. In 1937, this band performed the first jazz concert in New York City's most prestigious concert venue, Carnegie Hall, an indication of the high regard in which this precision ensemble was held.

"RIDING HIGH," COLE PORTER, BENNY GOODMAN ORCHESTRA

"Riding High" is based on the AABA song form that is typically 32 bars in length. In this instance, the form is doubled to 64 bars with each section being 16 measures in length. This piece can best be followed by tracking the reg-

Benny Goodman (foreground) and his orchestra

"Riding High," Cole Porter, Benny Goodman Orchestra		**LISTENING GUIDE**
CD 3:11		
00:00	Brief introduction	
00:05	A—16 bars	ensemble statement of "Riding High" theme alternation of brass and saxes
00:20	A—16 bars	repeat with different final cadence
00:36	B—16 bars	new statement, alternation of brass and saxes
00:51	A—16 bars	repeat
1:07	A—16 bars	improvisation based on A 8 bars clarinet, 8 bars trumpet
1:22	A—16 bars	more improvisation based on A 8 bars clarinet, 8 bars trumpet
1:36	B—16 bars	improvisation based on B 8 bars ensemble and clarinet, 8 bars ensemble
1:53	A—16 bars	more improvisation based on A 8 bars clarinet, 8 bars trumpet
2:08	A—16 bars	ensemble returns with A theme
2:15	Brief close	

ular groupings of measures that make up the structure. First, establish the beat; this is in a fast four, but you will probably find it easier to count in two (half as fast).

If your high school had a stage or jazz band, the basic concept came from the big band of the swing era. This fundamental group has witnessed significant style innovation through the work of musicians such as Duke Ellington, Stan Kenton, Charles Mingus, and Don Ellis. It is ironic that economics have caused the demise of most large jazz groups at a time when swing music and dancing is experiencing a renaissance.

CROSSROADS

MIXED MEDIA

John Adams (born in 1947) is a teacher as well as a composer. He has written music for both instruments and voices, including a highly publicized opera entitled *Nixon in China*. His compositions are emotional and full of energy.

"Short Ride in a Fast Machine" is written for two synthesizers and large orchestra, providing a third variant from the usual ensemble settings. It is also available in a very effective transcription for wind ensemble.

Minimalism, which you studied in Chapter 8, has turned out to be one of the predominant compositional techniques of the late twentieth century. Although the technique was probably created as a reaction against the complexity of serialism and some electronic music, its roots can be traced to world music. By the 1970s, both Steve Reich and Philip Glass, the two composers who are credited with beginning minimalism in music, were involved in the study of music of other cultures. Reich studied Balinese gamelan and African drumming in the United States, while Glass had firsthand exposure to the native music of North Africa, India, and Tibet. Both composers were seeking new means of organizing their music and came up with similar results by rejecting the traditional harmonic approach of Western music and substituting subtle variations of repeated motives and rhythms as an organizational method.

On the surface, a piece many seem repetitious or even uninteresting. But once the listener has adjusted to the tempo of this subtle musical change, a hypnotic, captivating effect is experienced that is very much the opposite of

LISTENING GUIDE	*Two Fanfares*, "Short Ride in a Fast Machine," John Adams
	CD 3:12

Section 1

00:00	opens with wood block pulse; series of increasingly complex rhythmic patterns
00:11	begin even note pattern: 3/2 = six quarter notes; flute riffs
1:06	quieter, horns enter; later bass drum accents
1:32	climax featuring horn glissandi, snare drum rim shots

Section 2

1:45	new section begins; characterized by foreboding bass pattern
2:12	climax featuring brass accents, bass drum, and tam tam
2:37	return of even note pattern

Section 3

3:00	wood block drops out, trumpet soli enters
3:20	climax featuring horns with "bells in the air"
4:03	tempo 1; return of initial material for close

our fast-paced everyday activities. This piece by Adams is cast in three large sections set off by major climaxes and style changes. The first two sections are made up almost entirely of rhythmic materials and the continuous pulse of the wood block. In the third section the wood block stops and an angular trumpet melody becomes the focus of attention. Adams described "Short Ride in a Fast Machine" in the following question: "You know how it is when someone asks you to ride in a terrific sports car, and you wish you hadn't?"

These three examples not only have allowed us to review diversity in large ensemble concert music but also have provided a window on the concept of pulse in music. In "Kebjar Taruna," the pulse you may have discerned did not greatly affect the structure of the music. In contrast, the pulse in "Riding High" gave you access to the musical structure. In the final example, a regular pulse with changing meters and revolving accents provided a precarious rhythmic "ride."

CROSSROADS

This chapter has provided a broad view of the variety that is found in large ensembles. Our focus now turns to specific ensembles, starting with the orchestra.

CHAPTER

Orchestra: The Evolution of the Classical Symphony

20

PRELUDE: THE RELATION BETWEEN INSTRUMENTAL GENRE AND LARGE FORMAL PATTERNS

Much of the music performed in contemporary recitals, chamber music and symphony concerts comes from the Classical and Romantic periods. Primary instrumental **genre** *(kind of piece)* during this 150-year period (1750–1900) include the sonata, string quartet, symphony, and concerto. The following chart should help you understand these genre.

Genre	Performed by	Usual Number of Movements
Sonata	solo instrument and piano (or piano alone)	3
String quartet	string quartet (2 violins, viola, cello)	4
Symphony	"symphony" orchestra (complement of strings, winds, and percussion)	4
Concerto	soloist (for example, piano or violin) and orchestra	3

Active Listening
CD 2:3

Work by Wolfgang Amadeus Mozart

CD 3:13

Work by Franz Josef Haydn

- Review the "Performed by" column in the chart above to make sure you associate the correct performers with each genre.
- Listen carefully to each selection.
- Is there a soloist?
- Is an orchestra performing? (This can be confusing when comparing a string quartet to an isolated section of some symphonies.)
- Identify the genre of the Mozart.
- Identify the genre of the Haydn.

Even though there are exceptions to these generalized descriptions, they should prove to be helpful guideposts as you listen to instrumental music through recordings and in the concert hall.

MOVEMENTS AND THEIR TEMPOS

Each movement has a typical tempo and formal pattern.

First Movement:	fast tempo, usually in sonata form; in the concerto the opening themes are usually stated first by the orchestra and then by the soloist.
Second Movement:	slow tempo, may be in sonata, ternary (three-part) or binary (two-part) form; sometimes theme and variations.
Third Movement:	moderate tempo, often in triple meter; minuet and trio (classical) or scherzo (romantic); ternary forms. (This movement is omitted from the concerto and sonata.)
Final Movement:	fast tempo, usually in rondo form.

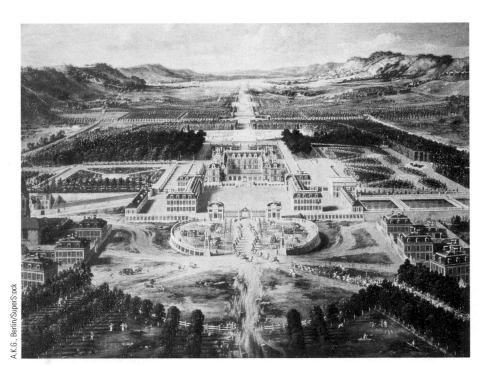

A.K.G., Berlin/SuperStock

Versailles Palace

Each of these formal designs will be described in detail and illustrated by a listening example in the subsequent discussions of the genre mentioned above.

ORCHESTRAL MUSIC

THE SYMPHONY

A **symphony** is a *work for orchestra that is usually in four movements and focuses on ensemble playing* rather than soloists Most often, the symphony is abstract: it does not project an extramusical idea or image. To avoid confusion, remember that the genre is called a symphony and the ensemble that performs it, an orchestra.

The longevity of the symphony's existence and the number of symphonies that have been composed make a persuasive argument for learning about the genre. From its beginnings in the late baroque, the symphony has enjoyed a continuous evolution up to the present day. To give you some perspective of the number of symphonies that have been composed, one catalog lists 12,350 works from the years c.1720 to 1810 alone.

The staying power of the symphony is due in part to the immense potential for variety that is inherent in the orchestra—a flexible ensemble in which strings, winds, percussion, and sometimes voices combine according to the expressive needs of the piece. At least as important to the popularity of this genre is the ingenuity of composers in continuously finding new and fresh ways to compose within the symphonic structure. A basic understanding of how the symphony evolved coupled with a knowledge of some conventions of symphonic composition will allow you to enjoy this primary vehicle for orchestral communication.

THE EVOLUTION OF THE SYMPHONY

In the late seventeenth century, the Italian word *sinfonia* (literally "together, sounding") referred to the title for opera overtures. In time, composers cast their *sinfonias* in three movements, with a fast-slow-fast pattern, and performed them as freestanding pieces. A more important contributor to the early history of the symphony was the *ripieno* concerto (the concerto, which will be discussed later, existed in three basic types during the baroque). Rather than featuring soloists or contrasting groups of players, the *ripieno*, or *tutti* concerto focused on all members of the ensemble, thereby approximating the texture of the early symphony. Also set in three movements, these works were almost always performed in a concert setting. Around 1740, Italian composers began writing opera overtures in a fashion that featured several characteristics of the new classical style:

1. A change from polyphonic to homophonic texture
2. A larger and more powerful orchestra
3. A greater use of gradual (instead of abrupt) dynamic contrasts
4. The use of contrasting themes in the first movement

Over the next few years, Italian composers such as G. B. Sammartini and German composers of the Mannheim court adapted these style characteristics to the symphony. Mannheim composers expanded the symphony to four movements by adding a minuet and trio before the last movement and used an incomplete version of sonata form in the first movement. With these changes, the classical symphony was complete in a somewhat embryonic form.

THE FIRST MOVEMENT—SONATA FORM

Sonata form is a *generalized, variable three-part formal design* that is usually *found in the first movements of symphonies, sonatas, concertos, string quartets, and overtures.* In a general sense, sonata form is analogous to the structure that is suggested for writing short papers in English classes: an opening paragraph that introduces the topic or subject matter *(exposition)*, a central section that develops those ideas *(development)*, and a restatement of the opening topic with a conclusion *(recapitulation)*. As in the case of reading a paper, it is important to remember the *theme* (thesis statement) of a sonata form in order to be able to follow

Courtesy of Michael Rosenfeld Gallery, New York, NY

First Theme,
Burgoyne Diller

the development and recognize the recapitulation and conclusion. While at first following a sonata form in an extended piece may seem like a daunting task, after a little practice you will find it very possible since the first theme is typically made very obvious, often at the very beginning of the movement.

SONATA FORM

Exposition

A slow introduction is optional.

Theme 1	memorable, in the tonic or home key (C, in C major, for example)
Transition	to the key of the second theme
Theme 2	contrasting, often slower; in the dominant key (G, in C major) or relative minor (a, in C major)
Close	optional **coda** or codetta: a musical afterthought
Repeat	typically, the entire exposition is repeated (this may be omitted in contemporary performances)

Development

Manipulation of themes 1 and/or 2. Themes may be

1. modulated, *changed to new keys,* which produces a feeling of instability and forward motion. Listening for statements of the theme at different pitch levels may help you identify modulation.
2. repeated.
3. sequenced, *repeated at successively higher or lower pitch levels.*
4. fragmented, *broken into parts.*
5. inverted, *performed upside down.*
6. in retrograde, *performed backwards.*
7. augmented, *made twice as long.*
8. diminished, *made half as long.*
9. reharmonized, *supported by new chords.*

Recapitulation

Follows the design of the exposition except

- the transition does not modulate to the dominant key. In order for the entire movement to seem finished, it must end in the tonic key
- theme 2 will probably sound lower than it did in the exposition.
- the recapitulation may be followed by a coda.

EINE KLEINE NACHTMUSIK, FIRST MOVEMENT, *ALLEGRO* WOLFGANG AMADEUS MOZART

The familiar *Eine kleine Nachtmusik* (first heard in Chapter 8) provides an ideal introduction to sonata form. Although it is actually a **serenade,** *a lighter, more compact work that is related to the symphony and the string quartet,* the first movement is similar to an early symphony and is easily identifiable as being in sonata form.

Active Listening
CD 1:6

Eine kleine Nachtmusik, First Movement, *Allegro,* Wolfgang Amadeus Mozart

Exposition

- Theme 1 opens the movement.
- Listen for the transition. It occurs after a softer section and is characterized by rising pitch levels at counter number 00:32.

- Theme 2 begins with a descending scale passage after a pause or rest. Although many composers use rests to set off formal sections, Mozart uses this technique in a very obvious fashion, making it easier to hear his formal patterns.
- Be sure to notice the closing theme that is used to end the movement.
- The exposition is repeated so you will have a second chance to hear all the themes.
- During the repeat, identify the counter numbers for theme 1, the transition, and theme 2.

Development

- After the repeat (and another rest), the development section begins with theme 1. Is theme 1 at the same pitch level or a higher or lower level?
- Immediately after the statement of theme 1, the closing theme from the end of the exposition is heard.
- This closing theme is stated on two additional pitch levels, indicating a key change (modulation back to the tonic). Since this is a more compact work, the development is very brief and leads directly into the recapitulation.

Recapitulation

- Follow the formal design as you did in the repeat of the exposition above. Is theme 2 at a lower pitch level than the exposition (remaining in the tonic)? Note that this difference changes the transition that precedes theme 2.
- The movement ends with a brief closing section.

CLASSICAL SYMPHONISTS

Wolfgang Amadeus Mozart (1756–1791) was one of three major composers of symphonies in the classical style. Mozart was a child prodigy, first as a performer with his sister Maria Anna and then as a composer, having written two symphonies by the age of nine.

In spite of his precocity, and the attention of his father, Leopold, who was devoted to his career, Mozart never received financial compensation that equaled the excellence of his music. He died at the age of 35 of natural causes, not as a result of the rumored poisoning by Salieri that was dramatized in the movie *Amadeus*.

Of Mozart's approximately fifty symphonies, forty-one are numbered. (Ludwig Köchel established the more systematic "K" identification system after

Young Mozart at the
keyboard, accompanied
by his father and sister

Giraudon/Art Resource, NY

Mozart's death.) Mozart's symphonies range from earlier works in three movements, which are related to the development of the symphonic form, to Symphonies 38 through 41, which are composed on a far grander scale and contain
much more sophisticated thematic development than *Eine kleine Nachtmusik.*

By contrast, Franz Joseph Haydn (1732–1809) spent most of his professional life in continuing employment as a composer and conductor at the Court
of Esterhazy. After the death of Prince Nickolas in 1790, Haydn's relationship
with Esterhazy became freer, allowing him to reside in Vienna and make several trips to London. As a "senior" composer, he became acquainted with
Mozart and the young Beethoven. When he became terminally ill, Napoleon
placed a guard of honor at Haydn's house in Vienna as a gesture of respect.

Haydn wrote approximately 104 symphonies, beginning with modest
works from the 1750s and ending with the 12 London Symphonies that were
written between 1791 and 1795 for public concerts in that city.

In his symphonies, Haydn consistently showed an interest in thematic
development and manipulation, often extending beyond the development section into recapitulations and expositions.

Classical composers more or less standardized formal patterns for the symphony. Beethoven, who we encounter at the beginning of the next chapter,
began composing in the classical style but soon started taking liberties with
classical forms.

Orchestra: The Zenith of the Symphony in the Nineteenth Century

BEETHOVEN: THE CULMINATION OF THE CLASSICAL SYMPHONY AND THE BEGINNINGS OF THE ROMANTIC SYMPHONY

The German composer Ludwig van Beethoven (1770–1827) is often thought of as the composer who bridges the classical and romantic periods of musical style. Born in Bonn, Beethoven was given early instruction in violin and piano and later learned to play the French horn. Under the guidance of his first important composition teacher, he studied the music of Bach. His later composition teachers included Franz Joseph Haydn. In addition to being a composer, Beethoven was a performer and conductor, making his first public performance as a soloist in one of his piano concertos in 1795. Unfortunately, by 1802 growing deafness was seriously impeding his work as a performer and conductor, and by 1824 his deafness was complete.

Traditionally, Beethoven's compositional output has been divided into three periods:

Through 1800: early period   most closely related to the classical style

1801–1814:   middle period   quasi-romantic in style, includes Fifth Symphony

1814–1827:   late period   most unconventional, innovative, and complex works, includes Ninth Symphony

Beethoven's Fifth Symphony is probably the most popular symphony of all time. It is an ideal work to study, since it retains the classical sonata form as an ideal, yet employs the experimentation and expansion of the formal design that are characteristic of the romantic style. The first movement is amazing in that a complex sonata form is based on the simple four-note, two-pitch theme that is most likely familiar to you.

Active Listening
CD 1:27

Symphony No. 5, First Movement, *Allegro con brio*, Ludwig van Beethoven

Exposition

- Like the Mozart piece, the movement opens with theme 1.
- The transition is a simple horn melody that is based on the rhythm of theme 1.
- The more lyrical theme 2 is almost immediately contradicted by an inverted version of theme 1 in the basses at counter number 2:15.
- In the repeat, identify the counter numbers of theme 1, the transition, theme 2.

Development

- The development opens with theme 1 in a different key.
- Several subsequent modulations can be heard at counter numbers 2:22 and 2:58.
- Theme 1 is also broken into fragments at counter numbers 3:04 and 3:14.

Recapitulation

- Beethoven breaks several "rules" of sonata form in the recapitulation.
- The first and most obvious is an oboe solo that is added.
- This movement should end here, but Beethoven adds a coda. This is the usual practice, but this coda is unusual in that it contains what sounds like continued development.
- The movement finally ends with theme 1 inverted.

CROSSROADS

By studying Beethoven's compositional sketchbooks we have learned that he carefully crafted his music through revision after revision. Mozart, who is known to have been a facile composer, wrote more than 40 symphonies in his brief 35-year lifetime. This compares to Beethoven's nine symphonies over a life span of 57 years. While some of this difference can be attributed to the much larger scope of Beethoven's symphonies, Beethoven's method of composing (along with his compositional goals) is partially responsible. Compositional method notwithstanding, creating music for a large group like an orchestra is a very private activity that is both laborious and time-consuming. Happily, recently developed computer programs allow composers to omit the slow process of hand-written scores and parts. Now a composer can "write" in full score on the computer and then have the computer play back the music and print out the score and individual instrumental parts.

This symphony retains the overall design of the classical sonata form. On the other hand, it leans toward romanticism in the expansion of emotional content, greater dynamic range, increased size of the orchestra, creation of relationships between movements, and overall length of the symphony.

ABSTRACT ROMANTIC SYMPHONIES

Many romantic composers used the symphony as a vehicle for personal expression and experimentation with orchestral color. These goals displaced the classical need to create a clear and balanced formal structure. The following list includes several of these composers, a comment on style, and a suggestion for further listening.

Franz Schubert	beautiful, lyrical themes	No 8, *Unfinished,* first movement
Felix Mendelssohn	colorful orchestration	No 4, *Italian,* first movement, sonata form
Johannes Brahms	conservative style	No 4, fourth movement, variations based on a chaconne (repeated) bass
Peter Tchaikovsky	best in lyrical movements	No 6, *Pathetique,* last movement (slow)

PROGRAM SYMPHONIES AND THE SYMPHONIC POEM

The composers in the preceding list represent the conservative faction of nineteenth-century symphonic composers. Their more progressive romantic counterparts seem to be united by a desire to represent the emotional: nature, dreams, visions, or the unattainable. Although this goal can be achieved in abstract instrumental music, these composers made the process more effective by the addition of a **program:** *some kind of description or story that was intended to be included in the concert program.*

To be sure, there are subtitles for the symphonies of Haydn and Mozart — some added by the composer and some added by later writers. Beethoven's Sixth Symphony, the "Pastorale," has a program that includes a musically illustrated "storm" movement. Using such points of departure, romantic composers developed more elaborate methods of illustrating programs in their symphonies.

Candle Dancers,
Emil Nolde

THE *IDÉE FIXE* IN *SYMPHONIE FANTASTIQUE* BY BERLIOZ

The *Symphonie Fantastique* by French composer Hector Berlioz (1803–1869) was first performed in 1830, just three years after the death of Beethoven. At the time of this performance of what turned out to be his most lasting work, the young Berlioz had finished studying at the Paris Conservatory and begun to establish himself as a composer. This symphony is based in part on his own life, for he had recently become infatuated with an Irish Shakespearean actress named Harriet Smithson. In the program that Berlioz provided, a young musician "sees for the first time a woman who embodies all the charms of the ideal being he has imagined in his dreams and he falls desperately in love with her." The *Symphonie Fantastique*, then, loosely represents the pursuit by Berlioz ("the artist") of the unattainable love, Harriet Smithson ("the beloved"). The "fantastic" element of the symphony is the series of dreams that the artist, who has taken opium, has about the relationship. For example, in the fourth movement, "March to the Scaffold," the artist believes his love is unappreciated and dreams he has killed his beloved and is witnessing his own execution. In the final movement, "Dream of the Witches' Sabbath," the beloved returns to take part in a devilish orgy ridiculing the dead artist.

Berlioz uses a theme he called an *"idée fixe"* to represent the beloved. With each appearance, the theme is transformed to represent a different vision. The following two excerpts are the initial version of the *idée fixe* from the first movement and the final version from the last movement, after the beloved has been killed and the artist executed. Listen to both excerpts remembering that the first depicts a beautiful young woman and the last describes the witch-like apparition of her appearing to the artist in his dream.

Symphonie Fantastique, **First Movement,** *Idée fixe,* **Hector Berlioz**

Active Listening
CD 3:14

Symphonie Fantastique, **Fifth Movement,** *Idée fixe,* **Hector Berlioz**

CD 3:15

- Is this musical transformation successful?
- Is the second melody still recognizable as a modified version of the first?

The practice of using one theme to unite several movements became more prevalent as the nineteenth century progressed. In a parallel development, Richard Wagner carried the process of using themes (which he called **leitmotifs,** or leading motives) to represent persons, places, or things to an extreme in his operas. At least as important in the music of Berlioz is his ability to use imaginative combinations of instruments to create highly dramatic music.

CROSSROADS

You heard the "Dies irae" theme in its original setting as part of the Mass for the Dead in Kyrie XI, in Chapter 12. Take a moment to review the text on page 74. A quick reading should suggest that it has more to do with the Day of Judgment and the possibility of asking for life after death than it does with death itself. However, as is the case in the *Symphonie Fantastique,* most symbolic uses of the theme use it to refer to death. In the example above, the artist dreams that his death has already occurred and that it is being satirized by the "Dance of the Witches' Sabbath" theme. In the movie *The Shining* the "Dies irae" is heard as Jack Torrence is driving up to The Outlook, a hotel where he has an interview for the position of caretaker. This statement of the theme is accompanied by screeches, howls, and electronic sounds, and stops when he arrives at the hotel. He is the only character who dies by the end of the film.

The "Dies irae" can be heard in a number of other concert works including Liszt's *Totentanz* (Dance of Death), Saint Säens' *Danse Macabre,* and Stravinsky's *Rite of Spring.* Pop groups have used both the theme and the text, and one "death metal" group even calls itself Dies Irae.

"DANCE OF THE WITCHES' SABBATH"

The fifth movement of the *Symphonie Fantastique* is in four sections, each with a subtitle. According to one theorist, the actual movement begins in the final two sections with the earlier sections serving as introductory material. Sections three and four comprise a loosely organized fugue that is modified by the programmatic conflict between two themes. The first occurs in section three, which represents a witches' sabbath round dance. This theme is pitted against the "Dies irae," the Gregorian chant from the Mass for the Dead.

LISTENING GUIDE

Symphonie Fantastique, Fifth Movement, "Dance of the Witches' Sabbath," Hector Berlioz

CD 1:28

Section 3, The Fugal Exposition

00:00	The "Dance of the Witches' Sabbath" theme is heard in all four voices.
00:28	Fugal episode involving theme fragments and other material
00:47	Restatement of fugal theme
1:03	Development
1:28	Restatement of theme followed by statements of "Dies irae" theme
2:00	Ascending and descending chromatic line leading to climax

Section 4

2:45	"Dance of the Witches' Sabbath" is combined in counterpoint with the "Dies irae." Each is then heard singly before the final demonic ending.
3:04	Transitional section
3:16	Augmentation (double note values) of Sabbath theme
3:50	New version of Sabbath theme; interrupted by "Dies irae"
4:00	Drive to the final cadence

A final interesting aspect of this work is the focus on depicting a fantastic and grotesque dream rather than a conscious, rational event. Later in the century, composers and visual artists became more interested in dreamlike, less representational topics and in providing opportunities for listeners and viewers to participate in the artwork by using their imagination. Listening to the entire *Symphonie Fantastique* will give you an ideal chance to use your imagination in this fashion. As a final note, in real life Berlioz neither took opium nor lost his beloved; he and Smithson were married not long after the first performance of the *Symphonie Fantastique*, although the marriage soon ended in divorce.

A type of program music that is more specific than the *Symphonie Fantastique*, is the **symphonic poem** (or **tone poem**): a *one-movement orchestral work that is based on a poetic or descriptive extramusical idea*. The poetic type is based on a poem, while the descriptive symphonic poem concentrates on describing a "noun" (person, place, or thing). Like the first movement of the symphony, these works were often in a modified sonata form. Franz Liszt, (1811–1886) a Hungarian composer who also wrote important piano music, can be credited with creating the symphonic poem.

A number of important composers wrote symphonic poems, and although these works are not as numerous as symphonies, they are frequently heard at orchestra concerts. The descriptive type of symphonic poem was favored by nationalist composers of the late nineteenth century. These composers sought to highlight and perhaps glorify their native country, often through a program that depicted important national places or events by the use of native folk melodies and rhythms. The symphonic poems listed below provide accessible listening.

Descriptive Symphonic Poems

Ma Vlast (My Fatherland)	1879	Bedrich Smetana
The Steppes of Central Asia	1880	Alexander Borodin
Finlandia	1899	Jean Sibelius
The Fountains of Rome	1917	Ottorino Respighi
Grand Canyon Suite	1922	Ferde Grofé

CORBIS/Bettmann

Liszt as a piano-winged hero destroying the dominance of rigid musical forms

Poetic Symphonic Poems

Les Preludes	1854	Franz Liszt
Romeo and Juliet	1870	Piotr Ilyich Tchaikovsky
Death and Transfiguration	1890	Richard Strauss
L'Après-midi d'un faune	1894	Claude Debussy
Till Eulenspiegel's Merry Pranks	1895	Richard Strauss
La Mer	1905	Claude Debussy

LATE ROMANTIC, POSTROMANTIC, AND TWENTIETH-CENTURY SYMPHONIES

The nineteenth century witnessed a dramatic growth in the size of the orchestra and the complexity and length of the symphony. The culmination of these trends can be seen in the symphonies of Austrian composers Anton Bruckner (1824–1896) and Gustav Mahler (1860–1911). Mahler's Eighth Symphony, subtitled the "Symphony of a Thousand," requires a huge orchestra, extra brass players, and men's, women's, and children's choirs for its performance. His Third Symphony is more than an hour and a half in length (most symphonies are less than an hour long). The strength of this music, however, lies not in size and scope but rather in the experimental use of tonality, the ingenious and sometimes sparing use of large orchestral forces, and the combination of a variety of styles in a single work.

The twentieth century saw a reaction to the excesses of romanticism in a return to smaller forces and the mirroring of earlier styles. Trends in music are often attributed to philosophy or idealism. In this case, however, one reason for reducing the size of the orchestra was quite practical: World War I had reduced much of Europe to ruins and made large performances financially and physically impossible.

Neoclassicism, when broadly interpreted to include the *return to any earlier styles other than romanticism,* describes the symphonies of several important early-twentieth-century composers. In addition to returning to smaller ensembles, the composers often used forms, terminology, and textures from earlier times. However, in almost all cases the musical language was contemporary.

Neoclassical Symphonies

Classical Symphony	1917	Sergei Prokofiev
Symphony of Psalms	1930	Igor Stravinsky
Mathis der Maler	1934	Paul Hindemith
Symphony in Three Movements	1945	Igor Stravinsky

Looking at the genre from a national perspective produces Witold Lutoslawski and Krzysztof Penderecki from Poland and Sergei Prokofiev and Dmitri Shostakovich from Russia. In the United States among the many nationalistic symphonists are Charles Ives, Aaron Copland, Samuel Barber, and Walter Piston.

As the twentieth century continued, an important change occurred when women composers began to receive recognition for their works. A case in point is Ellen Taaffe Zwilich, who was born in Miami in 1939 and educated at Florida State University and the Juilliard School, first received recognition in the 1970s for her *Symposium* and her String Quartet. A good example of a twentieth-century symphony is her Symphony No. 1, *Movements for Orchestra*, for which she was the first woman to receive a Pulitzer Prize in music, in 1983. Twentieth-century symphonists viewed the genre only as a basic framework for their compositions. Zwilich's symphony is in three movements instead of the usual four. Although earlier formal patterns are evident in this work, they are treated very freely. The third movement is in rondo form, which you remember from Chapter 8 involves the refrain idea with at least two returns of the opening A section (ABACA).

Active Listening
CD 3:16

Symphony No. 1, Third Movement, Ellen Taaffe Zwilich

* Identify the letter name for each of the following counter numbers:

00:00
1:12
1:36
1:50
3:17

* Are the returns of A exact repetitions of the original or does one evolve from the previous statement?
* Are the contrasting sections the same length as A?

Another important change in the symphony in the twentieth century was the interest in the genre by composers of non-European lineage. Such composers changed the flavor of the symphony by adding musical elements from their own cultural heritage.

William Grant Still (1895–1978) is acknowledged as the dean of African-American composers. His compositional background included some of the same influences enjoyed by Charles Ives. In 1916 he worked for W. C. Handy, the "Father of the Blues," and wrote the original band arrangements of Handy's most famous compositions, "Beale Street Blues" and "St. Louis Blues." This brief excerpt is an example of Still's blues background presented in "concert hall dress." The excerpt is fourteen measures long: a two-measure introduction and a twelve-measure blues pattern. It uses a call and response phrasing, as if the "call" is a question and the "response" is an answer.

Active Listening
CD 3:17

Afro-American Symphony, First Movement (excerpt), William Grant Still

- On the melodic score, do the following.

  Bracket each of the three phrases (as the introduction has been bracketed).
  Circle the "call" portion of each phrase and label with a letter "c."
  Circle the "response" portion of each phrase and label with an "r."

- Which instruments provide the call?
- Which instruments provide the response?
- Defend or contradict this statement: "This example of twelve-measure blues follows the aab form."

© Bettmann/CORBIS

William Grant Still

Although it has only been possible to scratch the surface of the symphony in this chapter, the vast number and diversity of works in the genre provide an almost limitless listening opportunity. Next we will consider the concept of the soloist, sometimes with orchestra and sometimes without.

CHAPTER

Soloists: With and Without Orchestra

22

THE SONATA

The word "sonata," from the Italian *sonare* (to sound), can be found in musical sources dating back to the thirteenth century and was customarily used in reference to some sort of instrumental music.

Initially, the baroque sonata in Italy could be dance or abstract music, for keyboard or ensemble, and for one to twenty-two performers. For example, Gabrieli's *Sonata pian' e forte* is an abstract ensemble sonata for winds and strings. One type of sonata that developed from this rather unfocused beginning was the ensemble sonata for one to four solo or melody instruments and accompaniment *(basso continuo)*. The most popular configuration for the ensemble sonata was the **trio sonata,** which consisted of *two soloists and basso continuo.* This title can be a bit confusing since a trio sonata actually required four players, with two musicians performing the continuo (often cello and keyboard). Similarly, a baroque solo violin sonata would require three players.

Because of a concern that only appropriate music be used in church, some sonatas used the distinguishing terms *da chiesa* or *da camera* in the title. A ***sonata da camera*** (chamber sonata) usually contained dance music and therefore was inappropriate for use in church. On the other hand, the ***sonata da chiesa*** (church sonata) was typically abstract and therefore was acceptable in religious settings.

The Sonata,
Marcel Duchamp

During the 1740s, composers began to concentrate on solo keyboard sonatas. As the pianoforte was developed during the classical period, the solo keyboard sonata became the piano sonata. Other sonatas involving keyboard instruments were either for piano and violin—which evolved into the violin sonata—or for piano, violin, and cello—which became the classical piano trio.

From the eighteenth century on, a **sonata** is a *work for solo instrument* that is *usually in three movements*. Sonatas for monophonic instruments (violin, for example) typically have keyboard accompaniment. To avoid confusion, remember that sonata may appear on a program to denote the genre defined above, while sonata *form* (exposition, development, recapitulation) is likely to be the formal design of the first movement of that sonata. The three movements of the classical sonata typically employ the formal patterns mentioned previously: first movement, *allegro* (a lively tempo), in a sonata form; second movement, slow tempo, in a sonata ternary, or binary form; third movement, *allegro,* in a rondo form.

Rondo form (mentioned in the previous chapter with respect to the Zwilich symphony) consists of the alternation of the opening section (A) with

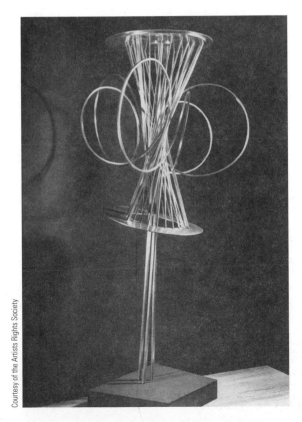

Rondo,
Hans Uhlmann

contrasting sections (B, C, D, and so on). Each repetition of A is in the original or tonic key, while the contrasting sections may be in other keys. Another way to think of rondo form is as an extension of ternary form.

Ternary Form: A B A

Rondo Form: A B A C A   or   A B A C A D A

Mozart's Piano Sonata No. 15 in C Major is one that has been played by many beginning to intermediate piano students. In fact, he subtitled it "little clavier sonata for beginners." It was, however, a late work, written in 1788 and published after Mozart's death. It is evident from this movement that Mozart was well aware of the latest developments in piano construction, including an improved hammer mechanism that would become standard in the future.

Active Listening
CD 2:3

Piano Sonata in C Major, Third Movement, Wolfgang Amadeus Mozart

- The movement opens with the A section. In the list below, identify the counter number each time there is a *full statement* of the A section in the tonic key.

  Opening statement of A — 00:00
  B (first contrasting section) — 00:18
  First return of A — _____:_____
  Second contrasting section — 00:52
  Second return of A — _____:_____

- Is the second contrasting section the same as B or different?
- If it is different should it be labeled C?
- Is it the same length as B?
- Which of the three sections of sonata form does this contrasting section remind you of?

As with the symphony, the sonata reached a high level of maturity with Beethoven. He wrote sonatas for violin, cello, horn, and piano. His thirty-two piano sonatas range from two to four movements; include traditional, expanded, and nontraditional forms; and are definitely intended for skilled professional performers. Although early romantic composers such as Schubert, Mendelssohn, and Weber wrote sonatas, interest in the genre declined after the death of Beethoven. Later romantic composers who carried on the sonata tradition include Schumann, Chopin, Liszt, and Brahms.

Sonatas have been written in the twentieth century for a much wider variety of instruments, with piano accompaniment. The establishment of numerous music schools and conservatories in the late nineteenth and early twentieth centuries created a need for solo recital literature for all instruments. Paul

Hindemith, a German composer who lived in the United States, initiated this trend by writing sonatas for nearly all orchestral instruments in the late 1930s and early '40s. Today, numerous sonatas and other solo works are available for every instrument.

THE CONCERTO: COMBINING SOLOISTS AND ORCHESTRA

Like "sonata" and "symphony," "concerto" went through several meanings before settling on the common practice: A **concerto** is *a three-movement work for soloist and orchestra.* One derivation of the term is the Italian *concertare,* meaning "to unite," as in joining together groups of instrumentalists and singers. Its Latin source means "to contend," which describes the opposition of soloist and orchestra found in the modern concerto.

Both ideas—opposition and unity—were common in musical thinking and practice at the turn of the seventeenth century at Saint Mark's Cathedral in Venice, where Giovanni Gabrieli (Chapter 5) and Claudio Monteverdi were employed. St. Mark's had two organs and two choir lofts, so it was natural for composers to separate musicians into two or even three opposing groups. Since string and wind players were readily available, it was common practice to add instrumentalists to the choirs or use them separately.

© SuperStock

Interior of St. Mark's Basilica, Venice, Italy

By the middle of the baroque period, three types of concertos were extant: the concerto grosso, the ripieno concerto, and the solo concerto. The concerto grosso featured a small group of soloists *(concertino)* pitted against a larger ensemble *(ripieno)*. The ripieno concerto featured the full ensemble and has been mentioned as a forerunner of the symphony. The last to develop was the solo concerto, which featured a single solo instrument with orchestra accompaniment. The six Brandenburg Concertos of Johann Sebastian Bach contain a compendium of characteristics of the baroque concerto. Although you learned in the ritual music unit that most of Bach's life was dedicated to church music, he did work for Prince Leopold of Cöthen from 1717 to 1723. It was during this time that these concertos were written and later dedicated to the Margrave of Brandenburg.

All of the Brandenburgs except No. 1 are in the typical (fast–slow–fast) three movements. Nos. 3 and 6 are ripieno concertos, while the other four are concerti grossi of varying descriptions. The instrumentation of the six concertos is varied and presents a kaleidoscope of instrumental colors. Some exhibit the traditional texture of opposing instruments, while others provide a texture that supports rather than contests the soloists. The first movement of the fifth concerto has an extended harpsichord solo (**cadenza**) like those that appear in the later classical concerto.

Brandenburg No. 2 is scored for natural (valveless) trumpet, recorder, oboe, and violin as the concertino with a string ensemble and harpsichord serving as the ripieno. An important technical device used in this piece is **sequence:** *repetition of a melodic fragment at a sequentially higher or lower pitch level.* Listen to the entire piece and answer the following questions. (A listening guide follows the questions.)

Active Listening
CD 3:18

Brandenburg Concerto No. 2, Third Movement, Johann Sebastian Bach

- Is the trumpet the dominant solo instrument, or do the other concertino instruments share in the solo responsibilities?
- Is the small group pitted against the large group, or does it serve primarily as an accompaniment for a contest of solo instruments?
- Is the texture predominantly polyphonic or homophonic or a combination of the two?
- Is this work divided into clearly defined sections of equal length like *Eine kleine Nachtmusik,* or are they less distinct?

If you answered these questions correctly, you have set the stage for understanding how the baroque concerto leads to the classical concerto and yet differs from it in several respects (see the following Crossroads).

During the classical period the concerto that featured a soloist, most often the violin or the piano, almost completely replaced the other types. As the solo

Baroque Concerto	**Classical Concerto**	CROSSROADS
Trumpet shares solo role	Trumpet is only soloist	
Contrast less clear	Contrast well-defined	
Primarily polyphonic	Primarily homophonic	
Less distinct sections	Well-defined, balanced sections	

Brandenburg Concerto No. 2, Third Movement,   LISTENING
Johann Sebastian Bach   GUIDE

CD 3:18

00:00   Trumpet enters with primary theme. Theme is in two parts; second part features sequence of a melodic fragment.

00:07   Oboe enters in imitation of trumpet.

00:30   Recorder enters at softer dynamic level.

00:46   Trumpet and oboe enter with theme.

1:05   Recorder with melody

1:15   Oboe with melody

1:30   All three instruments develop theme fragments.

2:03   Paraphrase of original theme; several instruments

2:37   Trumpet with theme to end

concerto became the preeminent type, a modified version of the first movement sonata form evolved. The result is sometimes called the double exposition: The orchestra presents the entire exposition, after which the soloist immediately re–presents it. Variations on this general plan range from abbreviating the orchestra's introduction to greatly condensing the soloist's exposition to the later idea of the soloist and orchestra presenting the exposition together. The first movement of the concerto acquired another difference from the other genres through the addition of a cadenza (unaccompanied solo) for the soloist at the end of the movement. Typically, the orchestra would cadence on a tonic chord and then the soloist embarks on an unaccompanied virtuoso solo that was often improvised. At the end of the cadenza the orchestra enters and ends the movement.

As in the other genres, the final movement of the concerto is most often a rondo form, adapted to the special needs of the soloist/orchestra relationship.

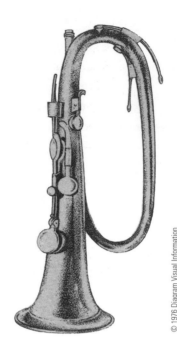

© 1976 Diagram Visual Information

Keyed trumpet

Haydn wrote the Trumpet Concerto in E-flat in 1796, in part because a keyed trumpet had been invented that could be played in a much wider range of tonalities than the natural trumpet.

Active Listening
CD 3:13

Trumpet Concerto in E-flat, Third Movement, Rondo, Franz Josef Haydn

- The movement opens with the orchestra stating the A section (counter number 00:00) and the B section (counter number 00:22).
- The soloist performs both A and B (counter numbers 00:38 and 1:07, respectively).
- The trumpet returns with the A theme.
- How would you describe the music that comes after this statement of A?
- After this section, the trumpet states the A theme, again followed by the B theme.
- Finally, the A theme returns in a closing section.
- What is the form of this rondo?

If you listened carefully to answer the question above you may have heard something that was based on A but sounded like development, a characteristic of sonata form. Here is how what we heard in the Haydn compares with rondo and sonata forms:

Haydn	A B :‖ A? (based on A) A BA
Rondo	AB A (C) ABA
Sonata	exposition/development/recapitulation (Th.1, Th.2)

Compared with rondo form, the Haydn has a modified return of A but no new contrasting section (C) after that. Like sonata form, it does have two themes and there is a development-like section (A?), but it ends with an incomplete statement of theme 1 (A). In fact, this is a form that is usually called **sonata-rondo:** a *hybrid form that mixes characteristics of rondo with sonata form.*

Although concertos continued to be written for other instruments, the violin and piano remained the most popular choices. Mozart wrote twenty-three concertos for piano whereas Beethoven composed five. Romantic composers in this genre include Mendelssohn, Schumann, Brahms, Grieg, Tchaikovsky, and Rachmaninov. As the century progressed, emphasis was focused on virtuoso performers like violinist Nicolo Paganini, whose showy performances led some to believe that he had supernatural powers. The piano concertos of Liszt and Chopin also follow this virtuoso trend. Romantic concertos remain a mainstay of contemporary orchestra programs.

Twentieth-century composers adapted the genre to their own musical language (Webern's Concerto for Nine Instruments) and to contemporary trends such as neoclassicism (Stravinsky's Concerto for Piano and Winds). A new type of concerto was the "concerto for orchestra," which featured various instruments and sections of the orchestra as virtuoso "instruments." Bartók's Concerto for Orchestra (1943), which you heard in Chapter 18, is the most popular example of this concerto type.

CHAPTER

Opera: Combining Voices with Orchestra

23

DEFINITION AND DESCRIPTION

Opera is *sung drama in which singers play the roles of the characters on a suitably decorated stage.* Operas are *accompanied by an orchestra* that is normally placed in a sunken space (the orchestra pit) between the stage and the audience. Optional components of opera include a chorus and dancers, both typically made up of "extras" in the plot.

OPERA PLOTS

Although a variety of terms describe types of operas, opera can generally be thought of in the same categories that apply to theater: comedy and tragedy, although words such as comic and serious are often substituted for the theatrical terms. The **libretto** or *text of the opera* is typically written by someone other than the composer and may be entirely new or, more likely, an adaptation of an existing literary work.

THE MARRIAGE OF FIGARO, WOLFGANG AMADEUS MOZART

Mozart and librettist Lorenzo da Ponte based *The Marriage of Figaro* (1786) on a French play by that name written by Beaumarchais about 1778 and first performed in Paris in 1784. The characters in the opera are Figaro, servant to Count Almaviva; Susanna, maid to Countess Almaviva; Count Almaviva; Countess Almaviva; Cherubino, the Count's page; Basilio, music teacher; Doctor Bartolo; Marcellina, his housekeeper; Antonio, the Count's gardener; and Barbarina, his daughter.

The opera opens with Figaro and Susanna planning to be married. However, the Count makes plans to take advantage of his feudal "right of the first night" with Susanna. Cherubino, the page, is infatuated with all women but

Cherubino (disguised as Susanna) singing to Susanna and the Countess

© Beth Bergman

If *The Marriage of Figaro* reminds you of a soap opera, you have drawn the right conclusion. Around the beginning of the twentieth century, opera was a popular type of entertainment in the United States. Early radio dramas capitalized on this popularity by copying the complexities of opera plots. Since advertising from soap companies supported these radio dramas, they became known as soap operas. It suffices to say that if you like the kind of plots you find in soap operas, you will also like opera.

particularly with the Countess. To make things more complicated, Figaro has an obligation to marry Marcellina unless he repays a debt to Doctor Bartolo.

The Marriage of Figaro does have its serious side, for underneath this almost farcical plot is a serious satire of the nobility. In the first act a group of peasants comes in singing a chorus thanking the Count for renouncing his "right of first night," making a strong social comment about this privilege. Moreover, Figaro consistently outwits the Count and in the end, wins Susanna.

MUSICAL NUMBERS IN OPERA

Most operas are made up of a series of musical numbers beginning with an overture. The **overture,** an *orchestral number* played before the curtain goes up, contains many of the main themes of the act and *serves as a musical introduction to the opera.* The drama of an opera primarily unfolds through the alternation of **recitative** *(basically free, speechlike singing)* and **aria** *(more structured and melodic singing with repeated words and recurring musical motives).* These two primary types of opera numbers evolved at the very beginning of opera in the opening years of the seventeenth century. The basic idea is that the recitative, with its simple style and easily understood text, carries the dramatic action forward. The aria, on the other hand, is a vehicle for reflecting on a single idea or emotion and provides the singer with an opportunity for displaying vocal talent.

In the second act of *The Marriage of Figaro,* Cherubino is wrestling with the emotions of impending manhood. Susanna and the Countess are both genuinely interested in his plight and gently poke fun at his immaturity. First, read the texts of both the recitative and the arietta (a shortened form of the aria). The interaction of the three characters in the recitative sets the scene for the reflective nature of the arietta. The simple chordal accompaniment of the recitative makes it easy for the words to be heard, while the lyrical nature of the arietta provides a vehicle for the expression of Cherubino's emotions. These recitatives and arias are played in a continuous fashion as they occur in the opera.

Active Listening

***The Marriage of Figaro,* Act II, Wolfgang Amadeus Mozart**

CD 3:19

Recitative, *"Quanto duolmi"*

Countess	I'm grieved Susanna, that that youth should have overheard the Count's follies: You just don't know . . . But why ever did he not come straight to me? Where's his song?
Susanna	Here it is: and when he comes, let's make him sing it. Hush, someone's coming: it's he. Come in, my gallant captain.
Cherubino	Oh don't call me by that horrid title! It reminds me that I am forced to leave a godmother so kind.
Susanna	And so beautiful!
Cherubino	(sighing) Ah . . . yes . . . indeed!
Susanna	(imitating him) Ah . . . yes . . . indeed. . . . You hypocrite! Make haste, sing to my lady the song you gave to me this morning.
Countess	Who wrote it?
Susanna	Look: he's blushing all over his face.
Countess	Take my guitar and accompany him.
Cherubino	I'm all a-tremble . . . But if my lady wishes . . .
Susanna	Yes, indeed she does . . . don't keep her waiting.

CD 3:20

Arietta, *"Voi che sapete,"* Cherubino

You ladies who know what love is, see if it is what I have in my heart.
All that I feel I will explain; since it is new to me, I don't understand it.
I have a feeling full of desire, which now is pleasure, now is torment.
I freeze, then I feel my spirit ablaze, and the next moment turn again to ice.
I seek for a treasure outside of myself: I know not who holds it nor what it is.

I sigh and I groan without wishing to, I flutter and I tremble without
  knowing why.
I find no peace by day or night, but yet to languish thus is sheer delight.
You ladies who know what love is, see if it is what I have in my heart.

Before the nineteenth century, recitatives were customarily accompanied
by a keyboard instrument and perhaps a violoncello, whereas arias featured
far more colorful and varied orchestral settings. The contrast between them
became less distinct in romantic operas.

Other types of musical numbers that occur in operas include the **duet,** *sung
by two singers,* and the **ensemble:** *a formal number for more than two singers in which
the characters express themselves both in alternation and simultaneously.*

COMIC OPERA

Comic opera features a *more or less humorous treatment of plot and a nontragic ending.* In different times and places, comic operas have varied somewhat in structure and have been identified by a variety of terms. For example, *The Marriage
of Figaro* is known as an **opera buffa.**

Because music traditionally unfolds in large lyrical formal structures, operatic scenes must have less text and less complexity of plot and characterization
than a stage play. In compensation, emotions are expressed more fully and, frequently, an important scene placed at the end of an act builds to a grand
ensemble-finale. This closing number is so named because it calls for the entire
company, including all or most of the principal characters and the chorus, to
sing together.

To keep the Count from pursuing Susanna, Figaro has written a letter to
the Count that suggests the Countess is meeting a suitor that evening. In this
brief scene, Figaro enters (in a fast tempo) hoping to rush through his wedding
ceremony. The Count enters in longer note values, effectively slowing down
Figaro's attack. Note that the meter changes to duple and the tempo slows
when the Count actually starts questioning Figaro about the letter. Figaro
steadfastly denies writing the letter and finally deflects the Count's questioning
at the end of the scene.

In meeting the dramatic needs of the text, the characters enter singly and
combine in duets, trios, and quartets. The vocal texture is sometimes polyphonic and sometimes homophonic and occasionally a combination of both. It
is remarkable that there is so much variety in a three-minute scene from an
opera that is several hours in length.

The Marriage of Figaro, Act II, Scene Ten, *"Signori di fuori,"* **Mozart**

- Fast, triple meter

Figaro	My lord and lady, the musicians are outside.
	You can hear the trumpeters and the pipers
	With the singing and dancing of your vassals.
	Let us hasten to celebrate our wedding!
	[he takes Susanna by the arm]

- Contrasting style, longer note values

Count	One moment: not so fast.
Figaro	The crowd is waiting.
Count	Before you go, remove a doubt of mine.

- All four characters making asides together results in quartet

Susanna, Countess, and Figaro [stage whispers]
          This is getting difficult, how will it end?
Count [stage whisper]
          Now I must play my cards carefully.

- Slower, duple meter

Count	Master Figaro, do you know who penned this letter?
Figaro	I've no idea.

Susanna, Countess, and Count
          You've no idea?

Figaro	No, no.

- Ascending line indicating a question

Susanna	Didn't you give it to Don Basilio?

- Imitation of ascending line

Countess	To deliver?

- Descending line (statement)

Count	You're deceiving me.

- Imitation of descending line

Figaro	No, no.

- Ascending line again

Susanna	You don't know about the gallant . . .

- Imitation

Countess	This evening in the garden . . .

- Descending line

  Count   You know now . . .

- Imitation

  Figaro   I've no idea.
  Count   In vain you seek a defense or excuse.
                 Your very face accuses you:
                 I can see you're trying to lie.
  Figaro   My face is the liar, not I!

- Duet, singing together

  Susanna and Countess
                 You sharpen your wits in vain;
                 We've revealed the secret,
                 There's no more to be said.
  Count   What's your answer?
  Figaro   Nothing, nothing.
  Count   So you admit it?
  Figaro   No, I don't, sir.

- Agitated, short note values

  Susanna   Hold your tongue, stupid,
                 This comedy must be ended.
  Countess   Hold your tongue, stupid,
                 This comedy must be ended.
  Figaro   Then to end it happily,
                 According to theatrical practice,
                 Let a marriage ceremony now follow.

- Lines sung together, women with lyrical lines, men independent, resulting
  in a quartet texture.

  Susanna, Countess, and Figaro
                 Oh my lord, do not refuse.
                 Grant their wishes.
  Count   Marcellina, Marcellina,
                 How slow you are in coming!

If you had difficulty following the action based on these changes in style, take heart; modern performances typically include English subtitles and the acting of the characters also provides some clues. Besides, reading the plot should verify the fact that this opera is similar in plot to most soap operas.

TRAGIC OPERA

Tragic operas are *serious works with unhappy or disastrous endings*, often involving the death of one or more of the main characters. Giuseppe Verdi's *Otello* uses the main characters and the basic plot of Shakespeare's *Othello* but transforms the structure of the play into that of Italian opera. By necessity the plot becomes more concise and the characters less complex. In compensation the language of music speaks directly to the listener's heart, and the scenes of interaction between the characters are enhanced by their singing simultaneously, in duets or in ensemble. As is traditional in romantic opera, the role of the heroine (Desdemona) is taken by a soprano, the hero (Otello) by a tenor, and the villain (Iago) by a baritone.

Verdi and his librettist Arrigo Boito eliminated Shakespeare's entire first act, choosing to open *Otello* with clearly separated pieces. The music of *Otello* flows continuously, helping the audience to believe in and assimilate the swiftly moving events of Act I: the storm, the victory celebration, the brawl, and the love duet between Otello and Desdemona. Conventional numbers remain, but now they are always absolutely integral to the drama. In Act II, for example, Iago's famous "Credo" (his assertion of nonbelief, which greatly clarifies his character and motivation) is expressed in an impressive, but quite traditional, aria. And when Otello's growing jealousy and loss of belief in Desdemona leads him to seek revenge, he and Iago express this decisive turn of events in a customary, act-ending, vengeance duet.

The great ensemble scene of the opera marks the high point of Act III. Here, one fully experiences the unique magic of opera. Rejected and reviled publicly by Otello in front of the Venetian ambassador and his retinue, Desdemona laments in a magnificently wide-ranging melodic line that must project through and float above the entire ensemble. Below, in their various lower vocal registers, Otello, Iago, and the ambassador (in fact, seven soloists altogether) simultaneously express their thoughts and feelings. Finally, two choruses complete the tableau by adding their observations of astonishment and pity.

By playing upon Otello's own weakness and inciting his jealousy, Iago has succeeded in turning him against Desdemona. In this ensemble, even as Iago arranges for her murder, she laments her unjust treatment.

Active Listening
CD 3:22

Otello, Act III Finale (excerpt), Giuseppe Verdi

- Desdemona falls to the earth and begins her lament.
- A chorus of women comments "have pity" while men exclaim "mysterious."
- The ensemble begins with four characters: Emilia, Cassio, Roderigo, and Lodovico.

- Desdemona joins them.
- Iago enters.
- Otello joins in; all seven characters participate.
- Otello rebukes Desdemona and the others cry out *"Orror"* (horror).
- Everyone quickly exits, leaving Iago and Otello on a bare stage.
- Otello, overcome by his rage, falls senseless to the ground and Iago sings in exultation over his prostrate body as the chorus (from offstage) sings: "Glory to the Lion of Venice!"

OPERA IN THE TWENTIETH CENTURY

While opera houses continue to focus on romantic works, operas composed since the nineteenth century have varied dramatically in style and plot. Perhaps the most successful opera composer of the 1980s was Philip Glass, an American born in 1937 whose style is rooted in the idiom called minimalism. Early compositions written in this style often featured a minimal amount of thematic material with little or no development, perhaps just occasional repetition in the midst of a forest of silence. Glass adopted repetition as his principal technique, but he forged a recognizable style (and pleased a large audience) by using diatonic chords rather than dissonant materials and by shaping them into coherent, if essentially static, large-scale patterns. To secure performances of his works and to build an appreciative audience, he toured the country with his own electronic ensemble.

Glass's reputation rests largely on three works: *Einstein on the Beach* (1976), *Satyagraha* (1980), and *Akhnaten* (1984). Each of them is centered on a great man, the second on events from the life of Gandhi, the third on an Egyptian pharoah who may have conceived the idea of monotheism. The two later works are considerably easier to comprehend in performance than the first. Although they do not unfold in straightforward chronological order, they clearly portray events from the principal characters' lives. The enthusiastic reception of these operas apparently lies in their manner of invoking a ritual, a quality that stems partly from the mysterious power of repetition and partly from their use of ancient languages (which are left untranslated for the audience by the composer's decree).

Glass's opera *Satyagraha*, completed in 1980, deals with Mohandas Gandhi's use of nonviolence to obtain the repeal of the "Black Act," which virtually enslaved the Indian population that lived in South Africa. Each of the opera's three acts is named after a historical figure who relates to Gandhi's struggle: Act 1 for Leo Tolstoy and Act 2 for Indian poet Rabindranath Tagore, both personal friends of Gandhi's and strong influences on his life. The third

Scene from
Satyagraha

act is titled "Martin Luther King, Jr.," a figure Glass viewed as an American Gandhi because of his nonviolent approach to solving social problems. In an effort to be authentic, he retained the original Sanskrit of the sacred text and used instruments that were native to both India and America.

The third act of the opera deals with the nonviolent Newcastle March, which brought about the repeal of the "Black Act." Glass broadens his musical language in *Satyagraha* to include more or less traditional arias with lyrical melodies. His accompanying instruments are common to both India and the United States.

In this final part Gandhi sings as his comrades sleep. Glass chose to represent the theme of the eternal expressed in the text by giving Gandhi an ascending melody that is repeated for the entire aria. Text sections are separated by instrumental interludes. Both the interludes and the accompaniment gradually increase in complexity, and it is through them that Glass achieves a dramatic climax at the end. Also note that the flute is added to the voice melody for the last entrances to add emphasis.

Active Listening
CD 1:3

Satyagraha, Act III, "Martin Luther King, Jr.," Part 3, Philip Glass

(The Lord said:)

I have passed through many a birth and many have you
I know them all, but you do not.

Unborn am I, changeless is my Self,
Of all the contingent beings, I am the Lord!
Yet by my creative energy, I consort with nature:
And come to be in time.

For whenever the law of righteousness withers away and lawlessness
    arises,
Then I do generate myself on earth.

I come into being age after age
And take a visible shape and move man with men
For the protection of good, thrusting the evil back
And setting virtue on her seat again.

As we close our discussion it is interesting to note that opera has enjoyed significant popularity in recent years, in part due to its visual nature. The band, a mainstay of music education in the public schools, has also experienced a renaissance of sorts in recent years. As someone who will undoubtedly vote on educational funding issues many times in the future, you should find some useful information about this unique organization and its music in the next chapter.

CHAPTER

The Band Idiom

24

THE EVOLUTION OF THE WIND BAND: FUNCTIONS AND MUSICAL STYLES

The band, an ensemble that is common in academic, community, and military settings throughout North America, is clearly derived from a European tradition. The word band probably evolved from the Latin *bandum*, which means banner. Medieval musicians often carried banners or suspended them from their instruments when riding on horseback. In the United States, **band** is commonly used to describe a *mixed wind and percussion group*.

In 1653, the first known band in the North American colonies was assembled in New Hampshire and consisted of oboes, recorders, and at least two drums. For a time, woodwind instruments were preferred because of the technical limitations of the natural brass instruments.

Brass Band, John Covert

Two important developments on the European continent were to have significant impact on the fledgling band movement in the United States. First, cymbals and the bass drum were permanent additions to the band as a result of Turkish influence (Mehter music, described in Chapter 14). The second development, the addition of valves to brass instruments, took place during the first quarter of the nineteenth century. Valved brass instruments had several advantages over woodwinds: A basic level of playing can be learned quickly, they are affected far less by temperature and humidity, and they can be played with gloves in cold weather.

By the middle of the nineteenth century brass bands flourished and woodwinds fell into disuse in bands. For marching use, over-the-shoulder brasses were designed so that the sound projected backwards to the rest of the parade. In concert settings this design meant that performers sat with their backs to the audience.

Patrick S. Gilmore, an Irishman who led a Union band during the Civil War, is usually credited with fathering the modern American symphonic band. Not long after the war ended, Gilmore assumed leadership of New York's Twenty-second Regiment Band and turned it into the leading professional band in the country.

The Triumphs of Maximilian I, woodcut by Hans Burgkmair

Courtesy of Dover Publications

   John Philip Sousa followed Gilmore with his own professional band and soon became the most important figure in the history of the American band movement. Sousa's concerts consisted of suites, rags, medleys, orchestral transcriptions, opera excerpts (with vocal soloists), and, of course, marches. The Sousa Band made regular tours of the United States and other parts of the world until Sousa's death in 1932.

   The popularity of professional bands fostered a growth in amateur ensembles supported by towns, fraternal organizations, and businesses. Town bands were so popular that some states passed laws that created special taxes to support free band concerts (in recent years, there has been a renaissance of the town band tradition, especially to provide summer concerts in public parks).

   After World War I the popularity of professional and amateur bands diminished due to the increased competition from radio, recordings, and movies. Given the decreased demand for performers, many returning military musicians found jobs as instrumental music teachers in the public schools. Even though there had been bands in some universities and public schools since the end of the nineteenth century, it is interesting that they became the primary genre of instrumental music education at a time when public interest in the professional version of the idiom was waning.

   Gustav Holst (1874–1934) was an English composer who wrote operas, songs, and choral and orchestral works. Perhaps his best-known piece is *The Planets,* a *Star Wars*-type piece that was originally written for orchestra but is

Union Army Band, Washington, D.C., 1865

available in a band transcription that you may have played in high school band. Holst's First Suite in E-flat for Military Band is reputed to be the first work in the twentieth century for concert band by a significant composer.

A **chaconne,** as Holst used the term, is a *type of theme and variations in which the theme is an ostinato (repeated) pattern.* In Chapter 9 this piece was used to demonstrate how using different instruments or instrumental combinations can create variety. Here the focus is on other musical elements that create variety in the form. Each bullet in the guide represents a statement of the theme.

Active Listening
CD 2:10

First Suite in E-flat for Military Band, First Movement, Chaconne, Gustav Holst

- Theme
- Countermelody added in the brasses
- Different countermelody in woodwinds
- Clarinets and trumpets in call and response motif
- Staccato (short) accents in trumpets and snare drum
- Obbligato in woodwinds
- Slower running bass line in trombones and tubas
- Clarinet countermelody
- Soft woodwind answering theme
- Theme varied

- Trumpets play varied theme with ponderous bass line
- Trombone plays varied theme with similar bass line
- Original theme returns, crescendo begins. Woodwinds with snare drums in the background.
- Theme with ascending countermelody; snare climax
- Low brass theme; trumpet countermelody
- Closing variation of theme, snare roll and bass drum
- Cadence

SYMPHONY IN B-FLAT FOR BAND, PAUL HINDEMITH

During the two decades after World War I, band clinics emerged and several band associations were formed. Both developments tended to foster improved quality in concert band performance. Similarly, marching bands, which were a regular part of university sporting events as early as the end of the nineteenth century, grew in size and stature as a result of clinics and band organizations. Although the band movement was somewhat curtailed during World War II, returning veterans once again added renewed energy to the field at the end of the war. More support associations were formed and, increasingly, the best composers were commissioned to write for band. Paul Hindemith (1895–1963), mentioned earlier as a composer of sonatas for almost every orchestral instrument, was a German composer who immigrated to the United States to avoid Nazi persecution.

Hindemith was on the faculty at Yale University and was asked by the United States Army Band to compose a work for one of its regular Washington, D.C., concerts in April 1951. The resulting three-movement symphony is primarily based on contrapuntal (polyphonic) writing.

A fugue is a contrapuntal composition comprised of an exposition followed by an alternation of episodes (development) and restatements of the subject. The *primary theme* or the **subject** is introduced in imitation in each voice part in the opening of the exposition. Like many twentieth-century composers, Hindemith uses the fugue form freely, creating an amalgam of compositional devices.

CROSSROADS

In this one movement Hindemith has connected with the baroque style (fugue), sonata form (second theme), the idea of themes moving from one movement to another (cyclic form, as in Berlioz' *Symphonie Fantastique*), and the coda that was used by Beethoven and others.

LISTENING GUIDE	Symphony in B-flat for Band, Third Movement, Fugue, Paul Hindemith

CD 3:23

Introduction

00:00   Opens with an 8-measure introduction that features the primary theme.

Exposition

00:15   Trumpets state the subject (theme) of the fugue and play at a faster tempo than in the introduction.

00:22   The second statement is shared by the trombone and the horn.

00:31   Instead of a compete third statement there is a partial statement in the woodwinds and one in the trombone. At this point the exposition dissolves into a combination of exposition and episode.

00:47   Fragments developed in the woodwinds.

1:00   Trumpet and trombone in *stretto* (close imitation)

1:13   The word *scherzando* appears in the score indicating a lighter style. Woodwinds enter at a slower tempo with a scherzo-like motif that returns later.

1:25   A second theme is heard in the bass clarinet and bassoon. This theme is used several ways including as a harmonization that features fragments of the original subject.

1:31   Fragment of the second theme used in imitation.

2:42   Scherzo-like motif returns.

2:56   Gradual slowing, and the music comes to an uncertain pause. The expectation at this point is a recapitulation of the opening material. Instead, Hindemith brings in themes 1 and 2 simultaneously.

3:45   Theme 1 from the first movement is added to the mix.

4:20   Theme 2 from this movement and the theme from the first movement are stated again.

4:36   The movement closes with a brief coda.

In 1952, Frederick Fennell founded the Eastman Symphonic Wind Ensemble as a new type of wind group that featured a flexible instrumentation of about forty-five players and with one player on a part as in chamber music. While it was promising that the best composers were being encouraged to write for band, Fennell recognized that since the sixteenth century, a great deal of music had been composed for wind and percussion groups ranging from fewer than ten to forty-five players.

Fennell's wind ensemble concept has expanded the realm of concert literature for band to include everything written for more than five or six wind players as well as music composed for military or symphonic concert bands. Composers in the former category include Haydn, Mozart, Beethoven, Liszt, and Ives. Much of the music of the latter type has been written since 1850, with the earlier works intended for military band. Rossini, Holst, Vaughan Williams, Hindemith, and Schoenberg wrote music for full band. Some composers, such as Mendelssohn, Tchaikovsky, Copland, and Stravinsky, composed for small wind groups as well as full band.

CHAPTER

25 Diversity in Small Ensembles

INDIAN CLASSICAL MUSIC

Though its lifeblood is improvisation, Indian classical music is based on very organized musical forms. The improvisation is musically sophisticated and takes place within carefully circumscribed patterns.

RAGA

Most simply, **raga** is *the mood*—the *rasa*—that is being conveyed by the music. In Indian music there are considered to be nine of these, the *Nava Rasa*. They are the Erotic, the Comic, the Pathetic, the Furious, the Heroic, the Frightful, the Disgusting, the Tranquil, and that of Wonderment. The term is also used in reference to painting, dance, and poetry and more broadly to all the fine arts, known as *sangita*. There are also specific ragas for different times of day, different seasons, and specific celebratory events.

A second meaning of **raga** is the *germinal melodic material used in improvisation in Indian classical music*. It has been said that it is "more than a scale and less than a melody." It is a succession of pitches ranging from as few as seven or eight to as many as fifty or more. A *raga* is generally considered to have both an ascending and descending form. Also, notes in the scale from which the *raga* is derived may be omitted (these often being the fourth and seventh scale degrees), creating a major pentatonic scale. This pentatonic scale is a familiar sound also found in Scottish folk music (for example, "Auld Lang Syne"), in Chinese music, and in some of the songs of the cowboys of the Old West (probably derived from the music of the American Indians). Mathematically, thousands of *ragas* are possible, but only about fifty are in general use.

These *ragas* are used as the basis for improvisation, the "making up" of more complex music in somewhat the same way as jazz musicians improvise on standard pop tunes or the "blues." These improvisations are done in a *form* also called the *raga*. Confusing? Just keep in mind the three definitions — mood, melodic pattern, and form — and it will help you appreciate the music more.

TALA

The rhythmic component of Indian classical music is called the **tala.** It is a *rhythmic cycle of beats (matras) that is divided into measures (angas)* by accenting various beats to create subdivisions of from one to nine beats. *Talas* consist of anywhere from 3 to 128 beats, although 7- to 16-beat cycles are the most common. One of the easiest for Western listeners to follow is the *tintal*, probably because it consists of a total of sixteen beats grouped in patterns of 4-4-4-4, resembling our 4/4 meter in the common four-, eight-, and sixteen-measure phrases encountered in most popular and folk tunes. The first beat of the entire cycle is called the *sam,* and often in performances in India the listeners clap their hands on this beat, clap more softly on the other beats, and wave the hand sidewise on the occasional weak beat. This gives them the feeling of being participants in the performance.

The form of these improvisations varies from one performer to another. One popular pattern consists of an opening section, the **alap**, which includes the *drone instrument sustaining one or two of the principal pitches of the raga, and the solo instrument* (a sitar, sarod, or shenai, all described below) *slowly playing the original melody* so that the audience may get in mind the "tune" that will be improvised upon. In more recent times, a violin or guitar might substitute as a solo instrument, both indicating Western influence.

After the opening section, the soloist begins improvising on the *raga* in the predetermined rhythmic pattern, the *tala*. Soon the drums — the *tabla* or *mridangam* — take up the rhythmic pattern, and the rest of the piece consists of a *series of improvisations on the rhythmic and melodic patterns introduced*. These sections are called **gats,** and in them there is a gradual increase in the intensity and musical excitement of the performance. This excitement is created by several means — an increase in the speed of the notes' occurrence (rhythmic density), moving into higher pitch range, an increase in the volume, and the addition of many ornaments.

In India, a single *raga* performance may last as long as three hours, but performances for Western listeners are usually much shorter. Even half an hour is considered taxing to our generally shorter attention spans. At festivals in India, all-night concerts are not uncommon, lasting from about 9 PM until dawn. Attending these festivals is not as taxing as might be imagined, because they are less formal than Western recitals and concerts (although not as unrestrained as rock concerts). The audience is sometimes quietly conversing, walking to obtain a cup of the ever-available tea, clapping lightly to the music, or even dozing.

In *Shenai Raga Bilawal* you will hear a complete miniature *raga* performance. The solo instrument is the *shenai*, a double reed aerophone (sounding like our oboe), and the drone is supplied by two larger instruments with the same timbre but of lower pitch. The sections of the form described earlier can be clearly heard, with their changing aspects including increased rhythmic activity and speed, and higher pitch level.

LISTENING GUIDE

Shenai Raga Bilawal, India

CD 4:1

00:00	The drone instruments enter first; *shenai* enters on the same pitch.
00:22	Slowly, the *shenai* introduces the primary melody in an unmeasured rhythm.
00:58	*Tabla* enter and establish a regular rhythm.
1:26	Brief fade-out
1:28	The *gats* sections begin at a faster tempo.
2:12	Solo becomes more complex.
3:00	Solo reaches increasingly higher pitch levels.
3:12	*Tabla* part becomes more complex.

The *sitar* and *sarod* are Hindustani instruments, plucked lutes, with a few important differences from each other. The *sitar* has a large gourd resonator while the *sarod's* resonator is carved from wood. While the *sitar* is fretted like the guitar, the *sarod* has no frets, permitting slides that are characteristic of its sound. The *sarod* is shorter than the *sitar* and has a parchment soundboard and metal fingerboard.

Both have several melodic strings, which are fingered to produce the melody, and two or three drone strings, which are not fingered and not even used if a drone is being supplied by another instrument. A dozen or so additional strings under the main strings vibrate sympathetically when activated when the main string that sounds the same pitch is plucked. This gives the instrument a characteristic resonance that is familiar to all devotees of Hindustani music.

RAGA TODI

This example offers the opportunity to hear the *sitar* and the *sarod* in close succession. In it you will hear the somewhat buzzy sound of the *sitar* alternating with the purer sound of the *sarod*. The recording, which is not a recent one, includes the performances of Ravi Shankar, *sitar*, and Ali Akbar Khan, *sarod*, both recognized as the acknowledged masters of their metier. The *raga* is *Todi*, a morning *raga* said to delineate a profound mood with a tinge of pathos.

Todi Raga, India	**LISTENING**
CD 4:2	**GUIDE**

00:00	*sarod*
00:08	regular rhythm established by *tabla*
00:38	*sitar*
00:48	*sarod*
00:58	*sitar*
1:14	more complex *tabla* part
1:24	*sarod*
1:42	*sitar*

SMALL GROUP JAZZ: AN AMERICAN CLASSIC

BOP

Bebop, or **bop,** employed complex harmony and required great technical facility of its players. Its tempos were very fast and discouraging to a swing era audience that loved to dance. However, for musicians who loved to listen, it was a very exciting style. The characteristic ensemble was a quintet with two players (usually sax and trumpet) on the frontline and a three-piece rhythm section. Typically, the opening and closing of a song featured the "horns" (wind instruments) playing in unison. Between the opening and the closing, lots of space was provided for improvised solos.

Even though he died at age 34, Charlie ("Bird") Parker is the most legendary of all jazz saxophonists and probably the greatest of all jazz improvisors. He and John Birks "Dizzy" Gillespie, who plays trumpet and piano on this recording, were at the center of the development of bop.

Like many improvised jazz works, this performance of "Koko" is in a type of theme and variations structure. However, thematic material from the

Charlie Parker
(saxophone) and
Dizzy Gillespie
(trumpet)

© Frank Driggs Collection

initial thirty-two bars is not used as the basis for variation. Instead, Parker uses the chord changes from the tune "Cherokee" for his solo. The opening thirty-two bars consists of the statement of an eight-bar theme followed by improvisation.

LISTENING GUIDE

"Koko," Charlie Parker: Charlie Parker, saxophone; Dizzy Gillespie, trumpet and piano; Max Roach, drums

CD 4:3

Theme

00:00	8 bars, trumpet and saxophone
00:07	8 bars, trumpet improvisation
00:13	8 bars, saxophone improvisation
00:19	8 bars, trumpet and saxophone

Parker saxophone solo—extended improvisation on "Cherokee" tune

00:25	Chorus 1—64 bars long instead of the usual 32
1:16	Chorus 2—64 bars
2:07	Drum solo by Max Roach
2:29	Restatement of the original 32 bars

At least as early as the flappers of the "Roaring Twenties," certain styles of dress and use of language became associated with types of popular music. During the history of rock music, we have experienced the leather jackets of the 1950s and the tie-dyed tee shirts and folk dresses of the 1960s, and a new fad with almost every change in rock style; our ears have been filled with the "let's git down" lingo of soul musicians and the rhythmic patter talk that led to rap. Similarly, the musicians and fans of bop developed a style of dressing and speaking that set them apart. Dizzy Gillespie was often thought of as a caricature of that appearance and talk. Dressed in a hip beret and a wild sport coat (often imitation zebra or leopard skin), wearing a goatee and spouting a line of jive, "the Diz" was the personification of the bop musician—and the model for the wolf in Steve Allen's clever little book, *Bop Fables*.

> "You know something?" little Red Riding Hood said, squinting suspiciously at the furry head on the pillow. "I don't want to sound square or anything, but you don't look like my grandmother at all. You look like some other cat."
>
> "Baby," said the wolf, "you're flippin'!"
>
> "No, man," insisted Red. "I just dug your nose again and it's too much . . . where's my grandma?"
>
> The wolf stared at Red Riding Hood for a long, terrible moment. "Your grandma," he said, "is gone."
>
> "I'm hip," said Red. "She's the swingin'est, but let's take it from the top again. Where is she?"
>
> (Steve Allen, *Bop Fables*, "Crazy Red Riding Hood," pp. 46–47)

It's interesting to observe the evolution of our language as it is affected by popular music. For instance, where our great grandfathers might have used the word "good," succeeding generations have used the word "hot," then "cool," then "bad," and recently, "phat."

COOL JAZZ

Cool jazz was a reaction to the "hot," hard-driving rhythms and complexities of bebop. The ensembles were larger than those used in bebop and *often included instruments not usually found in jazz*, such as French horn, oboe, and cello. The *emphasis was on subtlety*. Notes were attacked delicately and use of the

middle register of the instruments predominated. Many influences from classical music were felt in both compositions and arrangements.

"JERU," GERRY MULLIGAN

This selection is from an album entitled *Birth of the Cool* that features a nonet
(nine players) led by trumpeter Miles Davis and including trombone, French

---

**LISTENING
GUIDE**

"Jeru," Gerry Mulligan, Miles Davis Nonet

CD 4:4

00:00	The head (theme) in 32-bar song form—aaba
00:31	B section extended by Mulligan baritone saxophone solo
00:49	First chorus of improvisation featuring Miles Davis on trumpet
1:31	The next chorus features Mulligan and, for variety, the band plays the first four bars of each of the A sections while Mulligan improvises the second four bars.
2:31	The final 32 bars begin, but instead of repeating the opening theme, a combination of ensemble playing and solos brings the tune to a close.

Baritone saxophonist
Gerry Mulligan

Neal Peters Collection

horn, tuba, alto sax, baritone sax, piano, bass, and drums. Davis began his career playing bebop with Charlie Parker, but his personal evolution took him through many succeeding jazz styles, including jazz/rock fusion. The composer is Gerry Mulligan, who plays baritone sax on this 1949 recording.

Cool was followed by "hard bop" (a return of bebop in a very driving style), a piano style known as "funky," and an extension of that style known as "gospel jazz." Jazz has since incorporated elements of classical music to produce "third stream" music and abandoned itself to totally unrestricted improvisation in a style called "free form jazz." In the late 1960s, it combined with rock music to produce "fusion" and "jazz-rock," styles that are discussed later.

CROSSROADS

The pieces in this chapter come from two very different musical traditions. The Indian classical tradition is several hundred years old and jazz developed from African-American roots in the twentieth century. And yet they share some striking similarities.

- Each is a technically difficult music that requires of the performers a skill level that is developed through years of practice.
- Improvisation is a central feature of both traditions.
- Both make use of a regular rhythmic framework within which many individual details can change.
- Theme and variation is the formal design that unifies both of these styles.
- For both styles, the concert setting is somewhere between that of a rock concert and a symphony orchestra. Refreshments, conversation, and audience "participation" or physical reaction are part of both "scenes."

RECENT TRENDS

In an age of electronic and amplified sounds, a renaissance of traditional, acoustic jazz styles has begun. A family of very talented musicians from New Orleans seems to be leading this movement. The father, Ellis Marsalis, is a pianist who has performed with such diverse musicians as Ornette Coleman (free form) and Al Hirt (Dixieland). He is also a teacher. His musically conservative son, trumpeter Wynton Marsalis, uses his jazz responsibilities at Lincoln Center in New York City as a platform from which to advocate traditional acoustic jazz. His musically more liberal son, saxophonist Branford Marsalis, toured and recorded with Sting, but remains one of our finest performers of traditional jazz.

One of the fascinating things about jazz is that as new styles have developed, the old styles have not been abandoned but have continued to attract advocates, audiences, and performers—not as historical curiosities but as a vital means of musical expression. In his book *Enjoying Jazz*, Henry Martin states: "Jazz developed as a folk music, rapidly became a popular music in the 1920s, then finally established itself as a fine art by around 1950." This pattern of folk art to popular art to fine art is also found in the development of rock music.

26 Small Vocal Settings

One feature of vocal music as it has developed in the Western European tradition is its ability to reflect or to enhance the meaning of poetry. A fascination with such subtle projection of thoughtful or intimate words is characteristic of music composed for a solo singer or for a small vocal ensemble.

RENAISSANCE VOCAL MUSIC

With the Renaissance came an increasing attention to what an appropriate musical setting for a text might be. The generation of Josquin Desprez (ca. 1440–1521) began to write *chansons* and Italian songs with a flexibility of form that matches the varied forms of the poems and clearly reflects the meaning of the text. This interest in "word painting"—in musically illustrating the text—increased during the sixteenth and seventeenth centuries, and it produced some strikingly diverse musical results.

Two examples by Josquin show the range of possibilities. "Mille regretz" is a four-voice setting of a short French poem about leaving a loved one. The mood created in this *chanson* is one of sorrow. The musical setting blends a variety of vocal textures with lush harmonies to achieve an effective interpretation of the text.

Mille regretz de vous habandonner Et d'eslonger vostre fache amoureuse:	A thousand regrets to abandon you and leave your loving face:
J'ay si grand dueil et paine douloureuse,	I have such great sorrow and painful anguish
Qu'on me verra brief mes jous deffiner.	that my days will soon be seen to end.

IOSQVINVS PRATENSIS.

CORBIS

Josquin Desprez

Active Listening
CD 4:5

"Mille Regretz," Josquin Desprez

• set homophonically ending with a melisma	Mille regretz
• set homophonically	De vous habandonner
• in a descending pattern (2×)	Et d'eslonger
• polyphonically enlivened homophony (2×)	Vostre fache amoureuse
• homophonically (2×)	J'ay si grand dueil
• word painting, descending line represents painful anguish (2×)	Et paine douloureuse
• set polyphonically	Qu'on me verra
• set imitatively	Brief mes jous deffiner
• stated once	Qu'on me verra
• homophonically (3×)	Brief mes jous deffiner

"El grillo è buon cantore" is an Italian song that is set with light-hearted, rhythmic music. Like the previous example it is for four voices, but most often they sing together, obscuring the independence of line. This example is related to the *frottola*, which has a homophonic texture with the top voice dominating. It is cast in ABA form with ending lines of each section repeated.

"El Grillo," Josquin Desprez

- A stanza

El grillo è buon cantore,	The cricket is a good singer,
Che tiene longo verso,	Who sings a long note,

Call and response style; word painting to imitate cricket

Dale beve grille canta,	The cricket sings of drinking,
El grillo è buon cantore.	The cricket is a good singer.

- A stanza repeats
- B stanza—change of style to homophonic

Ma non fa com'gli altri uccelli	But he does not do like other birds,
Com' eli han cantato un poco,	When they have sung a little,
Van de fatto in altro loco:	Off they go somewhere else:
Sempre el grillo sta pur saldo,	The cricket stands firm,
Quando l'a maggior el caldo,	When it gets hotter,

Next line ends with melisma on amore

Al'hor canto sol per amore.	He sings for the love of it.

- A stanza repeats
  Last line repeats to end song

El grillo è buon cantore,	The cricket is a good singer.

The second line contains an obvious example of word painting. Can you identify it?

THE LIED

Coinciding with the rise of the piano during the late eighteenth century, there was an important flourishing of German poetry. Goethe and Schiller represented a high point in lyric poetry that was continued by the many romantic poets of the nineteenth century. These circumstances—the fine poetry and the means to give them musical expression—led to the marvelous outpouring of highly inspired songs that began with the compositions of Franz Schubert (1797–1828).

Schubert grew up in Vienna where Beethoven was carrying on the heritage of Mozart and Haydn. Although Schubert composed in the various instrumental genres developed by the three Viennese masters, his greatest and most enduring contribution to music was his development of the expressive qualities of the lied.

The German **lied** (song) is the *inventive, sensitive setting of poetry for singer and piano,* much as the sixteenth-century madrigal was for vocal ensemble. Schubert's more than five hundred songs mark the early masterworks in the genre. Schubert was able to match the melodies that he crafted carefully to a musical interpretation of the text in the accompaniment. This interpretation might range from something as simple as capturing the general mood of the poem to some explicit word painting.

Schubert's songs were on occasion quite dramatic. Goethe's ballad "Der Erlkönig" (The Erlking) tells of a father riding through the night carrying his sick son. The erlking, the king of the elves, talks to the child and eventually takes him; this, of course, represents the child's death. Schubert's imagination is at its best in this lied. The galloping of the horse is set out in the piano in fast repeated triplets and a sinister tune in the bass. The singer begins in the voice of a narrator. Throughout the song, however, the singer also represents the father, the son, and the erlking. Schubert gives the singer music appropriate to each character—high pitches for the son, low ones for the father, and one meant to be enticing or beckoning for the erlking. The accompaniment also changes from the frantic galloping to a gentler pattern in the major mode for each entrance of the erlking. The ending with its dramatic pause highlights the tragic conclusion. Before listening, read through the text and mark where each of the four characters is speaking: the narrator, the father, the son, and the erlking.

"Der Erlkönig," Franz Schubert

Active Listening
CD 1:8

Wer reitet so spät durch Nacht und
  Wind?
Es ist der Vater mit seinem Kind;
Er hat den Knaben wohl in dem Arm,
Er faßt ihn sicher, er hält ihn warm.

"Mein Sohn, was birgst du so bang
  dein Gesicht?"

"Siehst, Vater, du den Erlkönig nicht?
Den Erlenkönig mit Kron und
  Schweif?"
"Mein Sohn, es ist Ein Nebelstreif."

"Du liebes Kind, komm, geh mit mir!
Gar schöne Spiele spiel' ich mit
  dir.

Who rides so late through night and
  wind?
It is the father with his child.
He holds the boy in his arms,
He grasps him firm, keeps him warm.

"My son, why do you hide your face
  so anxiously?"

"Father, don't you see the Erlking?
The Erlking with his crown and
  tail?"
"My son, it is only a bit of fog."

"Dear child, come, go with me!
I'll play the prettiest games with
  you.

Manch bunte Blumen sind an dem
  Strand,
Meine Mutter hat manch gülden
  Gewand."

"Mein Vater, mein Vater, und hörest
  du nicht,
Was Erlkönig mir leise verspricht?"

"Sei ruhig, bleibe ruhig, mein Kind;
In dürren Blättern säuselt der Wind."

"Willst feiner Knabe, du mit mir
  geh'n?
Meine Töchter sollen dich warten
  schön;
Meine Töchter führen den nächtlichen
  Reih'n
Und wiegen und tanzen und singen
  dich ein."

"Mein Vater, mein Vater, und siehst
  du nicht dort
Erlkönigs Töchter am düstern Ort?"

"Mein Sohn, mein Sohn, ich seh' es
  genau,
Es scheinen die alten Weiden so grau."

"Ich liebe dich, mich reizt deine
  schone Gestale,
Und bist du nich willig, so brauch'
  ich Gewalt."

"Mein Vater, mein Vater, jetzt faßt
  er mich an!
Erlkönig hat mir ein Leid's gethan!"

Dem Vater grauset's, er reitet
  geschwind,
Er hält in Armen das ächzende Kind.

Many colored flowers are on the
  shore;
My mother has many golden
  garments."

"Oh, father, father, don't you hear

What the Erlking whispers in my
  ear?"

"Be still my child, be calm;
'Tis but the withered leaves in the
  wind."

"My lovely boy, will you go with me?

My daughters fair shall wait for you,

My daughters nightly revels do,

They'll sing and dance and rock you
  to sleep."

"Oh father, father, see you not

The Erlking's daughters in the dark
  place?"

"My son, my son, the thing you see

Is only the old gray willow tree."

"I love you, your form enflames my
  senses
And if you're not willing, I'll use
  force."

"Oh father, father, he grasps my arm!

The Erlking has harmed me!"

The father shudders, he speeds
  ahead,
He clasps to his bosom the sobbing
  child.

Erreicht den Hof mit Müh' und Noth:	He reaches home with pain and dread:
In seinen Armen das Kind war tot!	In his arms the child was dead!

Listen to the song.

- Can you hear the different characters represented by the singers?
- How do dynamic changes help separate the different parts of the text?
- How would you characterize the attitude of the father at the beginning?
- Does the father's attitude change during the song?
- How about the son and the erlking? Do their attitudes change?

CROSSROADS

The images created by each of the compositions in this chapter parallel the kinds of images that were being created by contemporary visual artists. The Renaissance pieces are representational: "Mille Regretz" describes real emotions and "El Grillo" provides a playful portrait of the cricket as a fun-loving insect. "Der Erlkönig," however, goes beyond a representational depiction of the story by symbolically describing the inevitability of death. "Der Mondfleck" goes further in describing an emotional state that is not normal, much like the states described by the expressionist painters of the time.

THE TWENTIETH CENTURY

During the late nineteenth and early twentieth centuries, songs were composed with accompaniment for either piano or orchestra. Mahler and Strauss both composed many songs for which they later provided orchestral settings of the accompaniment. An especially twentieth-century variation was the use of a small instrumental ensemble, rather than full orchestra, for the accompaniment.

Arnold Schoenberg (1874–1951) was an Austrian composer who grew up in the German romantic tradition. He was largely self-taught as a musician, but his inventiveness made him one of the great innovators in art music at the beginning of the twentieth century. He developed the twelve-tone technique of pitch organization that was both admired and reviled during much of the century. Schoenberg's need to develop this "serial technique" derived from his increasingly chromatic, nontonal music composed during the first decade and a half of the twentieth century.

Commissioned in 1912 to write some songs to poetry by Albert Giraud, Schoenberg made his musical statements more satisfying by including with

Pierrot, Pablo Picasso

piano four other instrumentalists: flute/piccolo, clarinet/bass clarinet, violin/ viola, and cello. His *Pierrot Lunaire,* Op. 21, is a cycle of twenty-one brief songs that are strange and evocative in their poetry and music. The singer does not actually sing these songs, but rather intones them in what Schoenberg called ***sprechstimme*** (speech-song), *a kind of singing without aiming at "real" pitches.* The complex interweaving of the instrumental lines echoes this unusual vocal effect, leaving an eerie impression on the listener.

Active Listening
CD 2:8

Pierrot Lunaire, "Der Mondfleck," Arnold Schoenberg

Read through the text before listening.

Einen weißen Fleck des hellen Mondes	With a snowy fleck of shining moonlight
Auf dem Rücken seines schwarzen Rockes,	on the shoulder of his black silk frock-coat
So spaziert Pierrot im lauen Abend,	so walks out Pierrot this languid evening,
Aufzusuchen Glück und Abenteuer.	seeking luck and adventure.

Plötzlich stört ihn was an seinem Anzug	Suddenly something disturbs him about his appearance
Er beschaut sich rings und findet richtig—	He looks around and then finds it—
Einen weißen Fleck des hellen Mondes	just a snowy fleck of shining moonlight
Auf dem Rücken seines schwarzen Rockes.	on the shoulder of his black silk frock-coat.
Warte! denkt er: das is so ein Gipsfleck!	Wait, he thinks, it's a piece of plaster,
Wischt und wischt, doch—bringt ihn nicht herunter	wipes and wipes, yet cannot make it vanish
Und so geht er giftgeschwollen weiter,	So, on he goes, poisoned with his fancy,
Reibt und reibt bis an den frühen Morgen—	rubs and rubs until the early morning
Einen weißen Fleck des hellen Mondes.	just a snowy fleck of shining moonlight.

- What can you deduce about Pierrot from this reading?
- Does the instrumental accompaniment illustrate the text in a general or specific way?
- Does it seem tonal? Does it seem directional?
- Notice that the singer illustrates the words *wischt* (wipes) and *reibt* (rubs) through rhythmic energy and vocal inflection.
- The first, seventh, and last lines of the text are the same. Are they the same musically?

CHAPTER

Small Instrumental Groups: Chamber Music

27

In the broadest definition, **chamber music** refers to *instrumental music written for a small number of players with one player on a part and the emphasis on ensemble rather than solo playing.* The term's derivation from the French *chambre*, meaning room, suggests that this music is often suitable for performance in a small, intimate setting. In fact, prior to the invention of radio, the primary access many people

The Family Concert, Jan Steen

had to instrumental music was home performance. Of the broad spectrum of styles of music that were performed in the home setting, the term "chamber music" refers primarily to Western art music.

Chamber ensembles are named according to the number of players and the instruments involved. With the exception of baroque music that employs the continuo process (described in Chapter 22), the words "duo," "trio," "quartet," "quintet," "sextet," "septet," and "octet" identify the number of performers and the number of parts. Thus, a string quartet is made up of four string players. In some cases, the instrumentation has also been standardized; in the string quartet, the instruments are typically two violins, one viola, and one cello (no string bass). Other common chamber ensembles and their instrumentation are listed below.

Piano Trio	**Piano Quintet**	**Horn Quintet**
piano	piano	horn
two strings	string quartet	four strings

String Quintet	**Brass Quintet**	**Woodwind Quintet**
two violins	two trumpets	flute
two violas	horn	oboe
cello	trombone	clarinet
	tuba	horn
		bassoon

As most broadly defined, chamber music dates back to the late Medieval and Renaissance periods, since some of the instrumental music was ensemble music with one instrument on a part. The trio sonata that was described in Chapter 22 is the primary form of chamber music in the baroque. Chamber music came into its own during the classical era with the creation of the string quartet. Since that time, the string quartet has continued to be one of the most important genres in chamber music.

STRING QUARTET

From time to time, Franz Josef Haydn (see Chapter 22) was invited to play in a string quartet at the country estate of his patron, Carl Joseph von Furnberg. It is for this setting that Haydn wrote what are probably the first "true" string quartets, in the late 1750s. The earliest quartets were light in character and in five movements instead of the four that later became standard. His later quartets are longer, more serious, and in four movements that employ the customary formal patterns and distribute thematic material equally to all four players. Mozart also composed string quartets, six of which he dedicated to Haydn.

Beethoven's sixteen quartets were written throughout his career. His early quartets show the influence of Haydn. The middle quartets are characterized

© Archivo Iconografico, S.A./CORBIS

Engraving of Franz Josef Haydn conducting a string quartet

by increased dramatic intensity, and the late quartets demonstrate complexity and great variety. Like some other genres, the string quartet declined in popularity during the romantic era. Nevertheless, Schubert and Mendelssohn, followed later by Dvořák, Schumann, Brahms, and Smetana, are romantic composers who chose to write string quartets. In the twentieth century, composers applied stylistic innovations to the quartet that were found in other works of the period.

Maurice Ravel (1875–1937) was a French composer whose unique style grew out of, yet away from, the impressionism of Claude Debussy. His string quartet, first performed in 1904, combines references to traditional formal patterns with harmonic and rhythmic language that was advanced for the genre at the time. In the last movement, "lively and agitated," the intense opening section in 5/8 alternates with more relaxed 3/4 sections that are based on the theme of the first movement. The alternation of sections in 5/8 and 3/4 suggests the possibility of a rondo form. This twentieth-century rondo, however, doesn't go much further in fitting the traditional design. The opening A returns three times in one form or another, alternating with 3/4 sections for a total of seven sections. The first return of A develops just a fragment of the original, while the second return combines the A theme with the lyrical B theme. The final statement of A is only part of what was heard at the beginning of the movement.

Active Listening
CD 1:11

String Quartet in F, Fourth Movement, *Vif et agité*, Maurice Ravel

- Identify the counter numbers of the seven sections of this movement.

    A —5/8 repeated note theme set off by fermatas (pauses)
      —repeated notes punctuated by *pizzicato* accents (string is plucked with the finger)
    B —slower 5/4 alternates with sections of 3/4
      —two themes, both transformations of themes from movement 1
      —theme 1
      —theme 2

CROSSROADS

Ravel composed this quartet in 1902–1903 as a young, relatively unknown composer. Some criticized the work as a rehashing of the quartet that Debussy had written in 1893. Faculty at the *Paris Conservatoire* thought the work was too experimental. Ravel submitted it to his teacher Gabriel Fauré, to whom it is dedicated, and he also found fault with the composition. Finally Ravel asked Debussy his opinion. Debussy declared, "in the name of the gods of music and in mine, do not touch a single note of what you have written in your Quartet."

Irene Young

Turtle Island String
Quartet

A′ —fragment of A, modulating in character
B′ —brief return of B-like material
A″—combines A and B themes
B″—theme 2 from first B above
    —theme 1 from first B
A —closing material based on A
    —statement of opening A theme
    —ascending triplet pattern to cadence

The string quartet remains popular among a small but intense segment of
the concert-going public. Active string quartets range from those that remain
focused on traditional literature to some, like the Kronos Quartet and the Turtle Island String Quartet, that blend the traditional literature with jazz and
folk styles.

MIXED CHAMBER ENSEMBLES

The string quartet, brass quintet, and woodwind quintet are homogeneous
chamber ensembles. (Because of its ability to blend with woodwind instruments, the French horn is included in the woodwind quintet.) Composers also
mixed instruments of different families, in part, to explore the greater technical
and timbral possibilities of the mixture.

Felix Mendelssohn (1809–1847) composed Trios Nos. 1 and 2 for violin,
cello, and piano. In a letter to fellow composer Ferdinand Hiller in August
1838, Mendelssohn wrote: "A very important kind of piano music of which I

The Three Shadows,
Auguste Rodin

am especially fond—trios, quartets, and other pieces with accompaniment—is quite forgotten now. . . . With that in mind, I recently wrote the violin sonata and one for cello, and I am thinking of writing a couple of trios." These trios, then, are examples of a composer's purposefully going back to an earlier style no longer in favor.

Both of Mendelssohn's trios are cast in the same four-movement form as the symphony. As is typical in the romantic era, the third movements are scherzos instead of the minuet and trio that was used in the third movement of classical symphonies.

These two third-movement designs have several basic commonalities: They are typically in 3/4 meter and they are customarily followed by a trio and then a repeat of the minuet or scherzo, which results in a ternary or three-part form. This use of the word "trio" originally referred to the fact that just three players performed the section marked trio in works for larger ensembles. In that sense, these are true trios. In music written after the baroque, it may imply a texture that is lighter than the preceding minuet or scherzo.

Third-Movement Form

Classical:	minuet	trio	minuet
Romantic:	scherzo	trio	scherzo

Differences in these two forms relate to the tempo and character of the music. The minuet developed during the baroque period in France as a dance. The minuets of the classical period were elegant and formal and consequently were usually performed in a moderately fast tempo. In contrast, the **scherzo** (literally "joke") *ranges from light and playful to vigorous and abrupt* and is *generally in a faster tempo* than the minuet.

Mendelssohn dedicated Trio No. 2 to the German composer Louis Spohr, and it is said that the two composers performed the work together. The scherzo departs from the norm in that it is in 2/4 meter. The first statement of the scherzo is repeated with some changes to the ending. The return of the scherzo after the trio is not an exact repetition in that it includes the trio theme. It is followed by a coda.

Trio No. 2 in C Minor, Third Movement, Scherzo, Felix Mendelssohn

CD 2:11

LISTENING GUIDE

Scherzo

00:00	Theme 1
00:18	Theme 2
00:31	Closing section
00:45	Theme 1
1:13	Theme 2
1:26	Extended closing section; different melodic material
	Ends with a statement of theme 1

Trio

1:46	Slower tempo, in dominant key; contrasting melodic material

Scherzo

2:30	Theme 1 (shortened)
2:42	Coda
2:56	Return of trio theme
3:26	Ends with material based on theme 1 in piano, pizzicato in strings

---

Conventional instrumental ensembles are easy to understand. As you have seen, chamber ensembles are identified simply by counting the number of performers. Electronic music is much more difficult to contend with. For example, a synthesizer can produce an "ensemble sound" of many different parts and yet it is a single "instrument." In the next chapter you will learn more about this unique contradiction.

CHAPTER

28

"Together" But Not an Ensemble: Electronic Music

For most of history, the art of music has relied exclusively on natural sources of sound: a vibrating object that creates sound waves in the air. The discovery of electricity led to the creation of devices that support conventional instruments (amplifiers), contrivances that simulate acoustic instruments (electronic organs), and machines that create sound electronically (synthesizers). Although all three of these categories of electronic inventions have had an impact on the music of the twentieth and twenty-first centuries, synthesizers have created more possibilities for new sounds than all the other technical developments of recorded history combined.

EARLY ATTEMPTS AT CREATING SOUND: ANALOG SYNTHESIS

Inventors had been interested in synthesizing sound since the beginning of the twentieth century. Between 1896 and 1906 American Thaddeus Cahill created a mammoth device called the Telharmonium. Although Cahill can be credited

Triple E, Noah Larsen

with inventing the first synthesizer, the Telharmonium, which weighed over 200 tons, was a financial failure because it relied on obsolescent technology. By the time the device was perfected, the vacuum or radio tube had been invented, making it possible to achieve the same result with much less cumbersome equipment.

A more successful invention was the Theremin, which was created by a Russian inventor of that name in the twenties. You play the Theremin by moving your hands above two antennae on the device. Theremins, which were being built as late as the 1970s, can be heard in the movie *The Day the Earth Stood Still* and on the Beach Boys' record *Good Vibrations*.

In Cologne, Germany, composers developed an electronic music studio in the early fifties. The goal of this studio was to extend the tradition of Schoenberg and Webern by providing composers with total control over the performance of their works through electronic means (again displacing the performer). The studio's three monophonic sound-generating devices were capable of producing several basic waveforms and white noise (random frequencies). Although these sound sources are primitive by current standards, using techniques for varying the envelope (the shape of the sound) and using filters and tape manipulation made it possible to produce complicated music. Ironically, the end result of the German compositional process was a tape recording—not a particularly exciting performance medium. The pronounced difference of opinion about natural versus electronic sound sources soon faded, and composers freely mixed the two.

Karlheinz Stockhausen, the most prominent of the Cologne composers, sought to provide for the traditional performance of his *Studie II* (1954) by creating a "score." His instructions to the performer, in this case a technician, are as follows: "This score of Study II is the first electronic music to be published. It provides the technician with all the information necessary for the realization of the work, and it may be used by musicians and lovers of music as a study score—preferably in connection with the music itself."

Another turn of technology, the invention of the transistor, allowed for the miniaturization of synthesizers. Within a decade, the tube-type synthesizers were going the way of the Telharmonium. Robert Moog was one of several inventors who developed compact synthesizers during the mid-sixties. When *Switched on Bach*, a synthesized record of the music of J. S. Bach, came out in 1968, "synthesizer" became a household word. Frank Zappa's *Freak Out* (1966) and the Beatles' *Sgt. Pepper's Lonely Hearts Club Band* (1967) both employed early electronic music techniques. When the most compact version of the Moog synthesizer was introduced in 1969, rock groups quickly adopted it as their electronic instrument of choice. From the late sixties onward there was a direct linkage between the inventors, technicians, and composers who created new technology and the music industry that served consumers of popular music.

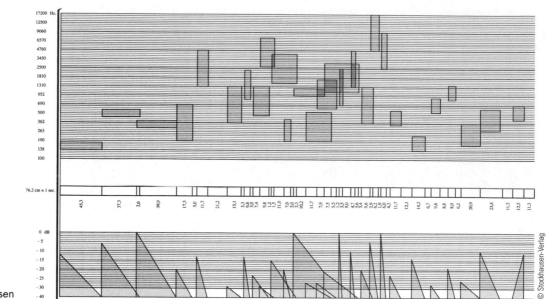

Studie II,
Stockhausen

© Stockhausen-Verlag

West Coast composer Morton Subotnick worked with inventor Donald Buchla on another version of the compact synthesizer. *Silver Apples of the Moon* (1967) is probably the first chamber music composition created specifically for the record medium. The composer took the title from a line of poetry by William Butler Yeats because he felt it represented the unifying musical idea of the piece; the idea appears in pure form at the end of Part II. This work is notable for the variety of synthesized tone colors, occasional sections that have a regular rhythmic pulse, and the interplay of melodic motives. It became a classical music bestseller and has been adapted for use by dance companies.

Active Listening
CD 1:12

Silver Apples of the Moon, Part II (excerpt), Morton Subotnick

- Vertical and horizontal sounds alternate; some are very high pitched
- "Faster," change in texture; some sense of forward motion; seems to start and stop
- Midrange sounds create an almost hocketlike quasi-melody
- Back to random sounds with accents; some lower sounds
- Becoming quiet and "slow" with high sounds; texture less dense
- More pointillistic, less dense material
- Lower sounds combined with high random sounds then softer
- Random sounds, some repeated; fade

The Phillips Collection, Washington, D.C.

Me and the Moon,
Arthur Dove

THE DIGITAL REVOLUTION
IN THE 1980S: MIDI AND CD-ROM

By 1980, both mainframe and personal computers were many times more powerful and much more compact than the first behemoth computers of the forties and fifties. The Synclavier had made real-time digital composing possible and made composing with the analog synthesizer a less desirable approach. Perhaps more importantly, the steady decline in price made PCs affordable to more and more people who would use them for musical as well as other purposes.

Although initial experiments connecting musical instruments (digital keyboards, and so on) to computers were successful, it was often necessary to reprogram the computer when changing from one instrument to another. The standard computer language called MIDI was created to solve the problem by allowing all MIDI musical instruments to interface with computers without reprogramming.

MIDI creates a series of instructions from the instrument to the computer memory that describes all aspects of a musical sound: envelope, pitch, dynamics, timbre, and so forth. This process of entering digital data and instructions into a computer is called *sequencing*. These instructions can then be played back through the MIDI device to the instrument to recreate the original sound.

More importantly, since individual aspects of the sound are described separately, they can be altered independently to shape the musical composition. For example, the pitch level could be changed while the other aspects of the sound remain the same. This process gives the composer far more control over detailed performance nuances than earlier electronic techniques allowed.

In practice, MIDI works like a recording studio in that up to thirty-two tracks can be entered into the computer memory. A variety of MIDI instruments, each offering an assortment of sounds, can be connected at once through MIDI to a computer. These two capabilities allow the composer to create relatively complex music while choosing from a diverse palette of sounds. The computer also allows music to be entered through an alphanumeric keyboard, and it can print the results in conventional music notation. The development of the PC and MIDI during the eighties and nineties has provided amateur musicians with access to all aspects of the composition process, regardless of their performing skills or knowledge of theory.

Morton Subotnick, whose *Silver Apples of the Moon* you just heard, created three imaginary ballets based on the novels of surrealist painter Max Ernst. The third of these, *All My Hummingbirds Have Alibis*, establishes a more-intimate setting for listening: a computer with CD-ROM drive. The CD-ROM contains not only the title work, but also *Five Scenes* (based on *Hummingbirds*), program notes, and descriptions of the performers, music, technology, and Ernst's career. The music is written for MIDI keyboard, MIDI mallets, computer, and digitally altered flute and cello sounds.

Five Scenes includes Ernst's artwork and a text choreographed by the composer to provide a "ballet of viewing." *Scenes* can be performed alone or with

CROSSROADS

Pure electronic music is rarely heard by itself, and when it is, it is often heard as natural or even instrumental sounds. However, the evolution of sound synthesis has had a marked influence on the world of music. In the introductory chapter to this unit on concert music, we heard *Short Ride on a Fast Machine* by John Adams. As you may recall, this piece used two synthesizers along with an orchestra. Listen to this work again and identify places where the synthesizer part is clearly heard. Also, you may want to listen again to Bela Fleck's arrangement of Aaron Copland's "Hoe Down" from the first chapter of the book. In this example, natural sounds (Western and world) were freely mixed with electronically manipulated and synthetic sounds to form a truly egalitarian aural tapestry. In both cases, your conclusion will probably be that synthetic sounds have become a normal part of the fabric of much contemporary music.

the composer's explanatory notes added to the screen. In sum, the CD-ROM provides the means to totally experience the artwork—from the full performance to "behind the scene" information about all aspects of the work.

TECHNOLOGY SINCE 1977

1977   Apple ll unveiled, first commercial digital recordings
1979   Sony Walkman introduced, first digital sampling instrument
1980   First sampled sound drum machine
1981   First CD produced, IBM PC introduced, MTV begins broadcasting
1982   MIDI standard introduced, Dolby surround sound
1983   MIDI introduced to the public
1984   Macintosh unveiled, first CD plant in U.S.
1987   First consumer DAT decks
1992   Sony introduces multimedia CD-ROM
1995   DVD introduced
1997   DVD audio standard developed

Although MIDI has become sophisticated enough to serve the needs of many musicians, some composers have continued to use larger, more powerful computers and programs like C–Music. While this approach provides some musical possibilities that are not available on MIDI–PC combinations, the

SuperStock

The Sleeping Gypsy,
Henri Rousseau

composition programs are much more difficult to learn and altering sounds is far more complex.

Pauline Oliveros directed the San Francisco Tape Music Center in the 1960s and was a pioneer in the development of electronic music. *The Lion's Tale* employs sampled gamelan sounds, which are used to create interwoven lines supported by polyrhythmic patterns. These patterns are repeated at speeds of up to 1800 times per second. The program that generates the patterns is capable of creating a new version of this composition at every performance.

LISTENING GUIDE

The Lion's Tale (excerpt), Pauline Oliveros

CD 1:4

Section 1

00:00	Gamelan sounds enter—repeated patterns; vague sense of duple meter
00:20	Sustained bass notes, slow midrange pattern; sense of 3
00:50	Repeated patterns layered; faster speed-faster sense of 3
1:05	Repeated notes, patterns and sustained sounds; slow 3
1:35	Low rumbling sounds; slowing, circular patterns added
1:53	Low pitch
2:06	Silence

Section 2

2:11	Gamelan sounds reenter; slow and very fast patterns
2:20	Exceptionally fast and slow patterns combined
2:31	Slower, almost metrical; polyrhythms
	Repeated bass notes, slowing
2:45	Very fast circular pattern added
	Slow polyrhythms with very fast 3 pattern added
3:07	Sense of 2 with fast upper-range patterns
	Layered patterns
3:22	Very slow low pitches and very fast patterns
3:45	Fade

Early Influential Styles in the United States

INTRODUCTION

As we enter the twenty-first century we find ourselves virtually surrounded by the music and entertainment industry. This industry intersects with our lives almost every waking minute. It's with us on the radio while we eat our breakfast, in the background while we work or study, on the CD player in the car; it annoys us in the elevator, stimulates us on MTV, soothes us in the dentist's chair, and on and on. If we were to try to count the elements of this multifaceted industry we would run out of fingers and toes long before we were done counting.

However, at the point in history where we begin our study of commercial and popular music, the second half of the nineteenth century, the music industry consists of only two significant elements: instrument manufacturing and music publishing. America was being entertained by the minstrel show, vaudeville, ragtime (the first truly American musical craze), and the wonderful songs and ballads of Stephen Foster.

SENTIMENTAL BALLADS AND STEPHEN FOSTER

The typical middle-class home of the nineteenth century had two gathering places: the fireplace for warming the body, and a keyboard instrument (usually a piano or a reed organ) for warming the soul. Most social gatherings, at home, church, or club, included singing. A favorite afternoon or evening pastime was the parlor recital that usually featured genteel ladies singing for an audience of family and friends. Songs of all types abounded, but most popular was the **sentimental ballad,** the lyrics of which *dealt with love and courtship* (successful and unsuccessful), or tear-provoking topics such as *natural disasters and human tragedy.*

Stephen Foster,
1826–1864

The first truly great American songwriter was Stephen Foster (1826–1864). During his short lifetime he produced about 150 songs, most of them either ballads or songs for the minstrel show. For Ed Christy and the Christy Minstrels, he wrote "Oh, Susanna," "Camptown Races," and "The Old Folks at Home." Foster's most famous sentimental ballads include "My Old Kentucky Home," "Beautiful Dreamer," and "I Dream of Jeanie." At the height of his career, he produced many wonderful songs, which are as lovely and touching today as they were then.

The music of Stephen Foster is not noted for rhythmic innovation or for harmonic originality. What sets his writing apart is the lyric expressiveness of the melody. This song is a wonderful example of that melodic lyricism. Foster dedicated it to his wife, Jane. We don't know how "Jeanie" became part of the song's title.

Active Listening
CD 4:7

"I Dream of Jeanie," Stephen Foster

- Both verses are in aaba song form.
- Using brackets at the beginning of the text lines, indicate the sections of the melody and then add the letter "a" or "b" to show the musical form of each verse.
- Most effective melodies have a melodic "climax," usually a note made most important through its length, volume, or pitch (high or low). In each verse, circle the word being sung when the climax is reached.

- The violin has three brief solo parts (one at the beginning, one between the verses, and one at the end). The last violin part is a very short codetta, which, in jazz, might be called a "tag." Name the other two parts using terms you've learned earlier in the text.

Lyrics (two verses)

I dream of Jeanie with the light brown hair,
Borne like a zephyr on the summer air;
I see her tripping where the bright streams play,
Happy are the daisies that dance on her way.
Many were the wild notes her merry voice would pour.
Many were the blithe birds that warbled them o'er:
Oh! . . . I dream of Jeanie with the light brown hair,
Floating like a zephyr on the soft summer air.

I long for Jeanie with the day dawn smile,
Radiant in gladness, warm with winning guile;
I hear her melodies, like joys gone by,
Sighing round my heart o'er the fond hopes that die;
Sighing like the night wind and sobbing like the rain,
Wailing for the lost one that comes not again;
I . . . sigh for Jeanie with the light brown hair,
Floating like a zephyr on the soft summer air.

Foster's life was a typical rags-to-riches-back-to-rags story, so common with the creative musician who has little knack for business. Found in his pockets when he died were only three pennies and thirty-five cents in Northern scrip (the currency used during the Civil War). Foster died just fifteen months before the war ended. Although he wrote many war songs, none has survived in the standard vocal literature.

However, that war did produce many songs that remain part of our musical heritage, including "The Battle Cry of Freedom," by George Root, and "The Battle Hymn of the Republic," an old camp meeting song to which Julia Ward Howe set patriotic words.

RAGTIME

There is some debate over who wrote the first published "rag." But the title "King of Ragtime" is given undisputedly to the African-American pianist and composer, Scott Joplin (1868–1917). He was playing piano in the Maple Leaf Club in Sedalia, Missouri, when a publisher named John Stark heard him improvising in a ragtime style. Stark asked him to write down the improvisation and the result, "Maple Leaf Rag," was published in 1899. It was tremendously successful, and the sheet music quickly sold over one million copies.

Although performed by many different types of ensembles, **ragtime** is essentially a *piano style*. It *combines happy, syncopated, banjo-like rhythms of the minstrel show* (usually in the right hand or treble part) *with even, stable rhythms* (usually in the left hand or bass part), *which emphasize the meter*. This combining of rhythms is unusual in European-influenced music but very common in African music.

Rags are typically made up of a sequence of sections that typically do not grow out of each other. Each may be repeated, and sections may return after intervening sections. In some ways this formal structure is parallel to the contemporary marches of John Phillip Sousa. In fact, the following rag is marked "march tempo" and includes a trio, which in a march involves a change of key and a contrasting style.

LISTENING GUIDE	"Maple Leaf Rag," Scott Joplin
	CD 4:8
00:00	A—16 bars repeated steady eighth-note pattern in the left hand (lower pitch) syncopated pattern in the right (higher pitch).
00:32	ascending, arpeggiated pattern
00:45	B—repeated descending pattern in the right hand
1:27	A—16 bars
1:48	C—Trio, repeated key change, repeated chords in the right hand
2:31	D—repeated eighth notes in the right hand followed by syncopation

Joplin wrote a total of thirty-nine rags. One of them, "The Entertainer," was at the center of a 1970s revival of ragtime because of its use in the movie "The Sting."

When "Maple Leaf Rag" was published in 1899, the limited recording techniques of the day had not yet been applied to popular music or jazz. In 1877, Joplin's contemporary, Thomas Edison, had invented a method of recording sound on metal, wax, or shellac cylinders. Edison envisioned this primarily as a method of preserving classical music and the spoken word. Two decades later Emile Berliner developed a method of recording in a disc format with a

In his book *Music in the United States*, H. Wiley Hitchcock pays tribute to this great composer of popular music:

> Joplin's rags . . . are the American equivalent, in terms of native style of dance music, of minuets by Mozart, mazurkas by Chopin, or waltzes by Brahms. They can be lovely and powerful, infectious and moving — depending on the skill of the pianist, for they are not easy music. . . .

Illustration of Scott Joplin from *The Entertainer*

standard speed of 78 revolutions per minute (rpm); because of better sound quality and ease of manufacture, the disc soon replaced the cylinder. For similar reasons, 45 rpm records replaced 78s during the 1950s only to be followed by the 33 rpm "LP" ("long playing"), various tape formats and digital compact disc formats through the end of the twentieth century. Recordings of popular and dance music were not commercially available until late in the first decade of the twentieth century, and the first jazz recordings weren't made until 1917.

However, the popularity of ragtime was spread by use of another technology. During the nineteenth century several mechanical devices were produced that "made music." The most popular of these was the player piano, which was a favorite form of entertainment from the 1890s through the 1920s. It is estimated that 205,550 player pianos were sold during 1923 alone. Piano players and player pianos spread the interest in ragtime music.

The player piano "played" itself, but a person was needed to pump the foot pedals that provide the power for the "player" mechanism. The sounds of a player piano were controlled by a piano roll. This long sheet of paper with perforations cut into it moved in front of the strings and hammers. The hammers and keys of the instrument were activated by a complicated system of air pressure and levers that were, in turn, controlled by the perforations in the piano roll.

Although many piano rolls simply reproduced the notes from sheet music, another, more complex approach used a device that cut the perforations as a pianist actually performed the composition. The recording you heard of "Maple Leaf Rag" was a performance by Scott Joplin, captured first on a piano roll and then transferred to a modern recording.

During this same period (late 1800s through about 1930), "Tin Pan Alley" became a significant force in American commercial music. "Tin Pan Alley" originated as a nickname for a street in New York City on which many publishers of popular music had their offices. But eventually the expression also came to describe a way of life in which producing, promoting, and marketing popular music was big business, reaping large financial rewards. Tin Pan Alley is where the music and entertainment industry of today began.

CROSSROADS

An interesting comparison can be made between the player piano of a century ago and modern electronic keyboards, which are capable of playing all or portions of a composition while the performer plays the melody or any other part he or she might wish. These keyboards are valuable for instructional purposes. At another level, drum machines and other percussive devices can provide the rhythmic accompaniment for professional musicians, supplementing (or sometimes replacing) a drummer. By employing MIDI to link together sound sources, a single musician can call upon a great variety of timbres. Musical instrument technology has made some amazing advances, but its function remains basically the same: to assist in fostering musical performance.

BOOGIE WOOGIE

Around the turn of the twentieth century, many African-American musicians moved to the large cities of the North. Chicago was a favorite destination and soon became the jazz center of the world. The marching-oriented New

The different forms of artistic expression often use the same vocabulary to describe or define the intangible aspects of their creations. For example, we have "Impressionists" and "Expressionists" in the visual arts, in literature, in poetry, and in music; the word "tempo" is often used to describe the activity in a painting as it is used to describe the pace of a piece of music. The Dutch artist Piet Mondrian was one of the founders of twentieth century abstract painting. His paintings were satirized in cartoons and imitated in grid-like fabric designs for clothing. However, his art was not simply geometric; his desire was to go beyond, to transcend expression that relies on the depiction of natural objects and make bold artistic statements that demonstrate a universal order. Two of his paintings, *Broadway Boogie Woogie, 1942–43* and *Victory Boogie Woogie* bear titles that make reference to the musical style. The unthinking observer might respond, "Mondrian could have called that painting anything," but he didn't! He had something specific in mind when he created that title.

CROSSROADS

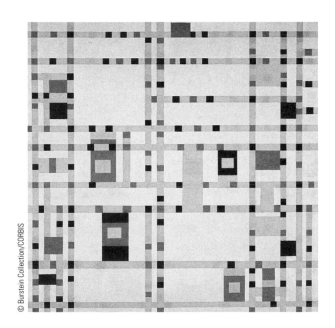

© Burstein Collection/CORBIS

Broadway Boogie Woogie, Piet Mondrian

- The primary characteristic of the boogie woogie piano style is the contrast between a strong, steady bass, played by the left hand, and a free, melodic melody, played by the right hand.
- What contrasts of line, color, shading, or shape may Mondrian have been considering when he selected the title *Broadway Boogie Woogie, 1942–43*?

Orleans Dixieland band became the dance-oriented Chicago Dixieland band. This style enjoyed wide appeal, especially among youthful audiences. Saxophone was often added to the frontline and piano and string bass to the rhythm section, replacing the banjo and tuba. As it evolved, the Chicago style developed a greater emphasis on improvised solos and an important rhythmic addition called the **backbeat** (*emphasizing beats 2 and 4 of the measure*). The backbeat is a primary element in rhythm and blues as well as in rock and roll.

An economic downturn caused nightclub owners to turn to entertainment that was less expensive than the six- or seven-piece Dixieland band. The choice was the solo pianist. Several piano styles had evolved out of ragtime. All of them featured a very forceful left-hand technique. One of these is boogie woogie.

Boogie woogie is *a solo piano style* that often uses the twelve-measure blues structure. Its most characteristic feature is *a powerful, repeated eight-note pattern (four beats per measure, subdivided into two notes on each beat) played by the left hand*. The expression "eight to the bar" (four beats times the two-note subdivision) is often used to describe this pattern, which, in traditional terms, might be called an ostinato. Above this pattern, *the right hand is free to interpret the melody or to improvise*. The contrast between the two hands is so striking that it can give the impression of two players. Meade "Lux" Lewis was one of the greatest performers in this style. The recordings of rock and roll performer Jerry Lee Lewis show the influence of boogie woogie.

"Honky Tonk Train," Meade "Lux" Lewis

This song, "Honky Tonk Train," uses the twelve-measure blues structure. As you recall from our earlier discussion of the blues, the twelve-measure pattern is divided into three four-measure sections called "phrases." The classical twelve-measure blues pattern follows an AAB form; that is, the first two phrases are similar to each other and the last phrase is different. This excerpt includes ten repetitions of the blues structure. In all ten repetitions, the last section or "B" has the same melody. This helps to mark the end of each statement of the blues structure.

LISTENING GUIDE	"Honky Tonk Train," Meade "Lux" Lewis
	CD 4:9
	00:00 A brief introduction, consisting of a rolled chord and a few high notes in the right hand
	00:02 Blues structure starts with left hand playing the characteristic boogie woogie pattern

These twelve measures are the initial blues statement:

00:20   Repeated "even-note" accents in right hand

00:37   Tremolo in right hand

00:53   Ascending broken chord patterns

1:11   Repeated short chord rolls

1:28   High broken chord rhythmic accents

1:44   Middle register chord accents

2:02   Yet another series of chord accents

2:19   Short runs up and down

2:36   Dissonant chords slowing to a close in the final B section

These early popular music styles laid the foundation for the wonderfully rich and diverse American popular/commercial music of today. In the next chapter we will study the beginnings of current pop music culture.

Country and the Birth of Rock

COUNTRY MUSIC

Country music *grew out of the folk ballads of the British Isles*, which were characteristically somber in mood. This somberness was perpetuated in the lyrics of country music, which often *dealt with lost love or cheating lovers*, with traditional values violated as well as upheld, with *disappointment and pain* more often than promises fulfilled. Song titles like "My Wife Ran Off with My Best Friend and I Miss Him" and "I Have Tears in My Ears from Lying on My Back in My Bed, Crying Over You" indicate that humor is present, but the old sadness hasn't left country music. A brief article in the November 23, 1992, issue of *Newsweek* entitled "Beware of Those Tears in Your Beers," reported on a year-long study conducted in forty-nine metropolitan areas. The study showed a direct relationship between radio time devoted to country music and suicide rate. Jokingly, the article asks, "What do you get when you play country music backwards? You get sober, get your job back, your dog and wife come home . . ." And as Richard Corliss wrote, there's "a pang in every twang. . . . misery loves country." (*Time*, March 11, 1996)

THE LONESOME COWBOY (AND COWGIRL)

Texas lies at the extreme western end of the "South" in which country music was born. In the 1930s, the romantic vision of the West and its lonesome cowboys was promoted in novels, movies, and song. Cowboy songs became part of country music as did an elaborate, brightly colored type of cowboy attire better fitted for the movies than for the range. Through his recordings and live radio broadcasts, Gene Autry became the most famous cowboy in the land. His movies established for decades the "good boy" image of the cowboy hero; his version of "Rudolph the Red-Nosed Reindeer" became one of the best-selling recordings of all time.

In 1935, Patsy Montana made music history by being the first woman to produce a big country hit: "I Want to Be a Cowboy's Sweetheart." Her easily recognized style was widely imitated and made her a star on the radio program, National Barn Dance, where she was part of a group called the "Prairie Ramblers." She was with that program until 1959.

In this arrangement, the basic strophic design of "I Want to Be a Cowboy's Sweetheart," is broken up by instrumental interludes and a vocal technique

---

CROSSROADS   What did Gene Autry, King Louis XIV, Jimi Hendrix, and Benjamin Franklin have in common? You guessed it! They all played the guitar. This instrument that plays such an important role in popular music today dates back some four thousand years to a Persian instrument called the "tar," meaning "string." In those days, it consisted of a string or two stretched over a resonating body such as a gourd or tortoise shell with a hunting bow or something similar used as a neck. In time, a wooden six-stringed instrument became standard, although there were many variations in both the number of strings and the size. Portability made the guitar a favorite among travelers; Christopher Columbus brought one to the Americas and it was the instrument of choice among settlers in North America. The explosion of country music through radio, recordings, and movies during the 1920s and 1930s inspired an American love affair with the guitar, which was encouraged by affordable prices made possible by mass production. All of this early interest had to do with "hollow body" instruments; "solid body" guitars were introduced during the 1950s. The most famous of these were the "Broadcaster," "Telecaster," and "Stratocaster" models made by Fender and the "Les Paul" made by Gibson. These instruments were made to produce sustained tone, free of distortion. Ironically, they are the instruments used by rock guitarists to create feedback and distortion. For the year 1999, the National Association of Music Merchants reported guitar sales of 1.3 million units valued at $762,000,000.

© Frank Driggs Collection

Patsy Montana

called yodeling that evolved in the Alpine regions of Austria, Italy, and Switzerland and dates back to the sixteenth century. It involves alternating between a natural tone (lower pitch) and a falsetto tone (higher pitch). This folk technique was used by popular and folk musicians in other parts of the world and was adopted by the cowboy singers of the American West.

"I Want to Be a Cowboy's Sweetheart," Patsy Montana

Active Listening
CD 4:10

- Instrumental introduction featuring fiddle
- Yodeling
- Stanza 1
- Yodeling
- Instrumental interlude (fiddle and guitar)
- Stanza 2
- Yodeling
- Repeat of Stanza 1
- Yodeling to end

Since Patsy Montana's success, the doors to country music stardom have been open to many fine female performers. One family produced three: Loretta Lynn, Crystal Gale (sister), and the current bard-ess of heartbreak, Patty Loveless (cousin).

BLUEGRASS

In the fall of 1939, Bill Monroe and the Blue Grass Boys joined the cast of the Grand Ole Opry, the weekly country music radio show broadcast from Nashville. Monroe enjoyed experimenting with different combinations of instruments, and by 1945 had settled on a combination with a very distinctive sound: fiddle, guitar, mandolin, five-string banjo, and string bass. This sound was widely imitated and was called *bluegrass* after the name of this innovative band.

The vocals usually take the form of solos or duets. In the duets, the harmony part is higher than the melody. Bluegrass tunes are also distinctive in that their tempo tends to be rather fast.

The instruments performing "Why Did You Wander?" are guitar, mandolin, banjo, fiddle, and bass. Like the previous example, the strophic structure is modified with instrumental interludes. However, in this piece a refrain is heard after the introduction and after each stanza of text. The refrain is set for vocal duet and each stanza is for solo voice. Alternating the featured instrument in the instrumental interludes adds further variety.

Active Listening
CD 4:11

"Why Did You Wander?" Bill Monroe and Lester Flatt

- Introduction—fast tempo, mandolin featured
- Refrain—vocal duet
- Interlude—fiddle solo
- Stanza 1—solo voice

Bill Monroe and the
Blue Grass Boys

© Frank Driggs Collection

- Refrain
- Interlude—banjo solo
- Stanza 2
- Refrain
- Interlude—fiddle solo
- Stanza 3
- Refrain
- Interlude—mandolin
- Refrain to end

During the 1970s, some bluegrass bands began to experiment with rock techniques and songs. The result has become known as *newgrass*. The perceptive listener has probably noticed that drums have not been used in either of the country music examples to which we have listened. Drums are not a part of traditional country music. However, as country music and rock and roll have intermingled, drums have become an integral part of the contemporary country style.

Pre-Rock Blues

The structure or form called **blues** was probably the most important of the many musical elements that combined to produce the "Rock Revolution" of the 1950s. As we have seen, blues is a twelve-measure pattern, divided into three sections called phrases. In classic blues, the lyrics sung in the first and second phrases are the same (or similar) and the lyrics to the third phrase are different. Another form that is important in rock, especially in country-related forms of rock, is the verse-chorus form. In this form, each statement of the chorus (also called "refrain") repeats the same words, but each statement of the verse (also called "stanza") has different words. Most often these verses are used to tell a story or to provide additional information about a topic.

The example that follows is interesting in that it combines characteristics of these two forms. It is a classic blues that follows the verse-chorus pattern (remember that "bar" is the same as "measure"), and note the words.

Active Listening
CD 4:12

"Hound Dog" (excerpt), Lieber-Stoller ("Big Mamma" Thornton)

- Chorus—12 bar blues structure
- Verse—12 bar blues structure
- Chorus—12 bar blues structure
- Guitar solo—36 measures (3 times through the blues structure)
- Verse—12 bar blues structure
- Chorus—12 bar blues structure

Elvis Presley made this song into a nationwide hit. His version is quite different from Thornton's. Comparing the two recordings will give your ears a chance to hear the differences between the blues and early rock and roll.

EARLY ROCK AND ROLL

Three categories or styles of commercial music *(pop, country western, and rhythm and blues)* came together in the mid-1950s to produce what has become probably the most important and influential of all popular music styles. Disc jockey Alan Freed named it "rock 'n roll"; we'll call it **rock.** Rock has produced so many substyles that it is virtually impossible to adequately describe them all in this limited space. Each substyle emphasizes one of the three categories listed above while including elements from the other two. *Two factors seem common to all of the rock styles: emotional vocal interpretation and a heavy emphasis on the beat — especially the backbeat.*

Historians have proposed different years, different performers, and different recordings to mark the beginning of rock and roll. Some suggest the R&B-oriented 1954 recording of "Sh-Boom" by the Chords. Others suggest 1955 and "Rock Around the Clock" by Bill Haley and his Comets. However, all agree that the "Rock Revolution" was underway by the time of Elvis Presley's 1956 recording, "Heartbreak Hotel." This was a big year for Elvis. Looking back, he said, "I was lucky. The people were looking for something different and I came along at just the right time" (Mick Farren, *Elvis in His Own Words*. London: Omnibus Press, 1977).

Very early in 1956 RCA purchased his contract from Sun Records, a small, independent, Memphis-based company. RCA unleashed its nationwide promotional forces, resulting in a series of hit recordings, including "Love Me Tender," "Don't Be Cruel," and "Hound Dog." On these recordings and the TV appearances that accompanied their release, Elvis displayed a type of raw, sensual energy that made him an immediate hit with teenagers and an immediate threat to parents and community leaders. "Critics loathed him; preachers called him sinful; . . . he was charged with obscenity . . . a Baptist pastor declared him 'morally insane.'" (p. 217. *All You Need Is Love*)

Elvis performed a kind of hillbilly music, with a sexy R&B-inspired vocal style, pop-oriented lyrics, electric guitar lead, and an emphasis on the beat. Buddy Holly, Roy Orbison, Jerry Lee Lewis, and many other stars performed in this style that became known as **rockabilly.** It was these sounds that influenced the Beatles and many other English groups.

Country Rock, Soul, and Other Styles

COUNTRY ROCK

During the early 1960s the larger rock audience in the United States moved away from country-influenced popular music and found enjoyment in the California beach sounds, various dance hits such as "the Twist," and "girl groups" like the Shirelles and the Supremes. However, in the coffee houses near college campuses (the gathering places for young intellectuals), folk-oriented music by performers of traditional folk music, such as Woody Guthrie, and original, socially oriented music by performers, such as Bob Dylan, became very popular. When the Beatles arrived in New York City in February of 1964, they set our popular music world on its ear. The Beatles' style was acclaimed as new even though their music was simply a combination of pop and rockabilly styles that the United States had exported to England a decade earlier. One of the reasons the Beatles enjoyed such long-term success was that they quickly absorbed the different kinds of music to which they were exposed and used them as if they were their own. They became very fond of Dylan's music and of the music of a new California-based group called "The Byrds," a country rock band in the tradition of Creedence Clearwater Revival, the Eagles, and many other bands that attracted quite a bit of attention from the mid-1960s through the 1970s.

This triangle—the Beatles, Dylan, the Byrds—produced a kind of synergy that is quite uncommon in popular music. In the TV documentary celebrating the twentieth anniversary of the release of "Sgt. Pepper," Roger McGuinn, leader of the Byrds, commented, "We became friends and we were transmitting [musical] messages across the Atlantic via records." Derek Taylor, press officer for the Beatles, responded "The Byrds took the best of Dylan and the best of the Beatles and synthesized it." As a matter of fact, it was a Dylan tune, "Mr. Tambourine Man," that became the first #1 hit for The Byrds.

"Mr. Tambourine Man" (Bob Dylan), The Byrds

Active Listening
CD 4:13

- Roger McGuinn opens the song on a twelve-string Rickenbacker guitar— a sound that became one of the characteristics of The Byrds' style.

- What elements do you hear in the recording that are country? Instruments? Form? Story line? Vocal tone quality?
- What elements do you hear that are rock?
- Compare the beginning and the ending. Does each use the same musical material? What names would you give to each of these sections?

SOUL

Although overshadowed by the "British Invasion," African-American performers were active during the early 1960s and a new, more sophisticated form of R&B was evolving. It was called **soul,** meaning it was *sincere and heartfelt.* Performances in this style often *included accompaniments featuring large brass, woodwind, and string sections, as well as backup vocal groups.* By the mid-1960s several cities were associated with slightly differing styles of soul: Memphis, where Otis Redding and Wilson Pickett were the big names; Chicago, with the Impressions and Curtis Mayfield; Philadelphia, which was known for the O'Jays and very sophisticated backup arrangements; and Detroit, where stars such as Smokey Robinson and Marvin Gaye recorded for the most famous of the soul-oriented record labels, Motown.

Marvin Gaye was raised in a gospel-singing church environment in Los Angeles and moved to Detroit in 1960. There he became part of the Motown "family" as a singer and songwriter and the husband of the sister of Berry Gordy, the label's founder. Gaye's very emotional, sensual, and sometimes almost despairing vocals helped to establish that part of the soul style. Released in 1968, "I Heard It Through the Grapevine" was his first #1 hit. The piece is set in a verse-chorus form, often used for telling a story, which is the case here: The verses progress through the story while the chorus repeats the basic theme of the song.

Active Listening
CD 2:7

"I Heard It Through the Grapevine," Whitfield-Strong (Marvin Gaye)

- The introduction sets the character of the song. An electronic keyboard establishes a repeated chord pattern over a subtle but growing pulse.
- Other instruments, both electronic and acoustic, enter.
- Vocal begins and the pulse becomes a driving beat, with a strong emphasis on the backbeat. What instruments do you recognize that contribute to the beat?
- The song begins with a verse. How many verses are there?
- What story is told by the verses?
- How many details of the story can you recall?
- The chorus begins with the title words, "I heard it through the grapevine." What high instruments accompany the backup vocal following the chorus?

Frank Driggs

Marvin Gaye

- Notice how the electric bass guitar makes a significant contribution to the aggressive rhythmic feel and still provides a strong foundation for the harmony.

INFLUENCES OF EASTERN MUSIC

During the mid- to late-1960s hippies became very interested in the apparent peacefulness and tranquility espoused by Eastern philosophies and religions. This interest took many young people to India, Pakistan, and other countries in that part of the world. During their travels these young people learned about the people and their music, and brought back with them an interest in these unusual-sounding melodies and rhythms.

George Harrison, lead guitarist with the Beatles, developed a special fondness for the *sitar*, a plucked string instrument from the Indian subcontinent, which has a large gourd for a body. Ravi Shankar, Harrison's teacher, made the instrument popular in this country.

PSYCHEDELIC AND HARD ROCK

The Beatles' *Sgt. Pepper's Lonely Hearts Club Band*, probably commercial music's most celebrated album, arrived in 1967. During that year, the "summer of love" was observed in San Francisco, a city in which music and drugs had merged to produce "acid" or "psychedelic" rock. Also in that year, a band named the Jimi Hendrix Experience became an instantaneous sensation after an appearance at the Monterey Pop Festival. Hendrix ended his performance by burning his guitar.

Jimi Hendrix was one of rock's most exciting and most imitated guitarists. Hendrix's death in 1970, at age 27, was one of rock's tragedies. The foundation of his style was the blues; his medium of expression was the electric guitar colored by the technologies of distortion and feedback. The Jimi Hendrix sound and the instrumentation of his band—guitar, bass, and drums: the "power trio"—were at the core of the hard rock style and of the heavy metal style that followed. As a *Guitar Player* (Sept. 1995) writer stated, "the story of electric guitar will be forever told in two parts: before Jimi and after Jimi."

CROSSROADS

Rock music and its stars have demonstrated a tendency toward self-destruction, as the drug-related deaths of Jim Morrison, Janis Joplin, and Jimi Hendrix, all around 1970, attest. In the same period, at the tragic Rolling Stones concert at Altamont, many in the crowd of an estimated 300,000 were physically assaulted and one person was murdered before the cameras of a documentary film crew. Ten years later eleven people died at a Who concert in Cincinnati, and a year later John Lennon was murdered. The message of rock seemed to encourage violence, sex, and drugs—shocking to parents and foreign to the popular music of people only one generation removed. This message has been carried to extremes by more recent groups such as Tha Dogg Pound, whose album "Dogg Food" *Newsweek* (Oct 9, 1995) described as "filled with profanity, misogynistic lyrics, graphic sex, and violence."

CALVIN AND HOBBES

The music of Jimi Hendrix and a British hard rock group called Cream led to heavy metal, which other British bands such as Led Zeppelin and Black Sabbath developed in their styles and bands such as Iron Butterfly, Van Halen, and others popularized in the United States. A number of substyles of metal evolved, including "glam" and "thrash."

JAZZ-ROCK/FUSION

Jazz and rock combined in two different ways. One, called **fusion,** is primarily *an instrumental style that includes extensive improvisation.* The trumpeter Miles Davis is associated with its beginnings. The other is known as **jazz-rock,** and *features a lead vocalist accompanied by horn (trumpet, sax, and trombone) and rhythm sections.* This recording of "Spinning Wheel," made in 1968, is an early example of the jazz-rock style. The form is AABA with an instrumental interlude between B and the return of A.

Active Listening
CD 4:14

"Spinning Wheel" (Thomas-Lipsius), Blood, Sweat and Tears

A   What goes up, must come down
       Spinning wheel, got to go round
       Talking 'bout your troubles it's a cryin' sin
       Ride a painted pony let the spinning wheel spin

A   You got no money, you got no home
       Spinning wheel, all alone
       Talking 'bout your troubles and you never learn
       Ride a painted pony let the spinning wheel turn

B   Did you find, the directing sign
       On the straight and narrow highway?
       Would you mind, a reflecting sign
       Just let it shine, within your mind
       And show you the colors that are real

• Instrumental break
A′   Someone is waiting, just for you
       Spinning wheel, spinning true
       Drop all your troubles by the riverside
       Catch a painted pony on the spinning wheel ride
• Instrumental break
• Trumpet improvisation
• Repeat last stanza (A′)
• Instrumental interlude with recorders imitates calliope sound of a carousel

CROSSROADS

A mobile is a majestic and yet delicate work of art. Hanging suspended in space with light reflecting from its surfaces, it brings to our eyes the sculptor's vision of the inner action of static and spontaneous elements. It consists of solid pieces hanging in a given spatial relationship with one another. The viewer's perception of the mobile changes as the angle or intensity of the illuminating light changes, or as the viewer changes perspective by moving around the work. Many mobiles move, rotating around the point from which they are suspended. This additional motion multiplies the ways in which the viewer can experience the relationships among the pieces of the mobile and enjoy the subtle combinations of light and shade on its solid surfaces. The creator of the work of art brings together two elements: the controlled and the uncontrolled.

This is very similar to the improvisation in jazz. The composer provides the basic structure of a piece: its melody, rhythm, and harmony—the static elements—and then around these structural parts the jazz performer improvises his or her line—the spontaneous element. It's this play of spontaneous against static, controlled against uncontrolled, that brings excitement and beauty to the jazz idiom.

Myxomatose, a mobile
by Alexander Calder

CORBIS/ARS, New York, NY

Active Listening
CD 4:15

"Spinning Wheel" (excerpt from live, improvised version), Blood, Sweat and Tears

- This excerpt was recorded live in 1991 and features the same musicians.
- Would you call this performance jazz-rock, fusion, or straight jazz?
- How does the improvisation change your perception of the "mobile"?

THE BLUES REVIVAL: COUNTRY AND ROCK BLUES

There's an old saying, "What goes around comes around." This has certainly been true of the blues. The blues (or its citified version, rhythm and blues) was there when rock started, experienced a revival in England during the 1960s, which led to great bands like the Rolling Stones and the Animals, and enjoyed a revival in the land of its birth during the 1980s. The use of heavily rock-oriented rhythm sections led to the term "blues rock"; the use of country instrumentation and country-style lyrics led to the term "country blues."

Rock and the blues have produced dozens of exceptional guitarists, far too many to list in this text. Jimi Hendrix would certainly be at or near the top. In a manner very similar to the way the 1967 Monterey Festival vaulted Hendrix into the spotlight, the 1982 Montreux Jazz Festival lifted the blues guitarist Stevie Ray Vaughan to a position of national attention. Strongly influenced by Hendrix and by his own brother, Jimmy (a prime mover in the U.S. blues revival), Stevie Ray developed a guitar performance style that was a unique blend of blues, jazz, rock, and country, a blend that audiences found to be very exciting. In 1990, he joined his brother to work on some projects with Bob Dylan and to tour with Eric Clapton. Unfortunately, his life was cut short when the helicopter that was transporting him to a Clapton concert crashed. He was 36 years old

Here, we listen to his "Ain't Gone 'N' Give up on Love." How's that for a country/western title? And yet, this is really a blues tune—one with some truly wonderful blues guitar playing! The overall form of this piece is a little unusual as compared to the blues structures we have considered in earlier chapters.

"Ain't Gone 'N' Give up on Love," Stevie Ray Vaughan

Active Listening
CD 4:16

- Four-measure introduction. The tempo is very slow and the beat is very heavy. The full harmonic background is played on a Hammond organ.
- Above this rich, energetic texture we hear the emotional guitar of Stevie Ray Vaughan, almost as if he were singing.
- A classic blues structure begins: twelve measures divided into three sections called phrases and separated by brief guitar fills. The first two phrases have the same words, "Ain't gone 'n' give up on love . . . ," and the third phrase has different words, "Every tear that I cry. . . ."
- Another twelve-measure section follows, again in classic blues structure. Identify the words that begin each phrase in this second blues structure.

Phrase 1

Phrase 2

Phrase 3

- An unusual section begins: ten measures in two-measure sections with the first eight measures building toward a climactic restatement of the title, "Ain't gone'n' give up on love" and leading to an extended guitar solo based on the blues structure.
- What vocal material (words and melody) follows the guitar solo to end the piece?

32 The Musical

Our curtain opens on the most important American contribution to the stage—the musical comedy, or more simply, the musical. It is frequently called the Broadway musical because so many theaters that produce this form of entertainment are located on or near Broadway in New York City. The **musical** comedy is distinguished from its higher-class cousin the operetta by its *down-to-earth characters and plots*, by its *colloquial spoken dialogue*, and especially by the *popular style of its songs*. Because Broadway theaters are so much smaller than opera houses, the musical can welcome captivating stage personalities regardless of their relatively untrained (and certainly unoperatic) voices.

It would be difficult to imagine a more appealing and flexible medium than the American musical. In dialogue, song, and dance, the musical tells a story in a musical language that lies open to all styles, from popular song past and present (including rock) to jazz, and from the Western operatic idiom to ethnic musics of the world.

DEFINITIONS AND BEGINNINGS

The American musical has its roots in the British musical farce (as transplanted to New York), in vaudeville (or revue), and in comic opera and operetta. In addition to its popular style of singing, it is distinguished from opera by its spoken dialogue and its reliance on comedy. Plots deal with the dreams and problems of everyday people, but they are loose enough to permit almost anything. For example, one outstanding early composer of musicals, George M. Cohan, always managed to include a patriotic number—for example, the popular "Yankee Doodle Boy," from *Little Johnny Jones* (1904).

The early musical comedy always regaled the audience with popular comedians, scantily clad women, and a few would-be hit songs—all of these strung casually on a loosely woven plot. Those seeking a more tight-knit story and classical singing found them elsewhere, in the distinctly different genre of the operetta.

KERN AND HAMMERSTEIN: THE MUSICAL COMES OF AGE

The American musical came of age in *Show Boat* (1927), written by Jerome Kern (1885–1945) and Oscar Hammerstein II (1895–1960), which is a unique synthesis of the genre's constituent elements. The songs are generally popular in style, some of them as captivating as the hit tunes of contemporaneous revues such as the Ziegfeld Follies. Nevertheless, like an operetta, the show is firmly integrated musically and dramatically and based on a solid, large-scale musical framework.

Show Boat, which is based on a novel of the same name by Edna Ferber, evokes American life over a span of almost fifty years. It does so by using a kaleidoscope of musical styles ranging from a nineteenth-century banjo tune and ragtime to operetta-like arias and duets. In addition, various styles of black music are heard, as in the poignant showstopper entitled "Old Man River." The plight of southern blacks is just one of the serious subjects not previously presented in musical comedy.

The composer of *Show Boat*, Jerome Kern, is generally regarded as foremost among the first generation of creators of the American musical. Historians of the genre celebrate his innovations, among them his creation of the contemporary love ballad and his use of jazz chord progressions. Music lovers treasure his traditional emphasis on catchy, popular melodies.

RODGERS AND HAMMERSTEIN: MUSICAL PLAYS

About this time, the Broadway musical began to enjoy the fruits of the partnership between composer Richard Rodgers (1902–1979) and lyricist Lorenz Hart (1885–1943)Their shows, sometimes referred to as musical plays, achieve an unprecedented integration of the fundamental elements of a musical:

- a book with somewhat believable characters and a real conflict (somewhat simplified to leave space for music and dance) that demands resolution,
- a viable subplot as a contrast and counterpoint to the main drama,
- song lyrics that reveal the inner feelings of characters,
- a comedic element (usually inherent in the characters and situations as opposed to being left to specifically comic characters and scenes).

A new era on Broadway began in 1943 with the premiere of Rodgers and Hammerstein's *Oklahoma*. The show's spoken dialogue and its songs alternate with a continuity that is effortless, and the action is nearly continuous. From its opening with an almost empty stage (unheard of in musicals) to its setting in the American West, to the importance given to the choreography of Agnes De Mille (who actually carried forward the story line in the Dream Ballet), *Oklahoma* established a model for the musicals that followed.

The songs, many of them still fresh and beguiling today, often contribute to the action, even as they help to delineate the characters. For example, the duet entitled "People Will Say We're in Love" outwardly seems to be just another exercise in the more or less standard verse and refrain form so common in musical comedy. Examined more closely, it provides a benchmark for the excellence of the partnership of Rodgers and Hammerstein. At the same time that the words of the song seem to indicate little attraction between the show's romantic but headstrong leads, the music clearly expresses their mutual attraction. Then, when the song has apparently ended, the music continues and the characters move in and out of dialogue and song to the end of the scene.

Oklahoma is a simple tale of country romance in which the beautiful farm girl, Laurey, is "keen" on the handsome cowboy, Curly. The course of their relationship is not running smoothly when they sing the duet "People Will Say

Laurey and Curly

© Frank Driggs Collection

We're in Love," describing all the ways they can devise to convince people they are not in love. The song begins with an introduction consisting of four lines: the first sung by Laurey, the second by Curly and the remaining two by Laurie. The refrain, which begins with the words "Don't throw bouquets at me," is in standard AABA form.

Oklahoma, "People Will Say We're in Love," Rodgers and Hammerstein

Active Listening
CD 4:17

- Brief instrumental introduction
- Four-line vocal introduction, moderate tempo, descending melody, characters alternate as described above. Laurey ends in rhythmically free style with a fermata.
- Laurey's refrain, AABA, slower tempo, more legato style
- Curley, four line vocal introduction
- Curley's refrain, AABA, as before; ends number

Oklahoma ran more than 2,000 performances in New York, an unprecedented number. Later successes by the same team included *Carousel* (1945), *South Pacific* (1949), and *The Sound of Music* (1959).

The late 1940s and 1950s proved to be a golden age for musicals, many of them still treasured and revived not just for their songs but because they are complete and interesting shows. Most of them, following the example of *Oklahoma,* were integrated musical plays. But now the door was open for new subject matter, ranging from goodhearted big-city lowlifes (Frank Loesser's *Guys and Dolls,* 1950) to plays fashioned from myth (Frederick Loewe and Alan Lerner's *My Fair Lady,* 1956), and even to full-blown tragedy (Leonard Bernstein's *West Side Story,* 1957).

THE MODERN MUSICAL

The 1960s and 1970s brought musicals on an even wider variety of subjects, including ethnic matters (Jerry Bock and Sheldon Harnick's *Fiddler on the Roof,* 1964), religion (Stephen Schwartz's *Godspell,* 1971), comic strip characters (Charles Strouse and Martin Charnin's *Annie,* 1977), and even a brothel (Carol Hall's *The Best Little Whorehouse in Texas,* 1978). Inevitably, given the musical's traditional link to popular styles, rock styles invaded Broadway, particularly in Galt MacDermot and James Rado's *Hair* (1967). Most rock musicals have been unsuccessful, but the reasons probably lie less with the musical style than with undue repetition, clumsily written books, and poor lyrics. A certain blurring of categories has taken place in rock musicals when, as in Andrew Lloyd Webber's *Jesus Christ Superstar* (1971), a show uses no spoken dialogue but, like an opera, is sung throughout.

The indeterminate territory between musical and opera (or operetta) has often attracted Stephen Sondheim (b. 1930–), the outstanding Broadway composer-lyricist of our time. Apparently willing to achieve commercial success only on his terms, he has tackled a variety of difficult subjects and sought to create a unique musical, lyrical, and theatrical style for each show. Acceptance of his works has sometimes been slow, perhaps because they lack comedy (as opposed to sophisticated wit) or because the musical style is complex. Few of Sondheim's songs can be extracted from their place in a show, and perhaps only "Send in the Clowns" (*A Little Night Music)* has been a true showstopper. But knowledgeable critics and connoisseurs have expressed heartfelt appreciation for his willingness to employ contemporary techniques and to deal with contemporary issues and ambiguities.

Sondheim's musicals range widely in subject, from operetta-like eloquence (*A Little Night Music,* 1973) to domestic life (*Company,* 1970), and from a seamy horror story (*Sweeney Todd,* 1979) to life in imperial Japan (*Pacific Overtures,* 1976). Several of his shows, including *Company* (1970) and *Follies* (1971), represent what has generally come to be called the *concept musical.* In the concept musical, one unifying idea lies at the heart of the show and determines every aspect of its style and production. Other matters, including the story, the characters, the stage design, even the music, play secondary roles.

In *Company,* for example, Sondheim deals with the difficulties of making relationships in contemporary society, a subject that is a far cry from the "happily ever after" couple portrayed in Oklahoma. It is probable that he was assisted in moving toward the idea of the concept musical in *Company* by the inspiration for the musical: a series of seven one-act plays by the actor George Furth. According to Joanne Gordon in *Art Isn't Easy: The Achievement of Stephen Sondheim* (p. 42), Sondheim said:

> A lot of the controversy about *Company* was that up until *Company* most musicals, if not all musicals, had plots. In fact, up until *Company* I thought that musicals had to have very strong plots. One of the things that fascinated me about the challenge of the show was to see if a musical could be done without one.

The show opens as a group of married couples with varying degrees of dysfunctional relationships throw a surprise thirty-fifth birthday party for Robert, the bachelor who serves as the principal character of the show. What follows is a series of snapshots of his relationships with his couple friends and with three different women. The goal of the couples is to see to it that Robert falls into the same trap they have fallen into and becomes part of their "company." At the same time, all are envious of his freedom. As the show progresses Robert begins to sense the value of a less physical, more mature relationship.

In Act 1, Scene 6 the couples try to fix Robert up with a variety of women. The scene opens with the "Bobby" refrain that recurs throughout the musical. The couples insistently attempt to contact Bobby, which hides their own inability to contact each other. The design of the number is based on the theatrical entrances of the characters as they perform singly, in duets and ensembles, sometimes as individuals or couples, and other times as husbands or wives. The various textures are also based the theatrical entrances as well as the need for emphasis and variety. The meter alternates between duple and triple while styles range from rock to a waltz.

Company, Act I, Scene 6, "Have I Got a Girl for You," Stephen Sondheim

Active Listening
CD 4:18

- "Bobby" rock beat with guitars. Husbands and wives individually vie for Bobby's attention (polyphonic texture).
- Couples ask Bobby to "come on over for dinner" (homophonic texture).
- Ends with sustained note on "love"
- Larry describes ideal "dumb" girl.
- Change to triple meter – in an ascending line he expresses own fantasies.
- Peter describes ideal "smart" girl.
- Triple meter and ascending line– expresses his fantasies
- Quintet: Larry, Peter, David, Paul, and Harry —"Have I got a girl for you" (polyphonic texture)
- Triple meter and ascending line —"Boy to be in your shoes what I wouldn't give" (in unison)
- Ends with "Marriage may be where it's been, but it's not where it's at!"
- Waltz: same characters "Whaddya like . . ." (in unison until the end)
- Whaddya wanna get married for?
- Repeat of last two lines

One of the most popular and long-lasting musicals of the late twentieth century was Michael Bennett's *A Chorus Line*. Bennett was a choreographer who worked on a number of shows during the 1960s. After several nominations, he finally received two Tony awards for *Follies* (1971), a show he choreographed and co-directed.

In *A Chorus Line*, Bennett's goal was to focus on the "gypsies," or chorus dancers, of Broadway. The book of the musical was developed through a series of workshops in which professional dancers shared their personal and professional experiences. Bennett, who served as director-choreographer, enlisted the services of Academy Award winner Marvin Hamlisch to compose the music. Bennett used a unique technique for *A Chorus Line* that he called cinematic staging. In essence, he assembled a series of procedures such as stage dissolves, montages, close-ups, and a bare stage with mirrors that gave the impression of a film.

The plot of *A Chorus Line* centers on a very diverse group of dancers—young and old, wealthy and poor, gay and straight, experienced and right off the bus—auditioning for a musical. Zach, who serves as director, tells the dancers that he wants to get to know them better, so one by one they tell of their experiences. By the end of the show, the cast is chosen, but all have empathy for each other because of the unique audition experience. *A Chorus Line* opened on Broadway and ran for fifteen years, closing in 1990 after 6,137 performances.

This opening is one of the most spectacular to occur on Broadway as the audition begins and dancers fly around the stage. Zach calls out steps and asks for different dances as the dancers express their hopes and fears. There is a conflict between the rhythmically exciting and forceful music of the dance and the lyrical melody of "I really need this job." Key and meter change help create variety, and the opening rhythmic figure in the piano is first in 4/4 and later reappears in 6/4. All of these musical elements combine to express the thoughts, hopes, and fears of the dancers.

Active Listening
CD 4:19

"I Hope I Get It," *A Chorus Line,* Marvin Hamlisch

Opening
- In 4/4. Zach calls out steps accompanied by piano playing a rhythmic figure that recurs throughout.
- Zach calls for a run-through, "5-6-7-8." Orchestra plays using rhythmic figure in 6/4-drum fill.

"I Hope I Get It"
- In 4/4. "I hope I get it . . . how many people does he need?" (A melody)
- Key change. "I really need this job." Tricia in a lyrical style (B melody)
- Zach calls for ballet combination—orchestra
- In 4/4. "I really blew it," based on the A melody
- In 6/4 *Tempo di Funk*. Orchestra uses rhythmic figure from opening with guitar. Changes to 4/4 when Zach speaks, then back to 6/4 for dancers. Zach calls boys first, then girls.
- In 4/4. "I think I got it . . . I hope I get it" (A melody)
- "I really need this job" (B melody)
- Cadences on A major chord with D# (#4th) added, making cadence inconclusive
- Paul enters on B melody with lyrical "Who am I anyway . . ."—the first personal reflection of the show.
- Evolves into "I really need this job" for conclusion

Despite the trend on Broadway toward mounting enormously expensive shows that have already proven to be successful on recordings and on other stages, there is undoubtedly still a place for the more traditional song-oriented musical with comedy and life-sized characters and maybe even a simple love plot. The number of revivals of such shows remains high, and the overall number of musicals produced at every level throughout the country seems to be increasing. Individuals who possess drive and talent will determine the future direction of the musical. As Richard Rodgers expressed it in his book *Musical Stages* (New York: Random House, 1975),

> One night a show opens and suddenly there's a whole new concept. But it isn't the result of a trend; it's because one, two, three or more people sat down and sweated over an idea that somehow clicked and broke loose. It can be about anything and take off in any direction, and when it works, there's your present and your future.

CHAPTER

Mixtures of Musical and Opera/Commercial and Concert

33

OPERETTA

Operetta is a form of *musical theater that is light and sentimental in character and contains music, spoken dialogue, dancing and other theatrical elements*. In the hierarchy of types of musical stage productions, it fits between opera and musical comedy. The term "light opera" is usually considered to be synonymous with operetta.

American operetta has as its foundation the French comic opera of the mid-nineteenth century and the Viennese operetta popularized by Johann Strauss and others. The Viennese-style operetta was very successful in New York City during the first quarter of the twentieth century. At the same time, an American variety of operetta was developing, one that was lighter than the European forms and less demanding for the singers.

Victor Herbert (1859–1924) composed the first notable works in this new style. An immigrant born in Dublin and trained in Europe, Herbert brought musical legitimacy to early American musical comedy and comic opera as well as to operetta. In their emphasis on romance and on happy endings, the operettas of Herbert established the American prototype of a genre that flourished until the Great Depression. One of his operettas, *Babes in Toyland* (1903), had such wide appeal that it later became a popular Hollywood film.

In *Naughty Marietta* (1910), another of Herbert's influential and popular operettas, all of the principal songs deal with various aspects of love, from the most sentimental to the most ineffable (as in our example). The attitude and style of this listening example reflect an earlier age and may seem naive or unrealistic to you. Be patient and remember that life probably wasn't simpler then, but it was different.

Active Listening
CD 4:20

Naughty Marietta, "Ah, Sweet Mystery of Life," Victor Herbert

- What do you think about the philosophy expressed in this once very popular love song?
- How do the rhythms, the pauses, and the ups and downs of the melody (called "melodic contour") strengthen the message of the lyrics?
- This piece is in an ABAC form, as indicated below:
  A "Ah, sweet mystery . . ."
  B "All the longing . . ."
  A "Ah, 'tis love and love alone . . ."
  C "'Tis the answer . . ."
- The climax or apex of both the melody and the words comes at the beginning of the "C" section. What makes this point feel like the climax?

During the time of Victor Herbert, attempts to broaden the appeal of operetta led producers to advertise some of their operettas as musical comedies. In truth, some shows lay between the two types, especially when the process of Americanization led to interpolation into operetta of songs originating on Tin Pan Alley. Nevertheless, the leading composers of the operetta for Broadway in the 1920s were the European-born and trained Rudolf Friml and Sigmund Romberg.

Romberg (1887–1951) was a remarkably versatile and productive composer. In addition to creating more than sixty shows over a span of forty years, he also found time to write music for films. His most popular operetta, *The Student Prince in Heidelberg* (1924) was made into a successful film. *The Student Prince* ran for more than 608 performances on Broadway at the same time as musicals much more popular in style by Jerome Kern and George Gershwin (discussed below) were packing theaters.

It should not be surprising that elements from each of these genres crossed over to the other. By the time the operetta went into a decline during the Depression, a number of its characteristics had become part of the musical. In the long run, musical comedy proved to be a more flexible medium than operetta, better able to assimilate new styles, especially the quintessential American style that came to be known as jazz.

GEORGE GERSHWIN:
JAZZ COMES TO BROADWAY

During the 1920s and early 1930s George Gershwin (1898–1937) brought the rhythms of jazz to Broadway. After serving as a teenage song plugger on Tin Pan Alley, Gershwin turned to writing songs for revues. The popularity of one of these songs, "Swanee," provided a big boost to his career when the popular Broadway singer Al Jolson introduced it in one of his shows. Gershwin next began to compose musicals, employing his younger brother Ira as his lyricist. Beginning in 1924 with *Lady Be Good,* they wrote a series of musicals in the madcap style of the period. Their last success was *Girl Crazy* (1930), noteworthy as the debut of Ethel Merman and for the song "I Got Rhythm," which has become a **standard** (a term meaning *an enduring popular song*) in both the popular and jazz repertoires.

The 1930s found Gershwin ambitiously undertaking new challenges in an attempt to synthesize classical techniques with his popular musical language. *Of Thee I Sing* (1931), a satirical political tale quite in keeping with the drastically altered mood of the Depression years, is raised by the composer to the level of comic opera after the model of the English musical theater team, Gilbert and Sullivan. *Of Thee I Sing* was the first musical to receive the Pulitzer Prize for drama. There remained one last triumph for the Gershwin brothers before George's untimely death in 1937.

In 1933, they began to collaborate with DuBose Heyward, setting his book, *Porgy,* to music. This project represents a rather unusual combination of ethnic backgrounds: composer and lyricist who were sons of Jewish-Russian emigrants, an African-American author, and a plot based on a unique Southern culture. When *Porgy and Bess* opened in 1935, it was billed as "An American Folk-Opera." Now recognized as a unique blend of elements from both opera and musical, *Porgy and Bess* originally received more praise from drama critics than from music critics.

Porgy and Bess is set in Catfish Row, a tenement area near Charleston, South Carolina. The plot centers on the crippled Porgy, who gets around on a cart pulled by a donkey, and Bess, mistress of the bully Crown. Crown kills a man in a gambling brawl and goes into hiding. In Crown's absence, Bess and Porgy fall in love. Crown returns to claim his woman, Porgy murders him and is put in prison. While Porgy is in prison, the drug peddler Sportin' Life persuades Bess to go to New York with him.

In Act 3, as he attempts to persuade Bess, Sportin' Life sings "There's a Boat Dat's Leavin' Soon for New York." It is an interesting combination of rhythm and blues, jazz, popular, and European classical elements. The form is a modified ternary with the opening A and B sections repeated and extended.

Sportin' Life
and Bess

LISTENING GUIDE   *Porgy and Bess,* Act 3, "There's a Boat Dat's Leavin' Soon for New York," George Gershwin

CD 2:6

Introduction

00:00   The bass clarinet plays a descending melodic line—a classical influence. Plucked string instruments accompany, accenting the second and fourth beats—a characteristic of rhythm and blues and rock.

A Section

00:08   Sportin' Life sings with muted trumpet duplicating the vocal line. Syncopation in the strings follows each vocal phrase and extends the 8-measure section by one measure.

Woodwind transition to a repeat of A melody.

00:27   A section repeats with new words.

B Section

00:48   Contrasting, darker style with strings duplicating first phrase, muted trumpet the second. Voice joins syncopation in second phrase.

1:04   B section repeats with new words.
Extended transition to A features pizzicato strings and vocalist intoning on one pitch.

Ends with descending tuba line and fermata with voice up an octave.

Return to A

1:34   Voice part in a modified, more popular style. Slows to close. Ends with increased tempo while Sportin' Life sustains high note and finally says "Come on Bess."

Although the musicals of the 1930s and early 1940s generally followed Gershwin's lead and made room for the rhythms and harmonies of jazz, the tighter musical and dramatic structure that had apparently been Gershwin's goal were seldom realized. The shows of Cole Porter, for example, despite their wonderful individual tunes, seem very much like revues to today's audiences. Their loosely woven plots serve simply as an excuse for the tunes and the dancing, so the songs live on but the shows are seldom revived. An exception is *Kiss Me, Kate* (1948), an adaptation of Shakespeare's *The Taming of the Shrew*, which has a stronger book than most Porter shows and just as many outstanding tunes.

WEST SIDE STORY: SHAKESPEARE IN THE TWENTIETH CENTURY

West Side Story (1957), composed by Leonard Bernstein (1918–1991), is an example of the musical variety possible in this form, as well as being another Broadway adaptation of a Shakespeare play, *Romeo and Juliet*. A classically trained pianist, conductor, and composer, Bernstein also possessed a strong love for and understanding of popular music styles. *West Side Story* includes totally integrated and compelling dance numbers, large-scale operatic ensembles, and songs in many popular music styles. Listen to the wonderful quintet entitled "Tonight," enjoying it at first for its sheer musical beauty.

The plot revolves around the cross-cultural love between Maria (whose brother, Bernardo, leads the Puerto-Rican gang known as the Sharks) and Tony (who has ties to a rival "American" gang, the Jets, which is led by a boy named Riff). The soaring "Tonight" melody was heard earlier in the show; its purpose then was to authenticate (as only music can) the love at first sight of

Photofest

"The Rumble"

Maria and Tony, despite the cultural barrier between them. The technique of *reusing a song heard earlier* is called **reprise**. When the "Tonight" melody returns in the "Quintet," the dramatic situation is totally different. Now the melody comes after a love duet ("One Hand, One Heart") and just before the fateful clash of the rival gangs. What better way to emphasize the threat to the happiness of the lovers than to contrast the "Tonight" theme with the music of the gangs?

But Bernstein does not settle simply for bringing the two themes into proximity. Instead, he raises the dramatic intensity to a higher level through a device achievable only in music. After the themes are heard individually, the composer combines them, allowing the audience to hear from all five principal characters and from the rival gangs as well—all at the same time. The clash is no longer simply a dramatic one; it is also powerfully represented in purely musical terms.

Active Listening
CD 2:2

West Side Story, Act I, "Tonight" Quintet, Leonard Bernstein

- After a brief instrumental introduction, the number opens with a bravura dialogue between Riff and Bernardo about an impending "rumble."
- Bernardo's girlfriend, Anita, follows, singing about her plans for a big evening.

- The tempo suddenly becomes twice as slow as Tony sings of his anticipated meeting with Maria. This is the return of the "Tonight" melody.
- A short instrumental interlude.
- Riff begins the "quintet," singing the same melodic material as at the beginning of this number.
- Riff's vocal line becomes a duet when Maria's singing of "Tonight" is added.
- We have a trio as Tony interjects short melodic fragments.
- Then a quartet as Bernardo adds his two cents.
- Finally, a quintet when Anita joins in.
- All of the combatants in the musical clash have entered.

As is often the case, *West Side Story* represents the combined creative efforts of several people. Jerome Robbins was the choreographer-director, and it was his idea to adapt Shakespeare's *Romeo and Juliet* to a twentieth-century, New York City setting. The modern version of the play was the work of writer Arthur Laurents. The lyrics were written by Stephen Sondheim. Sondheim, discussed in the previous chapter, has written both words and music for many Broadway musicals.

The composer, Leonard Bernstein, was the first American-trained conductor-composer to gain an international reputation as a classical musician. His thorough technical training as a composer enabled him to become one of the supreme craftsmen of the Broadway musical. *West Side Story* stands as a milestone in the history of the musical partly because of the exceptional quality of its music and dance. Even more important is the thorough integration of these elements into the story. As a successful setting of a tragedy, it reveals a new aspect of the ever changing nature of the musical.

Film Music

MUSIC'S ROLE IN FILMS

Imagine watching your favorite film without hearing the music that was composed to accompany it. Would the villainous might of Darth Vader and the evil emperor be adequately depicted simply through the dialogue and the realistic sounds called for by the action and the setting? Or does *Star Wars* in fact depend on music for much of its impact? Would your heart beat as wildly if *Psycho*'s deranged killer rushed at his terrified victims without the slashing sound of high stringed instruments?

If you have seen these films, you may well have found the affective power of the music greater than that of the visual images. Good film music brings to life the settings, situations, and characters of a film. It cushions the ordinariness of the lesser moments and heightens the emotional impact of the more significant ones. Bernard Herrmann, the composer of the music for *Psycho* and one of the best in this field, clearly summarized the importance of music in the movies in a *New York Times* article of June 4, 1945, entitled "Music in Motion Pictures."

> Music on the screen can seek out and intensify the inner thoughts of the characters. It can invest a scene with terror, grandeur, gaiety, or mystery. It can propel narrative swiftly forward or slow it down. It often lifts mere dialogue into the realm of poetry. Finally, it is the connecting link between celluloid and audience, reaching out and enveloping all into one single experience.

As a nonrepresentational art, music's impact is direct and immediate, whereas film must communicate indirectly through images. Music can instantly create an appropriate atmosphere for a scene, and it can indicate the emotional state of a character without any need for words. It is often used to supply continuity between scenes as well as unity among a series of short scenes. One of its most noteworthy uses is to indicate the passage of time between scenes. Music can also remind us of the past or give us warning of what is to come. In fact, music's ability to communicate elements beyond the actions depicted on the screen can be said at times to be manipulative, doing much more than merely intensifying the screen images.

At times, film music strongly asserts how one should react to events and characters in the film. A simple example would be the manner in which film villains, including such so-called animal villains as bears, mountain lions, and wolves, are musically distinguished from the heroes, quite apart from any actions visible on the screen. More complex is the use of music to canonize certain attitudes toward society, gender, and various social groups.

In the traditional school of film making, music always remains a subordinate art. Although it can contribute greatly to the unity of a film, it follows and supports the dramatic flow and message of the film rather than working out its own independent logic and structure as you would find in a concert piece such as a symphony. Since film music is not continuous, a composer must work on a small scale and cannot adapt the action to inherent musical rhythms and structures as in, for example, opera. Not only is there no need for logical musical form in a film, there is generally no possibility of it. It may be for this reason that so few composers from the world of concert music have involved themselves with films. Another reason that film composers have become a separate class of composer is the commercial aspect of most film making: The final artistic decisions (what to keep and what to edit out) are left to persons concerned first and foremost with the financial balance sheet.

A film composer ordinarily is brought into the picture after the film has been shot and cut, so he or she must be able to work quickly. Seldom do the director and the producer consult the composer until it is time to *decide upon the places where music will be heard in a film*. This process is known as **spotting,** and the *places chosen for musical background* are known as **cues.** The film composer sets to work on the basis of the cue breakdown. Working with a mechanical time keeper (the **click track**) or with closely measured units of elapsed time *(free timings)*, the composer must be able to synchronize the music with the film, down to the second. Just as important, the composer must be willing to see some of his or her music (perhaps its best moments) lost in the process of *dubbing* a film. It is during the **dubbing** that the *various tracks of dialogue, sound effects, and music are brought into a unified whole*.

The success with which composers subordinate music to the dramatic aspects of a film is one of the reasons why their music has not generally enjoyed an afterlife in the concert hall. Only in recent years have film composers enjoyed some success with concert arrangements of their film music. The stringent demands of the profession have often led film composers to imitate the styles of earlier composers such as Tchaikovsky, Rachmaninoff, and Richard Strauss and sometimes to borrow themes from their music, which is no longer protected by copyright.

Two principal kinds of music are heard in films. **Functional** (or background) music in films *is intended to bring the images more fully to life for filmgoers*. Most of the music supplied by a film composer is of this kind. *Music that originates within the film and that is heard by the characters* is called **source music** and is often drawn from folk, popular, or concert music. Although it is possible for music to be heard first in one situation and then the opposite—for example, to occur within the film as source music and then move to the background score—such shifts must be done with great care.

SOME OUTSTANDING FILM COMPOSERS

A comprehensive survey of music for films is yet to be written. Most film composers, by the nature of their profession, have been so prolific and eclectic that a brief summary is difficult. The reader wishing to delve more deeply into the subject is encouraged to examine one of the recent books on the subject, such as Royal Brown's *Overtones and Undertones* (Berkeley: University of California Press, 1994) or William Darby and Jack Du Bois's *American Film Music* (Jefferson, NC: McFarland & Company, 1990).

A considerable number of Hollywood film composers have been foreign born. Max Steiner was an early film composer who helped establish the late romantic European symphonic style in films. His credits number in the hundreds and include such well-known films as *King Kong* (1933) and *Gone with the Wind* (1939). Other composers in this style were Franz Waxman (*The Bride of Frankenstein*, 1935), Miklos Rozsa (*Spellbound*, 1945), and Dmitri Tiomkin (*High Noon*, 1952). Younger foreign-born composers of note include Maurice Jarre (*Lawrence of Arabia*, 1962), Nino Rota (*Romeo and Juliet*, 1968), Lalo Schifrin (*Dirty Harry*, 1971), and John Barry (*Goldfinger*, 1964).

Prominent American film composers include Alfred Newman (*Wuthering Heights*, 1939), Bernard Herrmann (*Citizen Kane*, 1941), Alex North (*A Streetcar Named Desire*, 1951), Elmer Bernstein (*The Man with the Golden Arm*, 1955), David Raksin (*Laura*, 1944), and Leonard Rosenman (*East of Eden*, 1955) More recently this group has featured Henry Mancini (*Touch of Evil*, 1958), Jerry Goldsmith (*Star Trek*, 1979), and John Williams (*Jaws*, 1975).

Readers familiar with Western concert music will miss the names of the great composers of the twentieth century in the lists above, but some of them have occasionally written for films. Among the ranks of foreign-born composers to work in films in their own countries are Darius Milhaud, Arthur Honegger, Sergei Prokofiev, Dmitri Shostakovich, Ralph Vaughan Williams, William Walton, and Benjamin Britten. In general, they have been fortunate in that film composing abroad does not mean loss of artistic reputation, as is often the case here in the United States. Two prominent American composers who have been involved in film scoring are Aaron Copland (*The Heiress*, 1949) and Leonard Bernstein (*On the Waterfront*, 1954). Copland, however, publicly disclaimed the title music for *The Heiress*, and Bernstein complained about alterations made in his music while the film was dubbed.

The career of Bernard Herrmann (1911–1975) offers an unusual view of music in the Hollywood film industry. Despite his reputation as an irascible, outspoken, and difficult man, Herrmann's talent and artistry placed him in a position to work on some famous films, with some very significant directors. Among these directors were Orson Welles (three films) and Alfred Hitchcock (seven films). Herrmann's approximately fifty film credits range widely in subject, from big-budget sentimental romance (*The Snows of Kilimanjaro*, 1952) to sleazy urban realism (*Taxi Driver*, 1976) and from hair-raising suspense (*Psycho*, 1960) to futuristic science fiction (*Fahrenheit 451*, 1966). His broad knowledge of musical styles enabled him to seek a unique sound for each of his film scores. For *The Ghost and Mrs. Muir,* he created eerie woodwind chamber music; brass and percussion sounds accompany *King of the Khyber Rifles;* and electronic sounds fill *The Day the Earth Stood Still.* Unlike most Hollywood composers, Herrmann always did his own orchestrations, feeling that this was an integral part of the music.

Herrmann's knowledge of the Western classical tradition was extensive, ranging back to the baroque (employed in *The Three Worlds of Gulliver*) and forward to the more dissonant styles of the twentieth century *(Psycho).* This expertise enabled him to borrow and imitate with somewhat more taste and skill than many other film composers. His intent was often to capture the inner feelings of the characters, regardless of the action on the screen, and to establish atmosphere and mood more by harmonic and instrumental means than by melodic ones. There are occasions on which Herrmann would seem to be going against the director's intention. In *Fahrenheit 451,* for example, the music occasionally succeeds in making certain characters and ideas much more attractive to the audience than do the images.

Although Herrmann generally preferred to write short cues, once again in opposition to the "wall-to-wall" scoring of some of his contemporaries, there were occasions on which he seized the opportunity to compose in larger units. The following statement by Herrmann concerning *Citizen Kane* is drawn from *Film Music Notes,* Vol. IV, #2 (1944), as quoted in Roy Prendergast, *Film Music: A Neglected Art* (New York: Norton, 1991, p. 56):

> The film was so unusual, technically, that it afforded me many unique opportunities for musical experiments. It abounded in montages, which were long enough to permit me to compose complete musical numbers, rather than mere cues to fit them. Mr. Welles was extremely cooperative in this respect, and in many cases, cut his film to suit these complete numbers, rather than . . . cut[ting] the music to suit the film.

It should be noted that both Welles and Herrmann were new to Hollywood at this time and that their affable working relationship had already been formed during years of working together in radio.

With Alfred Hitchcock, Herrmann was fortunate enough to encounter a second musically sensitive director who was able to appreciate how the composer matched his musical style to the unique style of the films. In *Psycho* (1960), for example, the highly dissonant major sevenths and minor ninths that support the moments of greatest tension are present in the opening prelude music and recur frequently thereafter. Another characteristic of the music for this film is an insistent ostinato (a repeated rhythmic figure) that is heard throughout, and is used very effectively in the scene in which the murderer is watching his woman victim through a peephole, just before the famous shower scene.

Herrmann's instrumentation is tailored especially for *Psycho* in that the composer's use of the strings was calculated to match the black and white medium of the film. By drawing upon the whole panoply of twentieth-century string techniques, the composer was able to provide a great deal of color as required in different dramatic situations. Norman Bates' mental state, for example, is depicted by the use of mutes and of extreme registers for the strings. For suspense, as when the detective enters the old house, Herrmann uses string harmonics and pizzicato strings, and then, during the murder, string glissandi. There is also use of such special string techniques as bowing near the bridge *(sul ponticello)* or near the fingerboard *(sul tasto)* of the violin. In fact, the composer developed a vocabulary of musical devices for creating suspense from film to film, always emphasizing harmony (mainly through highly dissonant intervals, but also through bitonality) and rhythm (through ostinato figures). Herrmann's favorite score in the Hitchcock series seems to have been *Vertigo.*

The music for *Psycho* is performed by a string orchestra. While this choice may seem to severely limit instrumental timbre, string instruments can produce a great variety of sounds and therefore are able to convey many emotions and moods. Each of the two musical cues used here is taken from a murder-

Janet Leigh, the
Psycho shower scene

related scene. In the shower scene, Norman Bates murders a beautiful young woman, Marian, while she is taking a shower. In the swamp scene, Marian's boyfriend, Sam, is searching for Arbogast, the detective hired to find Marian—and who has also been murdered.

Psycho (1960), Cues for the Shower Scene and the Swamp Scene, Bernard Herrmann

Active Listening

Shower Scene

CD 4:21

- Marian, begins her shower in silence—except for the sound of running water.
- The high, almost percussive, strings enter abruptly when Norman Bates attacks with a large butcher knife.
- The violins "attack" their notes in a manner similar to the stabbing knife.
- As Marian is dying, the focus of the agitated music shifts to the lower strings.
- Notice how the cellos "attack" their notes as the violins did earlier.

Swamp Scene

CD 4:22

- As the scene begins Sam is shouting Arbogast's name. The shout echoes across the swamp where Norman has hidden both of his victims.
- As Sam looks for Arbogast, the music enters with the high strings.
- When the visual image shifts to the murderer standing by the swamp, the musical focus shifts to the lower strings.
- What emotions are portrayed by the music from this scene?

THE RETURN TO SYMPHONIC FILM SCORES

The outstanding event of the last few decades of film composing has been the resurgence of symphonic film writing. Not unlike such classic adventure films as *The Sea Hawk* and *Robin Hood* are the modern films *Superman* (1978), *Raiders of the Lost Ark* (1981), *Indiana Jones and the Temple of Doom* (1984), and, of course, the *Star Wars* series. The composer of the scores for these films is John Williams.

After undergoing a traditional period of training in composition, Williams served a long film music apprenticeship with Alfred Newman, Dmitri Tiomkin, and others before making his own mark in films. His break came with the return of the big film epic and the opportunity to compose traditional symphonic music of a markedly romantic kind.

Although his scores may seem to be highly derivative of the music of Richard Strauss, Gustav Holst, and other postromantic composers, most moviegoers simply delight in Williams' brass-dominated marches and rhythmically stirring tunes. Even connoisseurs of music find considerable enjoyment in the traditional skill with which the composer develops his themes and uses them to enrich scenes in a film. An instance of this occurs when the main heroic theme of *Star Wars* (1977) serves as a counterpoint to the music accompanying Princess Leia's appeal to Ben Kenobi for assistance. The message is clear: There is still a place for traditional symphonic music and for concert music composers in films. The talents of John Williams—his ability to create memorable themes and even more significantly to develop them in the traditional symphonic manner—played a significant role in the return of the traditional symphony orchestra as background music for the big adventure films of the 1980s and 1990s.

LISTENING GUIDE

Star Wars, Main Theme and Princess Leia Theme, John Williams

CD 4:23

00:00	As the excerpt opens, the brass play a fanfare-like announcement of the beginning of the film.
00:09	Brass present the first statement of the heroic A theme.
00:27	The strings enter with the softer, contrasting Princess Leia B theme.
00:40	The B theme is extended by some figures in the brass.
00:50	French horns play the return to the A theme, punctuated by a strong chordal pattern.

Modern films often employ preexisting music, perhaps to avoid the added cost of a newly composed score. Examples are *Finding Forrester,* which uses the music of Miles Davis and others, and *O Brother Where Art Thou,* which uses a number of traditional folk songs in modern renditions. A movie that follows the traditional path of employing newly composed music is *Crouching Tiger, Hidden Dragon,* a film by Ang Lee, based on a book by Wand Du Lu. The music is composed and conducted by Tan Dun and features solos by cellist Yo-Yo Ma and orchestras and percussion ensembles from Shanghai. Throughout, Tan Dun combines Western and Eastern elements.

In the story line, Li Mu Bai, a great Chinese Zen warrior, decides to give up his treasured Green Destiny sword, stating that it "has not bred enlightenment, only sorrow." Li entrusts the sword with a dear friend, but shortly afterward, Jen Yu, a young warrior in training whose imminent arranged marriage would put an end to her aspirations, steals it. The plot of the movie unfolds in a series of love stories between the various characters, and ultimately centers on the recovery of this sword.

The listening selection, "Farewell," is heard at the end of the movie. Jen Yu journeys to a far-off mountain where she is reunited with her true love, Bo. Once there, Jen recalls a story that she was told earlier in the movie about a young man who falls over the side of the mountain in hopes that his faithful heart will make dreams come true. Jen asks Bo what he wishes for and then gracefully dives over the side of the mountain. Jen appears to float peacefully down the mountain in a meditative state. This mood is reflected in the music as the drumbeat stops.

Eastern and Western elements are evident in this example. The *erhu* solo and the Chinese drums balance Western elements such as the cello solo by Yo-Yo Ma, and the accompanying strings. The cello solo is a variation on the "Crouching Tiger" theme that is heard throughout the score, and the drum part is similar to those heard in the fight scenes.

There are eight repetitions of a melodic phrase in this example. As it progresses, the cello rises in pitch and the drum part becomes more intense while the Western strings remain constant in the background. The *erhu* interacts in a variety of ways with the cello.

Active Listening
CD 4:24

"Farewell," *Crouching Tiger, Hidden Dragon,* Tan Dun

- Cello enters with a variation of the original theme, accompanied by Western strings. The *erhu* enters at the end of this statement. Drum activity is minimal.
- The *erhu* becomes more prominent with a countermelody at a pitch level higher than the cello. Drum activity increases.
- Cello in the lower register while the erhu remains in the higher register.
- Cello rises to the upper register and interacts with the erhu. Drums more active.
- Cello upper register, more drum activity.
- More drum activity.
- Drums more intense.
- Drums stop, followed by quickening pitch oscillation that represents Jen's fall.

Film is an international medium, and films are produced in numerous countries throughout the world. In each country, film music reflects the native musical culture. In the next chapter, we will examine the evolution of such world traditions in popular music.

35 Evolving a Global Popular Music

POPULAR/COMMERCIAL TRENDS IN OTHER COUNTRIES

In the broadest sense of the word, types of "popular" music have existed in all cultures for centuries. These musics tend to be lighter in content and easily accessible, and to appeal to a broad spectrum of society. However, in our own time, popular music also has a commercial dimension. As was mentioned in Chapter 29, the commercial aspect of popular music in the United States was limited in the nineteenth century and grew dramatically in the twentieth century. In other parts of the world the commercialization of popular music happened at a much later time. The following piece originated in Egypt and is an example of music created to make a profit through the sale of copies. An ardent lover extols the attributes of a voluptuous girl named Salha. He describes in detail her curvaceous figure and sends greetings *(Salem Aleikem)* to all men who admire her.

Active Listening
CD 4:25

Mol Kaðð Tewela, Egypt

- Opens with an instrumental ensemble consisting of an *oud* (plucked lute), *kanun* (plucked zither), and violin, accompanied by the *ðarbukka* (drum) playing a rapid figure.
- Drum stops as a drone (sustained tone, usually in the low register) begins.
- Vocalist improvises a wordless *"taqsim"* in which the melodic pattern of the mode to be used is heard at a relatively slow tempo.
- Original tempo is resumed with both the instrumental ensemble and the vocalist performing.

BLENDING WORLD AND AMERICAN POPULAR STYLES

In pre-civil war Beirut (this city, the capital of Lebanon, was often called "the Paris of the Middle East" before the prolonged devastation from the mid-1970s through the '80s), a style of popular music was widely heard in the European-frequented cafes, casinos, and nightclubs, where it accompanied the gyrations of belly dancers. This popular music combined indigenous elements with considerable European-American influence, as evidenced in the next

Robert Washburn

Kanun and *oud* players

example. It is an interesting example of **acculturation**, which is *a mixing of native and foreign elements.*

One hears in this example the mixture of Arabic and European-American influences. This music is used to accompany the *debke,* a line dance popular throughout the Middle East. The instrumentation includes elements from both worlds.

Raksat el-Houria, Arabia

Active Listening
CD 4:26

- Lengthy introduction in Arabic style with Middle Eastern rhythms and melodies. Some are played on Arabic instruments, but Western instruments such as the accordion, percussion, and string bass are also used.
- Clarinet solo is obviously not performed on an Arabic instrument, probably showing the influence of Turkey and Greece.

Films are a popular form of entertainment in India, and hundreds are made each year. Most have considerable amounts of singing in them, and the songs are often released on CDs for individual sale. The musical style shows a variety of influences from traditional Indian folk melodies through American pop forms, Latin American rhythms, and Chinese scale patterns. Recently, such groups as Shakti and the vocalist Najma Naktar have shown an interest in a fusion of Eastern and Western styles. The song heard in the example, sung by the popular Najma, has many characteristics of a raga. Though devoted to singing *ghazals* (a traditional poetic form widely used in Muslim cultures), Najma and her producers use innovative techniques and modern instruments to make utterly contemporary, ethereal, and hypnotic sounds.

Active Listening
CD 4:27

Neend Koyi, India

- Begins with a drone over which the singer sings a wordless melody in an improvisatory style similar to the *alap* in a raga.
- Violin continues in a similar but somewhat embellished style.
- Tablas enter with a fast rock-influenced rhythmic pattern and a bass line that shows strong American pop influence.
- Voice reenters, this time with words and in a style that continues throughout the rest of the example with the accompaniment of American pop-style rhythms.

In recent years, Americans have come to associate the word "popular" with music that in some way comes from jazz and the blues, and their many derivatives, such as New Orleans jazz (Dixieland), swing, rock, country and western, and show tunes. The origins of jazz around the turn of the twentieth century, as we have discovered, were in the music of the slaves who were brought from Africa and combined their rhythms and melodic patterns with familiar tunes of the day. As jazz and its related idioms flourished and became more widely heard, they became popular in Europe and in Africa, the land of their origins. More recently they have become very popular in Japan and have influenced the popular music of many other cultures that have borrowed various characteristics—another example of acculturation.

In 1955, Bill Haley and the Comets carried American rock and roll to England. Since that time American popular music has been moving toward a position of worldwide dominance. American rock, soul, country rock, and hip hop can be heard in England, Germany, Japan, and many other countries. Of course, the vast distribution networks established by the commercial music industry have accelerated this process. It was natural for other countries to integrate stylistic features of American popular music into their own popular music heritage.

One of the most interesting and popular musical genres to come out of Africa in recent years is the blending of European-American popular idioms with African traditions. This process began in the 1950s in Ghana, when native musicians adopted the guitar to accompany their singing, and the music was called *highlife* or *palm wine* music. The first term came about through an association with the popular music of European colonists (various European nations remained colonial powers in Africa into the 1960s) and the second

referred to the relaxed, rural, acoustic guitar style associated with late afternoon drinking sessions at palm wine bars in the bush. Electric guitar bands
have largely replaced this style. Wind instruments were also employed at
times, probably obtained from the British military bands heard in the British
African colonies. A somewhat later but similar phenomenon occurred in Nige-
ria, where electronically amplified instruments, including the guitar, bass,
vibes, and the synthesizer (and at times traditional Western wind instruments)
are added to native African percussion. Traditional Yoruba rhythms are integrated with hymns, highlife, and Western popular music. This music is called
juju, a word of unknown origin.

The link with American jazz and popular music is strong, and characteristics of Caribbean and Latin American styles are very evident in many cases.
Two well-known artists in this idiom are Chief Commander Ebenezer Obey
and King Sunny Ade. Another Nigerian who achieved significant recognition
in Africa, as well as in the United States and Europe, is Fela Anikulapo Kuti
(usually called simply Fela). His rather flamboyant stage manner together
with his vocals, keyboard, and sax playing (along with the" suggestive" dancing of his twenty-some wives) resulted in widespread popularity. His lyrics
often were harshly critical of Europeans and Americans, music critics, and
African political figures. He ran for president in his country and also served
jail sentences for expressing his political views openly in his music and other-
wise. He referred to his style as *Afro-Beat.* **Afro-Pop** is another word often used
as *a generic term for all African popular music.* It is featured on a weekly broadcast
produced by National Public Radio.

Ebenezer Obey

The recordings of Obey are currently among the most popular of Afro-Pop. Obey's music is of interest because, in addition to exhibiting his own exciting guitar solos and singing, it combines strong African percussion passages (particularly the "talking drum" at the beginning of the example) with Western electrically amplified instruments, including the guitar, bass, and synthesizer. You will hear such a passage before Obey begins his vocal. Obey's texts are often of a serious, sometimes religious, nature.

Active Listening
CD 2:12

"Asiki Mi Ti To," Chief Commander Ebenezer Obey

- Introduction — African drums featuring talking drums
- Electric guitar vamp followed by flute entrance
- Solo and ensemble voice entrance "Asiki Mi Ti To"
- Instrumental interlude
- Text section — solo and ensemble voices alternate
- Drum interlude — talking drums
- Solo and ensemble voices
- Fade

Two centuries of slave trade brought African culture to the United States. In time, these African-American musics were brought back to an industrialized South Africa. The South Africans adopted some aspects of this African-American music, creating a new style that was then exported back to the

Talking drums

United States. This circular pattern of cultural exchange has become common in our time, and as means of communication continue to improve, the elapsed time between exchanges decreases.

Ladysmith Black Mambazo, a men's chorus led by Joseph Shabalala, has been a popular group in South Africa since the early 1970s. Their a cappella singing style, *isicathamiya*, was developed by Zulu workers who were transplanted to work in South African mines and factories. It combines Zulu music with African-American gospel, rhythm and blues and doo-wop. Paul Simon and Joseph Shabalala collaborated on "Homeless" for the *Graceland* CD and tour in 1986, effectively bringing this multicultural music to the United States.

This concludes the unit on popular music, a music that reflects the fact that we live in a popular culture. Part VII brings together all of the parts of the book by describing the various styles and functions of music in the immediate present and suggesting ways in which you can interact with these musics in the future.

36   The Contemporary Scene and Experiencing the Classics

MUSIC IN THE PRESENT

Many times, finishing a college course seems to mark the end of dealing with that particular content for the foreseeable future. However, arts courses offer the potential of beginning a process of applying what you have learned in a way that will lead to lifelong enjoyment. To assist you in getting started, these concluding chapters will provide information about music in present-day society along with a contemporary view of several types of music and suggestions about how to connect with them.

THE ARTS CLIMATE

A 1996 Harris poll provides some surprising information about the health of the arts community in the United States. At a time when federal and state bureaucrats are cutting arts funding because of a supposed decreased interest in the arts, an amazing 86% of the nation's adults participate in one or more of the arts. This figure is 33% higher than the usual participation in a presidential election. Similarly, arts attendance involves 86% of the population—a higher percentage than for paid sports events.

The poll also presents statistics that provide insight into popular trends in adult attendance at music events. Perhaps the most interesting category is classical music, which plummeted from 27% in 1987 to 23% in 1992. As you are about to discover, symphony orchestras made dramatic changes in marketing and repertoire in the early nineties, and in 1996 classical attendance had risen to 30%. Similarly, radical new directions in popular music during the same period apparently contributed to a decline in concert attendance from 57% in 1987 to 49% in 1996. Attendance at operas and musicals remained relatively constant at 23% of the adult population.

Data about attitudes toward government funding of the arts are also positive. Overall, 79% of Americans thought there should be local, state, and federal arts councils to foster the arts. Support for individual types of councils ranged from 57% for federal (down 2% since 1987) to 67% for local arts councils (up 4%). Of those surveyed, 56% indicated they would be willing to pay $10 more in taxes specifically for federal support of the arts. There was a consensus that government should not finance the arts entirely but provide seed money to encourage arts activities.

In addition to improving the quality of life, nonprofit arts agencies provide tremendous economic paybacks. A 1994 survey by the National Assembly of Local Arts Councils shows that arts agencies create 1.3 million jobs and $36.8 billion in expenditures. Tax revenues from nonprofit arts activities are $790 million at the local level, $1.2 billion for states, and $3.4 billion for federal coffers.

The National Endowment for the Arts (NEA) has been the prime mover in fostering the growth of the arts in the United States. Since its inception in 1965, it has awarded more than 100,000 grants to artists and arts organizations. With NEA support, there are now more than 3,800 local arts agencies, and state level agencies have increased from 5 to 56. At the same time, the number of large orchestras has risen from 100 to 230 and opera companies have grown from 27 to more than 120. Given this record of success it may surprise you to know that the NEA receives less that one dollar per person in federal support (remember that the Harris poll indicated that 56% of the adult population would be willing to give an additional $10 for the arts annually). Clearly, our national interest in the arts deserves greater financial support than that.

MARKETING MUSIC

Long-term value in music has always been decided by broad popular opinion over time. Beethoven's Fifth Symphony, for example, remains the best-known symphony of all time because it continues to be relevant for the widest segment of society. In the present day, however, short-term decisions about the popularity of music are only partially determined by the people. Because the marketing practices that were initially developed in popular music now seem to apply to all styles, you will find that understanding the current musical scene depends on some knowledge of music marketing practices.

The most important fact to learn about popular music marketing is that marketing (selling) is more important than music (which music is sold). For example, radio stations are not driven by playing a certain kind of music but rather by playing the kind of music that will attract the largest audience for their advertisers. Since the goal is to make the most money possible, music marketers strive to create and satisfy musical fads and fashions.

The three parts of the process—selection, processing, and marketing—are guided by a combination of "science" and intuition, for there does not seem to be a formula for producing a hit. The selection of recordings for processing in one sense means that someone is choosing music for you on the basis of economic rather than artistic concerns. The combination of the high cost of mass marketing and the uncertainty of predicting success dictates that more recordings be chosen for initial processing than will finally receive full marketing support.

Launching a fad or a fashion requires massive publicity that is way beyond the means of even the four giant recording conglomerates that control the industry. Accordingly, record companies are largely at the mercy of "free" venues such as radio networks, television talk shows, and computer web pages. The uncertainties of being able to choose the right product and connect with the buying public through appropriate publicity make the recording industry a high-risk venture. To improve the odds, most companies concentrate their resources on new releases by proven artists or new groups that are directly connected to popular interests or trends. As a listener, you should realize by now that much of the music you hear is not only beyond your control, but also beyond the direct control of the record companies.

Popular music marketing has grown from a low-budget, small record company to local radio station process to a highly complex, billion dollar, international enterprise. As you are about to learn, jazz and even classical music are now employing pop-marketing techniques with remarkable success. In addition to this continuous expansion, the industry has been revolutionized with each change of technology. As an example, inexpensive and portable tape players brought recorded music to cars and expanded the audience to include people in nearly all countries of the world. MTV created an entirely new market, and the compact disc dramatically improved sound quality.

Predictions are that CD-ROM and World Wide Web technology may alter the way we buy and enjoy music. The Napster controversy made it clear that the technology required to distribute music electronically is already in place. Computers also provide the access to diverse radio broadcasts and the means for music groups to market their own music. While it is probable that some of these circumstances will have changed by the time you read this, at the very least you should keep all of these developments in mind as you purchase listening equipment and packaged music.

A DIVERSE MUSICAL SPECTRUM

You live in what is perhaps the most musically egalitarian time in the entire history of music. Composers and consumers alike are open to more musical styles and cultures than ever before. This worldwide musical landscape is homogeneous in that Western and non-Western, high and low art, electronic

© Dave Parkhurst

Aurora Borealis

and acoustic, experimental and traditional, and the visual and the aural are routinely combined in musical works. At the same time, this infinite variety of musical choices provides for great diversity and variety.

THE EMANCIPATION OF THE COMPOSER

As K. Robert Schwartz noted in a recent New York Times article,[1] young, contemporary American composers "fall into two distinct camps." In one group are such composers as Michael Torke and Aaron Jay Kernis—composers "rooted in tradition, writing for ensembles of acoustical instruments like the orchestra and the string quartet, and retaining forms like the symphony and the concerto." Their goal "is to extend the classical heritage while informing it with the materials of American popular culture."

In Schwartz's "other group," are composers who "rejected conventional media and forms, and turned to small, flexible ensembles that incorporate electronic and computer technology." Having grown up on minimalism and rock, these composers seek to free themselves from classical traditions. Such composers as David Lang, Julia Wolfe, and Michael Gordon, who created the Bang on a Can Festival held in New York in the late 1980s and 1990s, "define

[1]K. Robert Schwartz, "Young Composers Shun Isms, Emulate Pop," *The New York Times*, June 30, 1996.

© Dan Rest

Laurie Anderson

a compositional esthetic that is . . . strident, gritty, and aggressive." Julia Wolfe emphasizes rhythm and repetition over harmony and melody, is dissonant, "dense in texture, dark in color, and . . . loud." David Lang describes his *Cheating, Lying, Stealing* as "a series of unreliable, imperfect repetitions" and, as such, it is a caricature of the minimalist technique. Although Lang makes more use of traditional harmonies than Julia Wolfe does, his music is likewise "supported by an aggressive backbone of percussion."

An extension of the second group is the composer who not only rejects the limitations of the classical heritage, but even the limitation of one art form. Performance artist Laurie Anderson has made a career of combining music with other art forms in live performance settings. Her *Nerve Bible* is a full-scale multimedia production that serves as a metaphor for the human body and mortality itself. For the performance, Anderson descends into view from above, hanging upside down from a rope. Her black costume responds to certain gestures with programmed sound effects ranging from computer sounds to amplified heartbeats. She is backed by computer characters Bruce and Agnes, whose images are projected on a 36-foot screen. Video screens display a wide variety of images having to do with the primary theme of mortality.

FREEDOM FOR PERFORMERS

The late-twentieth-century dissolution of artificial barriers between art and popular music and between Western and world music increased the opportunities for artists to cross over to other styles of music. From the business perspective, crossovers in live performance or on CD projects often allow the artist to reach an entirely new segment of the listening public. Similarly, collaborations with other artists provide for combining two or more distinct markets.

EXPERIENCING MUSICAL CLASSICS

OPERA ENJOYS A RENAISSANCE

At a time when symphony orchestras find themselves performing for aging, declining audiences, opera houses are often sold out to enthusiastic, younger crowds. For example, for the past eleven years the Chicago Lyric Opera has been at more than 100% capacity for all performances. According to the Lyric office, their current annual audience represents a more than 1,000% increase over their audiences of forty or fifty years ago.

Since the musical styles of symphonic music and opera are often similar, the recent attractiveness of opera must come from something other than the music. Undoubtedly, the decline in high school orchestras and music appreciation classes since the mid-sixties has made orchestral music much less accessible for much of the potential audience. Opera's visual nature, along with the potential of approaching an understanding through any of the several art forms that comprise it (drama, dance, artwork on sets, and instrumental and vocal music) provides much easier access for these audience members. Also, contrary to what many people believe, the average audience member usually finds opera plots attractive because of their soap opera or mythological character and the inclusion of those popular television commodities: sex and violence. In the last forty years, opera's intrinsic appeal has been heightened by an increasing emphasis on the visual aspects of the performance, with acting taking on a greater role in explaining the plot. Finally, English-language subtitles or super titles have been added to most professional productions, making the drama far easier to follow.

EXPLORING OPERA

Attending an opera may be the furthest thing from your mind. However, most classes that attend a professional production find it very enjoyable. Here are some suggestions to help you have a similar experience.

Choose the opera carefully. If you like musicals you might want to consider an initial work that is somewhere in between the two genres: *West Side Story, Porgy and Bess,* or something by Gilbert and Sullivan. Mozart's *Marriage of Figaro* or a comic opera might also suit your fancy. If you like tragic endings, try something from the standard repertoire like *Carmen, La Boheme,* or *Madame Butterfly.*

Attend a professional production. As a rule, any opera company in a major city should be of good quality. Asking a regular opera fan about a particular production or reading a review might also be wise.

Read the synopsis of the plot in the program. Even with exceptional acting and subtitles, the plot may be hard to follow without some prior knowledge.

Suspend your contemporary view of reality. It is very likely that you do this regularly when you attend movies. Because opera may include complex combinations of instrumental and vocal music, acting, and scenery along with conventions in the plot that may come from a very different time, you may need to have an even more flexible view of reality than you would at a movie.

SYMPHONY ORCHESTRAS: CRISIS AND RESOLUTION

As Bernard Holland has pointed out in *The New York Times,* "For the past 150 years, the American orchestra has been more or less the European orchestra adapted to this country's free-enterprise system. It has used European or European-inspired music to attract a like-minded audience and has offset the inevitable shortfall from ticket sales through the generosity of private citizens."[2] Henry Fogel, executive director of the Chicago Symphony, "accused the American orchestra business of promoting pretension in a country dedicated to unpretentiousness."[3]

In the 1960s and 1970s, orchestras in the United States experienced what seemed to be an unending expansion with community groups turning into fulltime regional symphonies and urban orchestras growing to international status. Because of an expanding economy and tax laws that allowed write-offs for donors, salaries and operating budgets grew dramatically. Many more symphony players received fulltime compensation, allowing them to devote all of their energies to the orchestra.

The ingredients that implied a bright future turned out to be a recipe for disaster. In time, tax laws changed and the economy slowed, leading to the failure of a number of mid-sized orchestras that could no longer meet payroll. Significant declines in arts teaching in the public schools, particularly school orchestra programs, meant fewer prospective audience members and orchestra players. As more and more players became fulltime, they withdrew from pri-

[2] Bernard Holland, "Survival of Symphonies: Radical Changes Urged," *The New York Times,* June 19, 1993, Arts section.

[3] Ibid.

vate teaching and other forms of community involvement. Composers' detours into electronic and experimental music that were often difficult for audiences to appreciate led to a dearth of popular new orchestral music.

In 1992, the American Symphony Orchestra League, a national organization made up of more than 850 orchestras, issued a report on the health of orchestras in the United States. The following year the league released a report recommending a variety of ways in which to improve the overall condition of the orchestra. Two sections, "Achieving Cultural Diversity" and "The Orchestra as Music Educator," caused immediate controversy. The cultural issue related to the largely white male personnel of most orchestras and a repertoire that is primarily Eurocentric.

After a year or so of debate, what appears to have happened is that individual orchestras began to make changes that were appropriate for their particular communities. Some successful marketing devices have been theme concerts, multimedia presentations at concerts, new concert times and lengths, a wider repertoire that includes some pop, jazz, and non-European music, packaging subscriptions with other arts or sports events, and reduced price or free "introductory" concerts.

In the area of education, the changes have been impressive; more than 300 orchestras have created relationships with their local public schools and there are a like number of youth orchestras, which have a minority population of 25%. A number of major orchestras have become involved with community music schools. As an example, the St. Louis Symphony purchased its own school that serves more than 3000 students with ensembles, private lessons, and theory classes.[4] Orchestras are also expanding traditional youth concerts and pre-concert talks. These educational efforts by symphony orchestras, coupled with the "National Arts Agenda" (which mandates music classes for all public school students), should dramatically improve the overall climate for symphony orchestras in the not too distant future. In fact, even the initial efforts made by orchestras seem to have helped, since a "recent Harris poll on participation in the arts shows attendance for classical music up 7% . . . from 1992 figures."[5] In conclusion, it appears that orchestras will thrive in the twenty-first century.

Exploring Orchestral Music

There are two obvious differences between the opera company and the symphony orchestra. First, the traditional orchestra concert lacks the visual and

---

[4] Bernard Holland, "A Prophet Finds Honor At Home," *The New York Times*, April 14, 1996, Sunday Edition, Section H.

[5] Karen Campbell, "The Future of American Orchestras May Be Bright After all," *The Christian Science Monitor*, July 16, 1996, Special to The Christian Science Monitor, Cincinnati, Music.

aural diversity found in opera, and, second, orchestras are working very hard at audience building. Here are some suggestions for selecting an orchestra concert.

Investigate your regional symphony orchestra. The information above indicates that there are a significant number of orchestras in the United States. Look for a Web page for the orchestra nearest you. Try to determine if the orchestra is among the more innovative: Are the program offerings varied and attractive? Do they offer preconcert talks or other ways of informing you about the music? And last but not least, what sort of student ticket prices do they have?

Look for a diverse program. Since orchestra concerts lack some of the visual interest of opera, finding a varied program could make this experience more interesting. Soloists or other special programming, such as a work for chorus and orchestra, are some possibilities. You may even like a concert with visuals or some other nonmusical addition.

Try to find a program that has at least one piece you know and like. This may sound daunting, but many people recognize and like Beethoven's Fifth Symphony, although a good number have not heard it in live performance. Also, consider some of the works covered in this text: *Symphonie Fantastique, Appalachian Spring,* or the *Afro-American Symphony.*

Learn about the music beforehand. Pre-concert talks are usually brief and are worth the extra time. Also, get to your seat early enough to be able to read the program notes.

Relax and enjoy. Our frenetic lifestyle can make it difficult to maintain focus on a concert length that was established more than a century ago. However, slowing down and enjoying some great music can be very therapeutic.

CHAPTER

37 Exploring Popular Music Styles

JAZZ, BLUES, AND WORLD MUSIC

A BLUES REVIVAL

As Phil Patton noted in *The New York Times,* "Beginning perhaps in 1990, when the complete works of Robert Johnson were issued on CD, setting half a million copies and winning a Grammy award a half century after the blues master

American Windows,
panels 1 (music) and
2 (art), Marc Chagall

died, the blues have been staging the latest of many revivals. Sales of blues records are up, the number of blues labels has increased, and the number of blues clubs in America has grown by half. . . ."[1] It is ironic that the blues, an alive and ever changing type of music that was created nearly a hundred years ago by disenfranchised blacks, should have sparked a revival. But the blues is capable of this sort of duplicity, having turned almost immediately after its founding into a democratic musical institution that could be acted upon by a society in flux.

The revival of the blues in the nineties has been marked by the growth of record sales; a proliferation of blues labels, blues clubs, and festivals; and by a considerable amount of controversy. Is it folk music or art music, a commercial venue or a tradition from the past, black history or music for the world? All of these issues seem to be involved in the *House of Blues* clubs founded by Isaac Tigrett, the former owner of the *Hard Rock Cafe* chain.

Tigrett anticipated the current revival by trusting the musical axiom that one style from the beginning of each century returns to prominence at the

[1] Phil Patton,"Who Owns the Blues?" *The New York Times,* November 26, 1995, Arts & Leisure section.

end. The focal point of $9 million Los Angeles *House of Blues* is a recon-structed cotton gin house from Clarksdale, Mississippi, where Muddy Waters had once worked as a hand. "The gin house's journey mirrored the move the blues have made . . . from juke joints to Hollywood"[2]—in this instance spark-ing charges of commercialism and exploitation against Tigrett by blues purists. In reality, initial investors did include the Harvard University Foun-dation and Disney; the holdings of this multimedia conglomerate include a syndicated radio show, a television show, a record label, a clothing line, and a Web site.

Also at issue was the selection of performers for the *House of Blues*. Patton quotes Francis Davis, author of *The History of the Blues:* "I've seen the House of Blues television show, but they never seem to have any blues on."[3] The truth is that since the first blues recordings in the twenties and thirties, record com-panies exploited blues artists. The amazing thing is the blues as a genre flour-ishes amid controversy and grows as musical styles and tastes change. It has been said that one must know all of the divergent blues styles that have evolved over the century in order to play this music well. Perhaps the beauty of the blues is that musicians who are so educated will be able to continue to weave fresh music regardless of the social, economic, or cultural changes that are to come.

EXPLORING BLUES

The description above suggests that the primary problem you might encounter in listening to blues is determining what generation you might be hearing. Since many of the original blues performers are no longer with us, performers you hear in concert are likely to be at least second generation. You may also be concerned about the authenticity of what you hear: Is it the real thing or some sort of blueslike commercial music? Although in the final analysis this distinc-tion may not matter, a little background work might be helpful.

Check out some recordings from your local library. Look for recordings of vaudeville-based blues singers like Bessie Smith or Ma Rainey. You might also look for some blues songs by jazz singer Billie Holiday. The music of Robert Johnson and Blind Lemon Jefferson represent early male blues musi-cians, and Memphis-based W. C. Handy, the composer of "St. Louis Blues," was influenced by European music.

Put the word "blues" in a search engine on the Web. You will find a significant list of sites including venues, artist pages, blues festivals, and sound sources.

[2] Patton,"Who Owns the Blues?"
[3] Ibid.

Find out who is performing before you attend. A description of the artists you are about to hear should help you decide whether you want to attend.

THE WANING AND WAXING OF JAZZ

Like the blues, jazz experienced a bit of an identity crisis in the last part of the twentieth century. In the sixties and seventies free jazz and jazz-rock fusion were two new styles that could have led to a new mainstream jazz. Many members of the traditional jazz audience, however, were either put off by the apparent lack of conventional structure in free jazz or the so-called selling-out aspect of jazz-rock. The result has been the decline of CD sales, the closing of some jazz clubs in the United States, and the migration of many artists to foreign markets. As Alex Ross pointed out in *The New York Times,* "Much as classical tonality returned to fashion in the 1970s and 80s, jazz has lately seen a conservative reaction and a retreat to essentials."[4]

Neoclassicism in jazz is the application of modern techniques to older styles and structures. For the most part, the return is to the chord changes, acoustic instruments, and structure of bebop with the addition of modern performance possibilities such as collective improvisation, variable formal structure, rhythm, and meter and the use of modal, tonal, or chromatic melodies. At the forefront of this movement is trumpeter Wynton Marsalis, who you have already heard performing the Haydn Trumpet Concerto.

Marsalis, who has studied both classical and jazz music, first gained national attention in 1984 when he issued two CDs, one classical (including the Haydn) and one jazz, and both won Grammy awards. In addition to recording, performing, and teaching, he currently directs the Jazz at Lincoln Center concerts and appears in the PBS *Marsalis on Music* television series. Wynton Marsalis seems to represent a new breed of jazz artist — well-educated, articulate, knowledgeable about several types of music, and much more astute about the business of music than his predecessors.

Saxophonist Joshua Redman, also the son of a jazz great, represents the next step in the creation of the new jazz artist, one who uses pop music corporate marketing techniques to forward his career. Redman said of himself, "My background is different . . . it made for a catch, 'The guy who went to Harvard, the would-be lawyer turned jazz musician.'"[5] After winning the Thelonius

---

[4] Alex Ross,"Talking Some Good, Hard Truths About Music" *The New York Times,* November 12, 1995, Sunday Edition.

[5] Peter Watrous, "Is Josh Redman a New Archetype?" *The New York Times,* November 20, 1994.

Monk Institute's saxophone award, Joshua Redman became an ideal commodity for a music marketer: the son of an important jazz saxophonist and an award winner on jazz's most popular instrument with an interesting personal story (Harvard grad gives up law school for uncertain career in jazz). The three albums Redman released sold more than 250,000 copies and his tour dates have exceeded 250 per year.[6] Unlike the pop music personality, the new jazz star is expected to make dramatic musical progress while maintaining a grueling marketing and performing schedule. Time will tell how many young artists are able to meet the demands of this new image.

Although it is uncertain how long neoclassicism in jazz will last, it does seem that this new breed of performers has restored virtuosic playing to the idiom. Also, like classical music, jazz appears to be moving into the musical mainstream by adopting systematic marketing techniques. The upshot may well be a group of well-known jazz stars playing a variety of styles and all available for your listening enjoyment.

Exploring Jazz

Like the blues, jazz encompasses a wide variety of musics. Traditional jazz is the original music of New Orleans, Kansas City, and Chicago. To some extent, this music can still be experienced in those cities, particularly in New Orleans. Swing, a big-band dance music that flourished between the two world wars, has recently experienced a renaissance. Modern jazz, roughly covering the second half of the twentieth century, includes styles such as bop, cool, fusion, and the new thing. These all precede neoclassic jazz, but all are available in some form in the present. Here are some ways to find the styles you like.

On radio or CD explore several of these jazz idioms. Here are some names to look for: traditional—King Oliver, early Louis Armstrong; cool—Miles Davis, Gerry Mulligan, Modern Jazz Quartet; bop—Charlie Parker, Dizzy Gillespie; fusion—Blood, Sweat and Tears, '70s Miles Davis, '70s Herbie Hancock; new thing—Ornette Coleman.

Listen to your local jazz station or surf the Web. Since many of the artists listed above are no longer with us, listen for clues, such as "cool jazz proponent," to help identify performers you want to hear. In major cities, check the newspaper to see who is appearing at local jazz clubs.

Attend a jazz festival. Putting "jazz festival" in a search engine will give you many choices in the United States and throughout the world. Inevitably, these are relaxed, fun events where you are likely to hear a variety of styles.

---

[6] Watrous, "Is Josh Redman a New Archetype?"

Check your university concert hall or music department. The music department is likely to have a jazz program, and both may bring in nationally known jazz performers from time to time.

WORLD MUSIC: MUSICAL ANTHROPOLOGY OR PART OF THE MELTING POT

The traditional Western view of music held that art music gradually evolved over centuries through the European style periods that we examined in earlier chapters. In the twentieth century, it has become evident that the creation of art music no longer follows this sort of evolutionary process and that music has become all-inclusive, international, and multicultural.

Walter Wiora, one of the few scholars to propose a new view of the history of music, suggests four ages of music, the last being "music in the technical and industrial age, spanning all countries of the world, uniting the heritage of all previous cultures in a kind of universal museum. . . ."

Perhaps because of the growing access to various world musics after World War II, new programs of study were developed to prepare students specifically for the study of world music. At that time, distinct, self-contained musical cultures existed in a number of places around the world. Through the research of ethnomusicologists and enhanced technologies that made instant communication possible, these musical cultures were shared around the world. Today, all world musics have been influenced by Western music and vice versa. The result is Wiora's united musical heritage—a circumstance that makes it possible to hear a sitar in a jazz quintet as well as in a traditional Indian classical ensemble. It is likely that you will hear world music in both of these contexts: blended with other musics and as a historical artifact.

EXPLORING WORLD MUSIC

While searching for ways to explore world music, keep in mind the musical anthropology/melting pot analogies. The truth is that a bit more anthropological work would make you much more effective in recognizing and appreciating the times when world music appears in the melting pot. Here are some ways to continue your research:

Investigate offerings on your campus. Many times music or multicultural study areas sponsor concerts and/or workshops featuring world music. If you have a particular interest in world music, consider taking a class.

Look for offerings by ethnic communities or organizations. In large cities, there are entire communities representing single ethnicities. In moderate-size cities often there are ethnic organizations (Americans from India, for example) that can steer you in the direction of authentic music.

Check your local library or CD store. Both should have some world music offerings. They may not have them divided into the melting pot/anthropology categories, so be careful to distinguish between the two.

Check the Web for other sources of music.

POPULAR MUSIC

RECENT SOCIETAL PROBLEMS AND MUSICAL REACTIONS

The eighties were a time of a freewheeling economy, two-income families, message-less mega pop stars, and growing youth and urban problems. When 1990 came, the results of these excesses were clear: permanently diminished economic opportunities, numerous broken homes, growing drug problems, the proliferation of street gangs, AIDS, and a poor urban society that was nearly dysfunctional. For millions of teenagers throughout the industrialized world, the answer to these issues was an explosion of popular musical styles that could be melancholy, violent, obscene, angry, physical, or a combination of the above. Groups such as Nirvana, Nine Inch Nails, Arrested Development, Pearl Jam, and Snoop Doggy Dogg created innovative music that was as relevant to segments of the world teen population as original rock was to American teens of the sixties.

Although punk rock is the root of many of these styles, they are far removed from the gospel-blues-country base of traditional rock. Computerized sounds or guitar bands that focus on distortion instead of chord progressions often displace the usual ensemble of guitars, bass, drums, and keyboard. For the most part, melody is replaced by rhythm. Dance music, from rave to reggae to disco, is an important part of the overall scene. In general, the songs tend to be cynical, abrasive, and noisy. A partial listing of styles of the early nineties includes rap, harsh rock, hip hop, trip hop, ambient house music, gangsta rap, industrial rock, grunge rock, techno, trance, jungle, and mope rock.

DIVERSE TASTES, SPLINTERING MARKETS

This multitude of styles responded to the varying geographical locations, classes, and inclinations of young listeners. The original rock audience, the baby boomers, was repulsed by this new music of angry messages, no melody, and electronic sounds. In addition, the recession and rising CD prices meant that the blind buying habits of the eighties were replaced by a more careful selection of albums for long-term listening. This more astute buying public also tended to make purchases from all of the available styles, rather that being allied to one particular genre or artist. In this environment, pop music marketers and radio stations could no longer concentrate on one album by an artist like Michael Jackson that would sell ten million copies. In short, the music was more relevant and marketers were forced to be more responsive to a diverse buying public.

Mellowing and the Institutionalization of Rock

In almost every instance of a radical change in musical style, a move back toward tradition soon follows. By 1995, some of the new popular music was slower, softer, and more positive in attitude. Hootie and the Blowfish topped the year's charts with a musical style and lyrics borrowed from the boomers. Groups like Urge Overkill, the Pizzicato Five, and punk rocker Nick Cave even show influence from 1970s pop songwriters like Neil Diamond and Burt Bacharach. Certainly the anger was not gone, particularly among women such as Alanis Morisette and Joan Osborne. Overall, however, the mood had softened and was even a bit reflective as the Grateful Dead disbanded after Jerry Garcia's death and the "The Beatles Anthology" was issued.

The Lilith Fair: A Sample Pop Music Life Cycle

In 1996 the Canadian singer Sarah McLachlan founded the Lilith Fair, a summer concert series featuring women. A run of four concerts in 1996 was followed by a thirty-five-city concert tour of North America in 1997. By the end of the summer 1999 tour McLachlan had decided to suspend the tour for the foreseeable future.

Although it may have been possible to continue the Lilith Fair for some years into the future, it is likely that it had run its course as a creative force in popular music. To be sure, it had achieved several important goals: dramatically enhancing the marketability of women in the music industry and adding to the mellowing of popular music. However, it also demonstrated a typical pattern in pop music—the degeneration of a relevant, issue-oriented music into a commercial enterprise.

Country Music Goes Worldwide

While rock and related forms of popular music were suffering an identity crisis in the early nineties, country went national and international, doubling its record market share in just two years. In fact, many of the new listeners were part of the rock audience who had become disenchanted with grunge, hip hop, and metal. For them, the less aggressive country style, with a clear text and conventional melodies, was a welcome relief.

Prior to this period of phenomenal growth, country had been a southern tradition centered in Nashville, Tennessee, and the Grand Ole Opry. The original Grand Ole Opry was a downtown location that supported regional radio broadcasts. Some years ago a new facility was built that added television and featured an adjacent theme park and the Opryland Hotel. Gaylord Entertainment Co., the owner of the complex, added impetus to the growth of country music by acquiring two cable television networks, CMT and TNN. The national distribution of country music led to a younger, more upscale image for country artists and to a revision of the traditional male and female country stereotypes.

The sexist images of the wild, macho, somewhat immature male and the strong, understanding female had actually been losing ground among southern country listeners prior to the nationalization of the genre. To appeal to the broader audience, the new male must be young, more understanding, and enlightened while the female is more liberated and assertive. Within these new points of view, country texts still concentrate on the social currents of American life, with the additional ". . . influence of contemporary concerns like feminism, the men's movement, the environment and AIDS."[7]

Very recently country music has experienced a backlash from adopting this homogenized style. Some traditional fans felt alienated, and some of the new middle-of-the-road fans lost interest after a relatively short period of time. Simultaneously, traditional recording studios have been challenged by artists who use home digital studios and by satellite radio stations. In reaction to all of this Nashville is diversifying by mixing other styles with what had been a straight country style.

POPULAR MUSIC AT THE PRESENT

At the beginning of the twenty-first century popular music seemed to be searching for an identity. Although rap and hip hop were principal styles, neither offered much in the way of innovation. And while a debate raged on whether rock was dead, it became clear that technology-driven music was a passing trend. In the midst of all of this, Paul Allen opened the $240 million Experience Music Project in Seattle, an interactive rock museum.

The trends that are evident seem to indicate that the postmodern idea is still in effect. Globalization continues to expand, and the "Top 40" can be expected to represent several countries. There has been a pronounced

---

[7] Billy Altman, "Country Just Ain't What It Used To Be," *The New York Times*, January 31, 1994.

Latin/Cuban trend in popular and jazz styles as evidenced in the success of the Buena Vista Social Club. Female performers have continued to expand their presence and influence in all popular styles. Crossovers and style mixes are prevalent, an important recent crossover being the movement of many Christian rockers to the pop genre. Radiohead's *Kid A* combines a variety of styles in a way that is reminiscent of Peter Gabriel's soundtrack to the film *Passion*.

The potential of entirely new music marketing systems evidenced by the Napster controversy and the uncertainty of the economy undoubtedly have something to do with the tentative pop music climate. It is also very likely that some very exciting and different musical offerings are on the horizon.

EXPLORING POPULAR MUSIC

The foregoing information should make it clear that popular styles are numerous, often interrelated, and constantly changing. Also, from the promoters' point of view, the goal is to make money not music. Making informed consumer decisions in this sort of climate is difficult indeed. Here are some questions you can ask yourself that may help.

Where is the group on the relevance-commodity continuum? Does the group you want to hear have a relevant message or has their music degenerated into a commercial commodity?

Is the work musically interesting? Does the group have fresh, new musical ideas or have they degenerated into popular "elevator" music?

Is it worth it—$60 per concert, $20 per CD? In both cases reviews in the newspaper might be helpful. For the CD, a music store with listening facilities may allow you to decide before you purchase whether or not this will be a lasting addition to you collection.

CODA

The musical form is complete and little remains to be said in the coda. As you leave at the end of the term remember that all music is for your enjoyment and enrichment. At this point, the information you have acquired should provide you with access to nearly any kind of music—the choice is up to you. And finally, the more effort you put into exploring music, the more rewarding the experience will be. Happy listening.

ENCYCLOPEDIA
AND KEY TO MUSIC SELECTIONS

ABA form   See ternary form.

a cappella   Vocal music that is not accompanied by instruments. *Ch. 13*

acculturation   A mixing of native and foreign elements. ♪ *Raksat el-Houria.* ♪ *Neend Koyi. Ch. 35*

Adams, John (1947–)   A teacher and composer who has written music for both instruments and voices, including a highly publicized opera entitled "Nixon in China." His compositions are emotional and full of energy. Adams' compositions frequently involved mixed media. ♪ *Two Fanfares,* Second Fanfare, "Short Ride in a Fast Machine." *Ch. 19*

adhan   The Muslim call to prayer. The adhan is sung five times a day from the top of minarets on mosques by a muezzin. ♪ *Adhan,* The *Muezzin's* Call to Prayer. *Ch. 12*

Afro-Pop   A generic term for all African popular music. ♪ "Asiki Mi Ti To," Chief Commander Ebenezer Obey. *Ch. 35*

alap   In Indian music, the drone instrument sustaining one or two of the principal pitches of the raga, and the solo instrument slowly playing the original melody so that the audience may get in mind the "tune" that will be improvised upon. *Chs. 25, 35*

allegro   A lively tempo; typically the tempo marking for the first and third movements of a sonata. *Ch. 22*

amjad   A bowed fiddle that is held vertically; a favorite instrument in Morocco. ♪ *El Baz Oichen. Ch. 17*

angas   The Indian term for measures. *Ch. 25*

angklung   A folk instrument from Bali made up of a set of numerous short bamboo tubes of graduated lengths loosely enclosed in small frames, a frame for each tube or a set of two tubes tuned in octaves. When the frames are shaken, the tubes rattle at definite pitches that are used to play melodies. ♪ *Segera Madu. Ch. 17*

aria   Structured and melodic singing within the opera using repeated words and recurring motives. ♪ Second Act, Arietta, "*Voi che sapete,*" *The Marriage of Figaro,* Mozart. *Ch. 23*

Armstrong, Louis "Satchmo" (1901–1971)   One of the most influential jazz musicians of the twentieth century. Known for his trumpet playing and "scat singing," he was also active as a bandleader, actor, and composer. ♪ "Back O' Town Blues," Russell and Armstrong. *Ch. 16*

arpeggio   To "run the chords"; the pitches of a chord played up and down in a sequence. *Ch. 5*

asymmetric meter   See irregular meter. *Ch. 3*

atonal   The term describing music in which no one note or chord within a piece of music feels like "home." ♪ Six Pieces for Orchestra, Anton Webern. *Ch. 5*

augmentation   A doubling of the original length of a theme during performance. *Chs. 18, 20*

Bach, J. S. (1685–1750)   A humble church musician from the baroque era who composed music primarily for use in religious services. His output of more than 300 chorales has served as a basis of harmony for more than 200 years. As cantor of the Thomas Schule in Leipzig from 1723 until his death, he was responsible not only for coordinating, and composing when necessary, the music of the four major churches of the city, but also for the education of the choirboys and the maintenance of the musical instruments. "Jesu, Joy of Man's Desiring," Cantata 140, First Movement, "Wachet auf." *Chs. 5, 13*

band   A term used in the United States to mean a mixed wind and percussion group. *Ch. 24*

baroque era   1600–1750. Historical period that corresponds with the invention of opera and the flourishing of independent instrumental music. Distinctions between opera, church music, and instrumental music and national styles, particularly Italian, French, and German, are characteristic of the music written between 1600 and 1750. *Ch. 10*

Bartók, Béla (1881–1945)   Twentieth-century composer who systematically collected folk songs from his native Hungary and either used them or new melodies he composed in the folk style in his compositions. Bartok is considered to be one of the first ethnomusicologists. By combining Hungarian elements with his own unique compositional style he introduced the flavor of the native music of his country to much of the world. Concerto for Orchestra, Fifth Movement. *Ch. 18*

basso continuo   Type of accompaniment found in ensemble sonatas. Often two instruments, such as the cello and keyboard, would perform the continuo. *Ch. 22*

Bay Psalm Book   The first book of Psalms to be printed in the British colonies. First published in 1640, it did not include music notation until the 9th edition (1698). *Ch. 14*

beats   Regularly spaced rhythmic pulses. ♪ "We Three Kings of Orient Are." ♪ "Stars and Stripes Forever." *Ch. 3*

bebop   A small group jazz medium that employed complex harmony and required great technical facility of its players. Its tempos were very fast. The characteristic ensemble was a quintet with two players (usually sax and trumpet) on the frontline and a three-piece rhythm section. ♪ "Koko," Charlie Parker, Dizzy Gillespie. *Ch. 25*

Beethoven, Ludwig van (1770–1827)   German composer who was born in Bonn. Often thought of as the composer who bridged the gap between classical and romantic style periods, Beethoven was often featured as a performer of his piano pieces and conductor of his symphonies. ♪ "Ode to Joy" melody, Finale, Ninth Symphony. ♪ Fifth Symphony, First Movement. *Chs. 4, 6, 21*

Berlioz, Hector (1803–1869)   French composer of the romantic period who used programs for his symphonies. ♪ *Symphonie Fantastique*, Movement Five, last movement, conclusion. *Chs. 6, 7, 21*

Bernstein, Leonard (1918–1991)   The first American-trained conductor-composer to gain an international reputation as a classical musician. His thorough technical training as a composer enabled him to become one of the supreme craftsmen of the Broadway musical. ♪ "Tonight" Quintet, *West Side Story. Chs. 7, 33*

Billings, William (1746–1800)   The most famous professional American musician during the last half of the eighteenth century. Billings was a singing master in Boston churches. ♪ "Chester." *Chs. 8, 9, 14*

biwa   A plucked lute added to the performance of gagaku when performed as concert music. *Ch. 11*

bluegrass   A type of music that uses the fiddle, guitar, mandolin, five-string banjo, and string bass.

The vocals usually take the form of solos and duets. In the duets, the harmony part is higher than the melody. The tempo tends to be rather fast. ♪ "Why Did You Wander?" Monroe and Flatt. *Ch. 30*

blues   Type of music that grew out of the "sorrow song" performed by African Americans after the Civil War. The blues are a vehicle for improvisation as well as a feeling or mood. ♪ "Mean Old Bed Bug Blues." *Ch. 16*

boogie woogie   A solo piano style that evolved out of ragtime that often uses the twelve-measure blues structure. Its most characteristic feature is a powerful, repeated eight-note pattern (four beats per measure, subdivided into two notes on each beat) played by the left hand. Above this, the right hand is free to interpret the melody or to improvise. ♪ "Honky Tonk Train," Meade "Lux" Lewis. *Ch. 29*

bop   See bebop.

Brahms, Johannes (1833–1897)   Nineteenth-century German romantic composer whose works combined the best of classicism and romanticism. He composed in almost every major medium except opera, including four symphonies, concertos, songs, piano and chamber music. ♪ "Wie lieblich sind deine Wohnungen," *A German Requiem. Ch. 15*

Britten, Benjamin (1913–1976)   Twentieth-century English composer of sacred music, operas, instrumental music, and solo and choral vocal music. ♪ War Requiem, "Dies irae" (excerpt). *Ch. 14*

bugaku   One category of gagaku. A type of Japanese dance music that has two principal forms, komagaku and togaku. *Ch. 11*

Cage, John (1912–1992)   Twentieth-century composer who is a major proponent of indeterminacy. ♪ *4' 33". Ch.8*

Cajun band   A band used to play Cajun music that is typically made up of a fiddle, concertina, guitar, triangle, and vocalist. *Ch. 16*

cantata   Literally means something that is sung. A type of seventeenth-century secular music related to opera that was integrated into the Lutheran church service. ♪ "Wachet auf" Cantata 140. *Ch. 13*

chaconne   A type of theme and variations in which the theme is an ostinato (repeated) pattern. ♪ First Suite in E-flat for Military Band, First Movement, Chaconne, Gustav Holst. *Ch. 24*

chamber music   Instrumental music written for a small number of players with one player on a part and the emphasis on ensemble rather than solo playing. The term is derived from the French *chambre*, meaning room, which suggests that this music is often suitable for performance in a small, intimate setting. ♪ String Quartet in F, *"Vif et agité,"* Maurice Ravel. *Ch. 27*

chance music (indeterminacy)   A formal design in which instructions or actions taken by the composer or performer result in an unpredictable musical outcome. ♪ *4' 33"*, John Cage. *Ch. 8*

chanson   A French song from the Renaissance written with flexibility of form that matches the varied form of the poems and clearly reflects the meaning of the text. ♪ *"Mille Regretz,"* Josquin Desprez. *Ch. 26*

chant   Monophonic music performed by singers that uses a limited range of pitches and flexible rhythms, often reflecting the rhythms of the words. ♪ Kyrie XI (Kyrie Orbis Factor). *Ch. 12*

chorales   The strophic religious texts associated with melodies that came to be used in the Lutheran tradition. *Ch. 13*

chord   Three or more notes sounded together. A component of Western harmony. *Ch. 5*

chord progression   Chords that systematically follow each other in a piece of music. An example is the twelve-bar blues. *Ch. 5*

chromatic scale   A scale made up of every pitch (black and white) in succession on a piano keyboard. *Ch. 4*

classical era   1750–1825. Musical period brought on by the Enlightenment's pursuit of "naturalness." The classical era ushered in a type of music that has been a staple of concert music ever since. Narrowly defined as high-quality or "model" music represented by the works of Haydn, Mozart, and Beethoven, classical music comes closest to being a truly unified, recognizable style. *Ch. 10*

colotomic structure   The entrance of certain instruments in the gamelan mark off the progress of the piece. ♪ *Kebjar Taruna. Chs. 3, 19*

comic opera   An opera featuring a more or less humorous treatment of plot and a nontragic ending. *Ch. 23*

commercial music   Music created for the primary purpose of generating revenue for the writers and performers. *Ch. 10*

compound meter   The simultaneous perception of two different levels of beat. ♪ "We Three Kings of Orient Are." *Ch. 3*

concertato   See concerto.

concertina   A small accordion used in Cajun bands. *Ch. 16*

concertino   A small group of soloists in the baroque concerto grosso. *Ch. 22*

concert music   Music intended primarily for the focused attention of the listener. *Chs. 10, 19*

concerto   (1) In the baroque era, music using voices and instruments together, performed "in concert" (together). *Ch. 13* (2) In the classical era and following, a three-movement work for soloist and orchestra. ♪ Third Movement, Trumpet Concerto in E-flat, Josef Haydn. *Ch. 22*

concerto grosso   A musical work featuring the concertino pitted against the ripieno. ♪ Third Movement, Brandenburg Concerto No. 2, J. S. Bach. *Ch. 22*

conductus   An early example of polyphony associated with music used during processions. ♪ *Ave Virgo Virginum. Ch. 12*

conjunct   Melodic motion in steps. *Ch. 4*

consonance   "Pleasing" sounds (intervals or chords). Provides resolution for dissonance. *Ch. 5*

continuo   A notated bass line performed by some melodic instrument (cello, bassoon, or other bass instrument) together with an improvised accompaniment usually "realized" from chord symbols by some keyboard instrument. *Ch. 13*

controllers   Instruments that do not create sound but trigger the actions of a computer synthesizer. These include guitar controllers, drum machines, keyboard controllers, wind controllers, and keyboard mallet controllers. *Ch. 9*

cool jazz   A reaction to the "hot," hard-driving rhythms and complexities of bebop. The ensembles were larger than those used in bebop and often included instruments not usually found in jazz, such as French horn, oboe, and cello. The emphasis was on subtlety. Notes were attacked delicately, and use of the middle register of the instruments predominated. ♪ "Jeru," Gerry Mulligan. *Ch. 25*

Copland, Aaron   (1900–1990)   An eminent American composer born of Jewish immigrant parents in Brooklyn. Elements of folk music are emulated throughout his music. ♪ "Hoe Down" from *Rodeo.*

♪*Appalachian Spring,* "Variations on a Shaker Melody." *Chs. 1, 2*

countermelody A secondary melody added to the melody that offers melodic interest when the primary melody is resting. *Ch. 16*

counterpoint A specific type of polyphony in which melodies are pitted against each other rather than simply combined. ♪"Tonight" Quintet, *West Side Story,* Leonard Bernstein. *Ch. 7*

country music A type of music that grew out of the characteristically somber folk ballads of the British Isles. This somberness was perpetuated in the lyrics of country music that often dealt with lost love or cheating lovers, with traditional values violated as well as upheld, with disappointment and pain more than promises. ♪"I Want to Be a Cowboy's Sweetheart," Patsy Montana. *Ch. 30*

da capo Literally, "from the head." A type of ternary form represented by the letters ABA. Da capo instructs the performer to return to the beginning of the piece to repeat the opening section (A). *Ch. 8*

da capo aria A type of ternary form used in operas, cantatas, and oratorios. *Ch. 8*

darbukka An Egyptian drum. ♪*Mol Kadd Tewela. Ch. 35*

debke A line dance popular in the Middle East. ♪*Raksat el-Houria. Ch. 35*

density An important element in the composer's use of sound. Takes into consideration volume, tone color, number of performers, and texture. *Ch. 7*

Desprez, Josquin (ca. 1440–1521) Generally considered the master composer of the Renaissance. His career included singing in Milan at the Cathedral and later the Ducal court, the Papal Chapel. He had a reputation as an outstanding singer and composer, and is best remembered for his motets. ♪*Ave Maria, gratia plena à 4. Ch. 13.* ♪"Mille Regretz." ♪"El Grillo." *Ch. 26*

development Follows the exposition in sonata form. Manipulation of themes 1 and/or 2 that usually includes frequent key changes (modulation) producing a feeling of instability and forward motion. Themes may be repeated, sequenced, fragmented, inverted, in retrograde, augmented, diminished, or reharmonized. ♪*Eine kleine Nachtmusik,* Mozart. *Ch. 20*

Dies irae A famous sequence (attributed to the thirteenth-century Thomas of Celano), which is well known for its melody and its association with death. It forms part of the Requiem Mass, or Mass for the Dead. *Ch. 12*

diminution A halving of the original length of a theme during performance. *Ch. 20*

disjunct Melodic motion in skips. *Ch. 4*

dissonance Sounds (intervals or chords) that are "unpleasing" to our ears. Dissonance serves a very useful purpose in that it implies musical activity (tension), and moving from dissonance to consonance provides resolution (rest). *Ch. 5*

dodecaphonic All twelve notes—black notes and white notes on the piano—are employed equally. The harmony of this music was based on a predetermined ordering of the twelve notes of the chromatic scale rather than on triads and seventh chords. *Ch. 5*

Dorsey, Thomas A. (1899–1993) An important composer of early gospel music. He began his musical career as a blues pianist, accompanying the famous blues singer "Ma" Rainey and writing some rather risqué songs for her. ♪"Hide Me in Thy Bosom." *Ch. 14*

dotara A plucked four-string long-necked lute whose body is carved from a single piece of wood. Common in Hindu folk music. ♪*Bhatiali. Ch. 17*

drums Percussion instruments in which the sound is produced by the vibration of a stretched piece of skin or plastic (a head). *Ch. 9*

duet In opera, a musical number featuring two singers. ♪Second Act Finale, Scene Ten, "Signori di fuori," *The Marriage of Figaro,* Mozart. *Ch. 23*

duggi A pair of drums similar to the tabla but less exact in pitch, and bells. Common in Hindu folk music. ♪*Bhatiali. Ch. 17*

dung-chen A long copper natural (unvalved) trumpet used to accompany Buddhist ritual music such as the chant. ♪*Tshetro Jineh. Ch. 12*

Dvořák, Antonín (1841–1904) A nineteenth-century nationalist composer who chose to represent the United States and his native Bohemia in his music. He was known for his symphonies and chamber music. ♪Symphony No. 9, *From the New World. Ch. 18*

dynamics The loudness or softness of sounds. *Ch. 6*

ensemble (1) Instruments and/or voices that perform together. *Ch. 9* (2) In opera, a formal number for more than two singers in which the composer has the characters express themselves both alternately and simultaneously. ♪ Second Act Finale, Scene Ten, "Signori di fuori," *The Marriage of Figaro,* Mozart. *Ch. 23*

ethnomusicologist   A specialist in the study of music of specific cultures. *Ch. 18*

exposition   The opening section of sonata form. Consists of the following: (A slow introduction is optional) Theme 1, Transition, Theme 2, closing material; coda is optional; typically, the entire exposition is repeated. ♪ *Eine kleine Nachtmusik,* Mozart. *Ch. 20.*

flat four   Each beat of the measure (four beats per measure) receives about the same amount of stress or accent. ♪ "Back O' Town Blues." *Ch. 16*

Fleck, Bela (1958–)   A New Yorker of Hungarian descent who plays a composite pop folk jazz on the banjo. ♪ "Hoe Down" from *Rodeo. Ch. 1*

flexible rhythm   Rhythm that is patterned after words or dance movements and complex rhythmic practices of non-Western cultures. ♪ Kyrie XI (Kyrie Orbis Factor). *Ch. 3*

folk music   Music that communicates on a direct personal level and is readily accepted by a large percentage of a population. Folk music is characterized by the anonymity of its creators, its performance by amateurs, and its oral tradition. *Ch. 10*

form   The overall design of a musical work that can be heard by the listener. ♪ "The Star Spangled Banner," Francis Scott Key. *Ch. 8*

forte   The dynamic marking for loud. ♪ Fifth Symphony, First Movement, Ludwig van Beethoven. *Ch. 6*

Foster, Stephen (1826–1864)   The first truly great American songwriter. During his short lifetime he produced about 150 songs, primarily divided between ballads and songs for the minstrel show. Popular works include "Oh, Susanna," "Camptown Races," "The Old Folks at Home," "My Old Kentucky Home," "Beautiful Dreamer," and ♪ "I Dream of Jeanie." *Ch. 29*

fragment   A part of a theme. *Chs. 18, 20*

frontline   In a jazz band, the three instruments that stand out front, nearest the audience. *Ch. 16*

frottoir   A rub-board. *Ch. 16*

fusion   One way that jazz and rock can be combined. An instrumental style that includes extensive improvisation. *Ch. 31*

Gabrieli, Giovanni (c. 1555–1612)   The greatest Venetian composer of the very late Renaissance. He is one of the first composers to indicate on the score what specific instruments should perform. Gabrieli wrote compositions for string and brass instruments and voice. ♪ *Canzona in echo duodecimi toni à 10. Ch. 5*

gagaku   "Elegant music." The principal musical style of Japanese court music; it was traditionally administered through an official music bureau. Exists in several categories: bugaku, komagaku, and togaku. *Ch. 11*

gamelan   A large ensemble consisting of a number of drums, gongs, xylophones, metallophones, and sometimes a flute and a hammered zither. Gamelans may vary in size from three or four instruments to more than twenty. There are family gamelans, community gamelans, and professional gamelans. These ensembles are common in Java and Bali. ♪ *Segera Madu* ♪ *Kebjar Taruna. Chs. 17, 19*

gats   In Indian music, a series of improvisations on the rhythmic and melodic patterns introduced. *Ch. 25*

genre   Term used to describe the kind of piece, such as sonata, string quartet, and symphony. *Ch. 20*

Gershwin, George (1898–1937)   American composer and pianist. Often collaborated with his brother Ira on songs and was influenced by jazz and popular styles. Important instrumental works include *Rhapsody in Blue* and *An American in Paris.* ♪ "There's a Boat Dat's Leavin' Soon for New York," *Porgy and Bess. Chs. 9, 33*

ghazals   A traditional poetic form widely used in Muslim cultures. *Ch. 35*

Gillespie, Dizzy (1917–1993)   Important modern jazz trumpeter and the personification of the bop musician. ♪ "Koko." *Ch. 25*

Glass, Philip (1937–)   An American composer whose style is rooted in minimalism. Glass adopted repetition as his principal technique, but he forged a recognizable style (and pleased a large audience) by using diatonic chords rather than dissonant materials and by shaping them into coherent, if essentially static, large-scale patterns. Glass is considered to be the most successful opera composer of the 1980s, and his reputation rests largely on three works: *Einstein on the Beach* (1976), *Satyagraha* (1980), and *Akhnaten* (1984). ♪ *Satyagraha.*

Chs. 1, 8. ♪ Act III, "Martin Luther King, Jr.," Part 3, *Satyagraha. Ch. 23*

glissando   Sliding between pitches. ♪ "Et surgens," *St. Luke Passion,* Krzysztof Penderecki. *Ch. 15*

Handel, George Frideric (1685–1759)   German baroque composer who studied in Italy and spent the later part of his life in England. He was an accomplished violinist and harpsichordist who often conducted from the keyboard. Although he is an almost exact contemporary of Bach, he made his living through producing performances of his music. He wrote and conducted operas in London for a number of years and then changed to the oratorio when opera was no longer lucrative. ♪ "The People Shall Hear," *Israel in Egypt,* Part 2. *Ch. 15*

harmony   The vertical dimension of music. A Western concept popularized in Europe during the ninth century. ♪ *Canzona in echo duodecimi toni à 10,* Giovanni Gabrieli. *Chs. 5, 12*

Haydn, Franz Josef (1732–1809)   Austrian classical composer who spent most of his career in the employ of the aristocracy but had two productive seasons in London later in life. Haydn wrote more than 100 symphonies and some of the first mature string quartets, as well as some important vocal works. ♪ Trumpet Concerto in E-flat, Third Movement. *Ch. 22*

Herbert, Victor (1859–1924)   Composer of the first notable works in the new operetta style. An immigrant born in Dublin and trained in Europe, Herbert brought musical legitimacy to early American musical comedy and comic opera as well as to the operetta. ♪ "Ah, Sweet Mystery of Life." *Naughty Marietta. Ch. 34*

hichiriki   A double-reed instrument used for the performance of gagaku. The hichiriki sounds like an oboe. ♪ *Hyojo Netori. Ch.11*

highlife music   The blending of European-American popular idioms with African traditions. This began in the 1950s in Ghana when native African musicians adopted the guitar to accompany their singing. *Ch. 35*

Hindemith, Paul (1895–1963)   A German composer who immigrated to the United States to avoid Nazi persecution. He was on the faculty at Yale University and wrote a series of sonatas for wind instruments and pieces for band in addition to orchestral

music. ♪ Third Movement, Fugue, Symphony for Band. *Ch. 24*

hindewhu   A one-note flute used by the Pygmies. *Ch. 17*

hocket style   A musical style in which melody notes are distributed among several players or singers. *Ch. 17*

Holst, Gustav (1874–1934)   An English composer who wrote operas, songs, and choral and orchestral works. Perhaps his best-known piece is *The Planets,* a *Star Wars*-type piece that was originally written for orchestra. ♪ First Suite in E-flat. *Chs. 9, 24*

homophonic   A type of texture made up of a prominent melody supported by chords. ♪ "Mean Old Bed Bug Blues," Bessie Smith. *Ch. 7*

idée fixe   The theme used by Berlioz to represent the beloved in *Symphonie Fantastique.* ♪ *Symphonie Fantastique,* Berlioz. *Ch. 21*

imitation   Occurs when each voice enters, one after the other, singing the same musical line in an overlapping fashion. ♪ *Ave Maria, gratia plena à 4. Ch. 13*

indeterminacy (chance music)   A formal design in which instructions or actions taken by the composer or performer result in an unpredictable musical outcome. ♪ *4' 33",* John Cage. *Ch. 8*

interval   The distance between two notes sounded together or one after the other. Intervals are named by counting the number of letter names between and including the two notes. *Ch. 5*

introit   The first part of the Mass Proper that is sung on Christmas Day. ♪ *Viderunt omnes . . . iustitiam suam. Ch. 12*

inversion   An upside down version of a theme. *Chs. 18, 20*

irregular meter   Patterns of twos and threes grouped in an irregular fashion. ♪ String Quartet in F, Maurice Ravel. See also asymmetric meter. *Ch.3*

jazz   A style of music developed in the late 1800s. Elements of jazz include a lilting beat called "swing," a characteristic rhythm called syncopation in which "offbeat" accents create a breakup of the regularity of beat, and improvisation. *Ch. 16*

jazz-rock   One way that jazz and rock can be combined. This musical style features a lead vocalist accompanied by horn (trumpet, sax, and trombone) and rhythm sections. ♪ "Spinning Wheel," Blood, Sweat and Tears. *Ch. 31*

jazz standards   Songs usually associated with jazz. *Ch. 19*

Joplin, Scott (1868–1917)   Black pianist and composer known as the "King of Ragtime." ♪ "Maple Leaf Rag." *Ch. 29*

juju   The integration of traditional Yoruba rhythms with hymns, highlife, and Western popular music. *Ch. 35*

kakko   Japanese drum. *Ch. 10*

kalangu   An African "talking drum." *Chs. 9, 35*

kanun   An Egyptian plucked zither. ♪ *Mol Kadd Tewela*. *Ch. 35*

khamaj mode   A mode like our major scale with a lowered seventh scale degree. ♪ *Bhatiali*. *Ch. 17*

komagaku   A type of bugaku derived from Korean and Manchurian sources. The dancers wear primarily green costumes. *Ch. 11*

koto   A Japanese zither added to the performance of gagaku when performed as concert music. Also used for the performance of kabuki. *Chs. 11, 32*

Kyrie eleison   The first Ordinary text of the Mass. ♪ Kyrie XI (Kyrie Orbis Factor). *Ch. 12*

leader-chorus   A type of spiritual sung in a way resembling the call-and-response type characteristic of African singing that is exemplified by successive patterns of a soloist singing a line of text and a group response. ♪ "I Want to be Ready." *Ch. 16*

leitmotifs   Themes used by Richard Wagner to represent persons, places, or things in his operas. *Ch. 21*

Lewis, Meade "Lux" (1905–1964)   American jazz pianist known for promoting the boogie-woogie style in the late 1930s. ♪ "Honky Tonk Train." *Ch. 28*

libretto   The text of an opera. The libretto is typically written by someone other then the composer and may be entirely new or more likely an adaptation of an existing literary work. *Ch. 23*

lied   In the nineteenth century, an inventive, sensitive setting of poetry for singer and piano. ♪ "Der Erlkönig," Franz Schubert. *Ch. 26*

lining out   A method of instruction in which the song leader speaks or sings a line or two of a song; that portion of the song is then repeated by the congregation. *Ch. 14*

liturgical music   Music that plays a prescribed role in religious ritual. ♪ *Adhan*, The *Muezzin*'s Call to Prayer. *Ch. 12*

liturgy   The official words, actions, music, and other behavior that constitute a religious ceremony. *Ch. 10*

major scale   The most common scale in Western music. An example would be C major, all of the white notes on the piano keyboard from one C to the next. ♪ "Joy to the World." ♪ "Twinkle, Twinkle Little Star." *Ch. 4*

matras   The Indian term for beats. *Ch. 25*

melismatic   Text setting in which many notes are sung for each text syllable. *Ch. 12*

melodic contour   The characteristic linear pattern or shape of a melody. ♪ "The Star Spangled Banner." ♪ "Here Comes the Bride." ♪ "Amazing Grace." ♪ "Twinkle, Twinkle Little Star." ♪ "Joy to the World." *Ch. 4*

melody   A succession of musical tones organized in a meaningful fashion. *Ch. 4*

Mendelssohn, Felix (1809–1847)   German romantic composer of symphonies, organ, piano and choral music. Served as a conductor and pianist throughout Europe and in England. ♪ Trio No. 2 in C Minor, Third Movement. *Chs. 9, 27*

meter   Beats that are grouped into regularly recurring patterns, normally with a stronger accent on the first note of each pattern. ♪ "We Three Kings of Orient Are." ♪ "The Star Spangled Banner." *Ch. 3*

Middle Ages   600–1450. The longest period in Western music. Characterized by monophonic music related to the Catholic church. *Ch. 10*

MIDI   Musical Instrument Digital Interface. An industry standard system of communication for digital instruments, computers, and synthesizers. *Ch. 9*

minimalism   The use of limited musical materials in a texture that features few (minimal) changes in rhythm, melody and harmony. ♪ Act III, "Martin Luther King, Jr.," Part 3, *Satyagraha*, Philip Glass. ♪ *Two Fanfares*, Second Fanfare, "Short Ride in a Fast Machine," John Adams. *Chs. 8, 19*

minor scale   The second most common scale in Western music. An example is A minor, all of the white notes on the piano keyboard from one A to the next. ♪ "We Three Kings of Orient Are." *Ch. 4*

minuet   A musical form generally found in third movements. The minuet is typically in 3/4 meter and is customarily followed by a trio and then a repeat of the minuet that results in a ternary or three-part form. *Ch. 27*

modulation   The process of key change. This generally involves a chord progression that creates the sense of a new key. ♪ "Jesu, Joy of Man's Desiring," J. S. Bach. *Chs. 5, 18*

monophonic   Literally, "one sound." Texture made up of a single melody. *Ch. 7*

Monroe, Bill (1911–1996)   American performer who coined the term bluegrass. ♪ "Why Did You Wander?" *Ch. 30*

Montana, Patsy (1914–1996)   Early American country music singer. ♪ "I Want to Be a Cowboy's Sweetheart." *Ch. 30*

motet   A polyphonic setting of sacred Latin texts. ♪ *Ave Maria, gratia plena à 4. Ch. 13*

Mozart, Wolfgang Amadeus (1756–1791)   Prolific classical composer from Salzburg. Mozart was a child prodigy as a performer on clavier and as a composer. He wrote symphonies, sonatas, concertos, choral music, and operas during his short lifetime. ♪ *Eine kleine Nachtmusik. Chs. 2, 5, 8* ♪ Piano Sonata in C Major, Third Movement. *Chs. 8, 22* ♪ Second Act, Recitative *Quanto duolmi, Susanna,* and Arietta, *"Voi che sapete," The Marriage of Figaro. Ch.23* ♪ Second Act Finale, Scene Ten, *"Signori di fuori," The Marriage of Figaro. Ch. 23*

mridangam   A type of Indian drum. *Ch. 25*

muezzin   The singer of the adhan. He praises the greatness of Allah and chants texts from the Koran, the book of Islam. *Ch. 12*

Mulligan, Gerry (1927–1996)   Jazz baritone saxophonist in the "cool" style. ♪ "Jeru." *Ch. 25*

music   Sound organized in time. *Ch. 1*

musical   A form of musical entertainment that features down-to-earth characters and plots, colloquial dialogue, and popular style song. *Ch. 31*

musical notation   A graphic representation of music in which every line and space between the lines represents a musical note. ♪ "Joy to the World." ♪ "Here Comes the Bride." *Ch. 4*

nationalists   Those composers who emphasized national elements in music. *Ch. 18*

nava rasa   In Indian music, the nine moods. They are the Erotic, the Comic, the Pathetic, the Furious, the Heroic, the Frightful, the Disgusting, the Tranquil, and that of Wonderment. *Ch. 25*

neoclassicism   Used to describe the compositions of a number of important twentieth-century composers. The return to any earlier style other than romanticism. However, in almost all cases the musical language was contemporary. ♪ Symphony No. 1, Ellen Taaffe Zwilich. *Ch. 21*

obbligato   An independent melodic accompaniment. ♪ "Back O' Town Blues." *Ch. 16*

Oliveros, Pauline (1932–)   Twentieth-century composer, performer, author, philosopher whose music involves improvisation, electronic sound sources, ritual, myth, and meditation. ♪ *The Lion's Tale. Chs. 1, 6, 7, 27*

opera   A sung drama in which singers play the roles of the characters on a suitably decorated stage. ♪ Second Act, Recitative *Quanto duolmi, Susanna,* and Arietta, *"Voi che sapete," The Marriage of Figaro,* Mozart. *Ch. 23*

operetta   A form of musical theater that is light and sentimental in character and contains music, spoken dialog, dancing, and other theatrical elements. American operetta has as its foundation the French comic opera of the mid-nineteenth century and the Viennese operetta popularized by Johann Strauss and others. ♪ "Ah, Sweet Mystery of Life," *Naughty Marietta,* Victor Herbert. *Ch. 34*

oratorio   The first religious substitute for secular entertainment. Texts, although based loosely on the Bible, were freely poetic plays or libretti. In Latin oratorios there was frequently a narrator. It soon took on the structure and dramatic character of a religious opera but without the customary sets, costumes, and acting. ♪ "The People Shall Hear," *Israel in Egypt,* Handel ♪ "Et surgens," *St. Luke Passion,* Penderecki. *Ch. 15*

orchestration   The process of choosing instrumental combinations for a band or orchestral work. ♪ *Symphonie Fantastique,* Last Movement, Hector Berlioz. *Ch. 6*

ordinary   A Mass text appropriate for many occasions; some are even called for every time a particular type of service is performed. ♪ Kyrie XI (Kyrie Orbis Factor). *Ch. 12*

organum   The earliest example of harmony. A melody accompanied by a second part that moves parallel to it at a specific interval. ♪ "King of Heaven, Lord of the Wave-Sounding Sea," Organum with parallel fourths. *Ch.5*

oud An Egyptian plucked lute. ♪ *Mol Kadd Tewela. Ch. 35*

overture An orchestral number that occurs before the curtain goes up, contains many of the main themes of the act, and serves as a musical introduction to the opera. *Ch. 23*

Palestrina, Giovanni Pierluigi da (ca. 1525–1594) Next to Josquin Desprez, the most important composer of the Renaissance. Lived in Italy and participated in reforms of the Catholic Church that resulted from the challenges of the Protestant Reformation. Associated with the highest level of the development of polyphonic a cappella church music. ♪ *Missa Papae Marcelli*, Kyrie. *Chs. 7, 14*

palm wine music The blending of European-American popular idioms with African traditions. This began in the 1950s in Ghana when native African musicians adopted the guitar to accompany their singing. The term comes from the relaxed, rural, acoustic guitar style associated with late afternoon drinking sessions at palm wine bars in the bush. *Ch. 35*

Parker, Charlie "Bird" (1920–1955) The most legendary of all jazz saxophonists and probably the greatest of all jazz improvisers. He was at the center of bebop music. ♪ "Koko." *Ch. 25*

Penderecki, Krzysztof (1933–) Avant garde Polish composer whose work is characterized by constant experimentation and a focus on unusual sonorities. He experimented with electroacoustic music and composed music for almost every genre and medium. ♪ "Et surgens," *St. Luke Passion. Ch. 15*

pentatonic scale A scale limited to five pitches from the named seven (for example, the five black notes on the piano). ♪ "Amazing Grace." *Ch. 4*

piano The dynamic marking for soft. ♪ Fifth Symphony, First Movement, Ludwig van Beethoven. *Ch. 6*

pitch The most basic component of melody; the highness or lowness of a sound. *Ch. 4*

polyphonic A piece of music made up exclusively of interwoven melodies. ♪ *Missa Papae Marcelli*, Kyrie, Palestrina. ♪ "Tonight" Quintet, *West Side Story*,

Leonard Bernstein. ♪ *Ave Virgo Virginum à 3. Chs. 7, 12*

polyrhythm The simultaneous use of two or more different rhythms. *Ch. 3*

Porter, Cole (1891–1964) American composer and lyricist. ♪ "Riding High." *Ch. 19*

program In the nineteenth century, a description or story that was intended to be included in the concert program. ♪ *Symphonie Fantastique*, Hector Berlioz. *Ch. 21*

proper A Mass text appropriate only to a specific day (for example, Easter Sunday) or to a season (for example, Lent). *Ch. 12*

Psalter Book containing prose and poetic translations of the Psalms of David. *Ch. 14*

quarter-tones Pitches smaller than the half-steps of the piano. ♪ "Et surgens," *St. Luke Passion*, Krzysztof Penderecki. *Ch. 15*

raga (1) The mood conveyed by the music, the rasa. In Indian music there are considered to be nine of these, the Nava Rasa. *Ch. 25* (2) The germinal melodic material used in improvisation in Indian classical music. It has been said that it is "more than a scale and less then a melody." (3) The form in which improvisations are done in Indian music. ♪ *Shenai Raga Bilawal.* ♪ *Todi.* ♪ *Neend Koyi. Chs. 25, 35*

ragtime A piano style that combines happy, syncopated, banjolike rhythms of the minstrel show (usually in the right hand or treble part) with even, stable rhythms (usually in the left hand or bass part), which emphasize the meter. Scott Joplin is known as the "King of Ragtime." ♪ "Maple Leaf Rag," Scott Joplin. *Ch. 29*

range In a melody, the distance from the highest note to the lowest note. ♪ "Joy to the World." ♪ "Twinkle, Twinkle Little Star." *Ch. 4*

Ravel, Maurice (1875–1937) A French composer whose unique style grew out of, yet away from, the impressionism of Claude Debussy. ♪ String Quartet in F. *Chs. 3, 27*

recapitulation The last major section in sonata form. The recapitulation follows the design of the exposition except that the transition does not modulate to the dominant key but instead stays in tonic. Therefore, theme 2 will probably sound lower than it did in the exposition. May be followed by a coda. ♪ *Eine kleine Nachtmusik,* Mozart. *Ch. 20*

recitative   Free, speechlike singing through which the drama of the opera unfolds. ♪ Second Act, Recitative *Quanto duolmi, Susanna,* Mozart. *Ch. 23*

reharmonization   A theme that is supported by new chords. *Ch. 20*

Renaissance   1450–1600. Historical period that corresponds to those intellectual movements in literature, architecture, and painting that arose in Italy by the fourteenth century. The development of music printing at the turn of the sixteenth century contributed to the preservation of much of this music. *Ch. 10*

reprise   The technique of reusing a song heard earlier. *Ch. 33*

retrograde   A backwards version of a theme. *Ch. 20*

rhythm   The temporal organization of sounds in music. ♪ "Der Erlkönig," Franz Schubert. *Ch. 3*

rhythmic density   The amount of rhythmic activity in a piece of music. ♪ *The Lion's Tale,* Pauline Oliveros. *Ch. 7*

rhythm section   In a jazz band, instruments such as the tuba, banjo, and drums that provide the bass part, the chords, and the beat. *Ch. 16*

ripieno   A large ensemble featured in the ripieno concerto. *Ch. 22*

ripieno concerto   A late-seventeenth-century musical form. This type of work focused on all members of the orchestra rather than featuring soloists or contrasting groups of players. Ripieno or tutti concerto was set in three movements and approximated the texture of the early symphony. *Chs. 20, 22*

ritual music   Music used in carrying out a specific, observable kind of behavior based on established or traditional rules. *Ch. 10* ♪ Giraffe Curing Ceremony, Bushmen, Africa. ♪ *Hyojo Netori,* Japan. ♪ Mehter music, Turkey. *Ch. 11*

rock   The type of music resulting from the combination of pop, country/western, and rhythm and blues in the mid-1950s. Two factors seem to contribute to the rock styles: (1) emotional vocal interpretation and (2) a heavy emphasis on the beat, especially the backbeat. ♪ "Hound Dog," Lieber and Stoller. *Ch. 30*

rockabilly   A kind of hillbilly music with a sexy rhythm and blues-inspired vocal style, pop-oriented lyrics, electric guitar lead, and an emphasis on the beat. *Ch. 30*

Rodgers and Hammerstein   Twentieth-century American composer and lyricist who collaborated on musicals such as *Carousel, South Pacific, The King and I,* and *Oklahoma.* ♪ "People Will Say We're in Love," *Oklahoma. Ch. 32*

romantic era   1825–1900. A reaction to musical classicism; a time when the romantic spirit pervaded the arts (an emphasis on nature, extreme emotionalism, and the like). Romantic music explored extremes—musical miniatures alongside of grand opera. *Ch. 10*

rondo form   A formal pattern in which the opening section returns after each new section of music. A rondo typically has a minimum of five sections and can be represented with the letters ABACA. ♪ Piano Sonata in C Major, Wolfgang Amadeus Mozart. *Ch. 8*

rub-board   Also called a frottoir. Resembles a corrugated metal washboard and is worn like a baseball umpire's chest protector. When "rubbed" or scraped with metal picks it adds a novel and dominant rhythmic sound. *Ch. 16*

ryutiki   A type of flute used for the performance of gagaku. ♪ *Hyojo Netori. Ch. 11*

sampler   A device that takes successive digital snapshots of a natural sound over time. *Ch. 9*

sangita   The nava rasa as applied to the fine arts. *Ch. 25*

sansa   Also called a mbira. An African instrument with metal keys fastened to a wooden resonator. *Ch. 3*

sarod   A Hindustani plucked lute carved from wood. The absence of frets permits slides that make up its characteristic sound. The sarod has melodic strings that are fingered to produce the melody and two or three drone strings that are not fingered and usually not used if a drone is being supplied by another instrument. ♪ *Todi. Ch. 25*

scales   Sequences of pitches. *Ch. 4*

scat singing   Singing nonsense syllables and improvising with the voice as if it were an instrument. *Ch. 16*

scherzando   An indication to perform in a lighter style. ♪ Third Movement, Fugue, Symphony in B-flat for Band, Paul Hindemith. *Ch. 24*

scherzo   A musical form generally found in third movements. The scherzo is typically in 3/4 meter and is customarily followed by a trio and then a repeat of the scherzo that results in a ternary or three-part form. ♪ Scherzo, Piano Trio in C minor, Felix Mendelssohn. *Ch. 27*

Schoenberg, Arnold (1874–1951)   Composer who is credited with founding the second Viennese School by developing atonality and 12 tone serialism. ♪ "Der Mondfleck," *Pierrot Lunaire*. *Chs. 9, 26*

Schubert, Franz (1797–1828)   Viennese composer who composed in the various instrumental genres developed by the three Viennese masters, Mozart, Haydn, and Beethoven. However, his greatest and most enduring contribution to music was his development of the expressive qualities of the lied. ♪ "Der Erlkönig." *Ch. 26*

Schuman, William (1910–1992)   Twentieth-century American composer who wrote for band among other idioms. ♪ "Chester," *New England Triptych*. *Ch. 18*

sentimental ballad   A popular nineteenth-century song common in parlor recitals. The songs dealt with love and courtship (successful and unsuccessful), or tear-provoking topics such as natural disasters and human tragedy. ♪ "I Dream of Jeanie," Stephen Foster. *Ch. 29*

sequence   A theme or melodic fragment that is repeated at successively higher or lower pitch levels. ♪ Third Movement, Brandenburg No. 2, J. S. Bach. *Chs. 20, 22*

sequences   Paired verses of text sung to single musical phrases. ♪ "Dies irae." *Ch. 12*

sequencing   The process by which digital data necessary to play back MIDI sequences and files are stored in a computer. *Ch. 9*

serenade   A lighter, more compact work that is related to the symphony and the string quartet. ♪ *Eine kleine Nachtmusik*, Mozart. *Ch. 20*

seventh chord   The second most popular chord in Western harmony, consisting of four different notes structured in thirds. C-E-G-B is a seventh chord. *Ch. 5*

shakuhachi   A Japanese end-blown bamboo flute. *Ch. 32*

shamisen   A Japanese three-stringed plucked lute. *Ch. 32*

shenai   A double reed aerophone (sounding like our oboe) used in Indian music. ♪ *Shenai Raga Bilawal*. *Ch. 25*

sho   A wind instrument used for the performance of gagaku. The sho sounds like a harmonica. ♪ *Hyojo Netori*. *Ch. 11*

sinfonia   Literally, "together, sounding." A late-seventeenth-century term referring to the title for opera overtures. *Sinfonias* were cast in three movements, with a fast-slow-fast pattern, and were a forerunner of the symphony. *Ch. 20*

sitar   A Hindustani plucked lute fretted like a guitar with a large gourd resonator. The sitar has melodic strings that are fingered to produce the melody, and two or three drone strings that are not fingered and usually not used if a drone is being supplied by another instrument. A dozen or so additional strings under the main strings vibrate sympathetically when activated by playing a main string that sounds the same pitch. ♪ *Todi*. *Ch. 25*

skip   Disjunct melodic movement that omits one or more notes in the scale. ♪ "Here Comes the Bride." *Ch. 4*

slendro scale   A five-tone (pentatonic) scale, roughly corresponding to the black keys of the piano. ♪ *Segera Madu*. *Ch. 17*

Smith, Bessie (1894–1937)   Early American blues singer. ♪ "Mean Old Bed Bug Blues." *Chs. 1, 7*

sonata   From the eighteenth century on, a work for solo instrument that is usually in three movements. Sonatas for monophonic instruments (violin, for example) typically have keyboard accompaniment. The three movements of the classical sonata typically employ the following formal patterns: first movement, allegro, in a sonata form; second movement, slow tempo, in a sonata, ternary, or binary form; third movement, allegro, in a rondo form. ♪ Third Movement, Piano Sonata in C Major, Mozart. *Ch. 22*

sonata da camera (chamber sonata)   In the seventeenth century, a chamber sonata usually containing dance music, making it inappropriate for use in church. *Ch. 22*

sonata da chiesa (church sonata)   In the seventeenth century, a church sonata that was typically abstract, making it acceptable in religious settings. *Ch. 22*

sonata form (1) A type of ternary form. *Ch. 8* (2) A generalized, variable, three-part formal design usually found in the first movements of symphonies, sonatas, concertos, string quartets, and overtures. The three parts of the sonata include the exposition, development, and recapitulation. *Ch. 20*

sonata-rondo form A hybrid form that mixes characteristics of rondo with sonata form. ♪ Third Movement, Trumpet Concerto in E-flat, Josef Haydn. *Ch. 22*

Sondheim, Stephen (1930–) Important contemporary composer of musicals. ♪ "Have I Got a Girl for You," *Company. Ch. 32*

soul Meaning sincere and heartfelt. A type of R&B that often included accompaniments featuring large brass, woodwind and string sections, as well as backup vocal groups. *Ch. 31*

spiritual The first combining of African and European elements. Texts filled with yearning for eternal peace and earthly freedom are set to melodies and harmonies learned in the shared religious experience and given the urgency of the African rhythmic drive. ♪ "I Want to be Ready." *Ch. 16*

sprechstimme A twentieth-century type of singing created by Arnold Schoenberg in which the singer does not actually sing the pitches but rather intones them without aiming at "real" pitches. ♪ "Der Mondfleck," *Pierrot Lunaire*, Arnold Schoenberg. *Ch. 26*

standard A term meaning an enduring popular song. *Ch. 33*

step Conjunct melodic movement to an adjacent note in a scale. ♪ "Twinkle, Twinkle Little Star." ♪ "Joy to the World." *Ch. 4*

Still, William Grant (1895–1978) Considered the "Dean" of African-American composers. Trained in the western European tradition, he integrated African elements into his works. ♪ Afro-American Symphony. *Ch. 21*

stretto Overlapping entrances of the theme in close imitation. ♪ Third Movement, Fugue, Symphony for Band, Paul Hindemith. *Chs. 18, 24*

string instruments Instruments in which the sound is generated by a vibrating string. The string may be bowed, plucked, or struck to begin the sound. The five basic types of string instruments are bows, lyres, harps, lutes, and zithers. ♪ Trio No. 2 in C Minor, Third Movement, Felix Mendelssohn. *Ch. 9*

strophic form A song in which each stanza of text is sung to the same music. *Chs. 8, 12*

subject The primary theme in a fugue. ♪ Third Movement, Fugue, Symphony for Band, Paul Hindemith. *Ch. 24*

surna A double reed wind instrument used to accompany Buddhist ritual music such as the chant. *Ch. 12*

swing The most popular jazz style of the twentieth century. Swing is based on large ensembles of ten or more musicians who play written arrangements that incorporate improvised solos. ♪ "Riding High." *Ch. 19*

syllabic Text setting in which most syllables in the text are sung to a single note. *Ch. 12*

symphonic poem A nineteenth-century one-movement orchestral work that is based on a poetic or descriptive extra-musical idea. *Ch. 21*

symphony A work for orchestra that is usually in four movements and focuses on ensemble playing rather than soloists. Most often, the symphony is abstract and does not project an extramusical idea or image. *Ch. 20*

syncopation The result of rhythms contradicting the underlying metric pulse, often by not lining up with the "strong" pulses that create meter. ♪ *Kebjar Taruna. Ch. 3*

synthetic instruments Instruments in which the sound is produced electronically, rather than by the vibration of some natural material. *Ch. 9*

tabla A type of Indian drum. *Ch. 25*

tala The rhythmic component of Indian classical music. It is a rhythmic cycle of beats (matras) that is divided into measures (angas) by accenting various beats to create subdivisions of from one to nine beats. ♪ *Shenai Raga Bilawal.* ♪ *Todi. Ch. 25*

taqsim In Egyptian music, an improvised, wordless vocalization in which the melodic pattern of the mode to be used is heard at a relatively slow tempo. ♪ *Mol Kaðð Tewela. Ch. 35*

tempo The speed of the beats. ♪ "Stars and Stripes Forever." ♪ "We Three Kings of Orient Are." *Ch. 3*

ternary form The simplest of formal patterns, represented by the letters ABA. Examples of ternary form include da capo and sonata form. *Chs. 8, 12*

texture The balance between the vertical (harmonic) and horizontal (melodic) realms in a given musical work. *Ch. 7*

theme (1) A melody that serves as the primary "horizontal" building material for a piece. ♪ Ode to Joy Melody, Ludwig van Beethoven. ♪ Third Movement, Fugue, Symphony for Band, Paul Hindemith. *Chs. 4, 24* (2) The "thesis statement" of a sonata.

theme and variations A formal design in which an original idea is stated and then repeated a number of times, with each repetition a variation of the original material in some way. Typically, there is a return to the original material toward the end of the variations to bring closure to the work. *Ch. 8*

timbre The color of sound. ♪ *The Lion's Tale*, Pauline Oliveros. ♪ *Symphonie Fantastique*, Hector Berlioz. *Ch. 6*

tintal An Indian tala that consists of a total of sixteen beats grouped in patterns of 4-4-4-4, resembling our 4/4 meter in the common four-, eight-, and sixteen-measure phrases encountered in most popular and folk tunes. *Ch. 25*

togaku A type of bugaku that contains elements of Indian and Chinese music. The dancers wear red costumes. *Ch. 11*

tonal density The number and kinds of voices and instruments being employed in a piece of music. ♪ *Symphonie Fantastique*, Hector Berlioz. *Ch. 7*

tonality The sensation of a particular chord being "home" and other chords functioning in relation to that chord. ♪ "Jesu, Joy of Man's Desiring," J. S. Bach. *Ch. 5*

tone clusters A group of adjacent pitches sounded simultaneously. ♪ "Et surgens," *St. Luke Passion*, Krzysztof Penderecki. *Ch. 15*

tonic The main note of the melody. *Ch. 4*

tragic opera A serious opera with an unhappy or disastrous ending, often involving the death of one or more of the main characters. ♪ Finale, *Otello*, Verdi. *Ch. 23*

tremolo Repeating the same note very rapidly with a change of bow direction for each note. *Ch. 18*

triad The basis of Western harmony. A chord consisting of three different notes. *Ch. 5*

trio sonata In the baroque period, the most popular configuration for the ensemble sonata, consisting of two soloists and basso continuo. *Ch. 22*

tshetro jineb An invocation to the Buddha of Boundless Life, an example of ritual music. ♪ *Tshetro Jineb*. *Ch. 12*

tutti concerto See ripieno concerto.

Twentieth Century 1901–2000. Characterized by diversity of musical idiom, performance opportunities, and audiences. *Ch. 10*

unmetered rhythm See flexible rhythm. *Ch. 3*

Verdi, Giuseppe (1813–1901) Important composer of nineteenth-century Italian opera. ♪ *Requiem*, "Dies irae" (excerpts). *Ch. 15* ♪ Finale, *Otello*. *Ch. 23*

verse-refrain A song in which the action is told in a series of verses with a refrain after each. ♪ "I Want to be Ready." *Ch. 16*

Webern, Anton (1883–1945) One of a group of twentieth-century composers who wrote music described as atonal and dodecaphonic. ♪ Six Pieces for Orchestra. *Ch. 5*

Western Plains Indians ♪ Sioux Grass Dance. *Ch. 2*

whole-tone scale A scale that uses every other pitch (black and white) in succession on a piano keyboard. *Ch. 4*

wind instruments Instruments in which the sound is produced by a vibrating column of air. Categories include flutes, reeds, cup mouthpieces, free wind. Wind instruments that are used in Western music are commonly divided into two subgroups: woodwinds and brasses. ♪ First Suite for Band, Gustav Holst. *Ch. 9*

word painting The use of musical devices to illustrate the text. ♪ "The People Shall Hear," *Israel in Egypt*. *Ch. 15*

Zwilich, Ellen Taaffe (1939–) American composer who was the first woman to win the Pulitzer Prize for composition. Symphony No.1, Third Movement. *Ch. 21*

zydeco Cajun music combined with country rhythm and blues. The piano and accordion sometimes replace the traditional button accordion for greater facility, and the sax and drums are often added. *Ch. 16*

INDEX

CREDITS

Chapter 1

1: © Teresa Heintzman   5: Photo by Herb Snitzer/Frank Driggs Collection

Chapter 2

7: Courtesy, National Museum of the American Indian, Smithsonian Institution, photo by Fred Nahwooksy   11: Concert program courtesy of James Major

Chapter 3

13: © 2003 Salvador Dali, Gala Salvador Dali Foundation/Artist Rights Society (ARS), New York, Bettmann/Corbis   15: Poplars on the Epte, by Claude Monet, Tate Gallery London/Art Resource, New York

Chapter 4

19: Excerpt from score of "We Three Kings," public domain   20: Excerpt from score of "Joy to the World," public domain   21: Excerpt from score of "Here Comes the Bride," public domain   22: Grant Wood, Joslyn Museum, Omaha, Nebraska/SuperStock

Chapter 5

25: Excerpt from score of "King of Heaven, Lord of the Wave-Sounding Sea," Giovanni Gabrieli (ca. 1555–1612), public domain

Chapter 6

33: Georgia O'Keeffe, American, 1887–1886, Blue and Green Music, 1919, oil on canvas, 8.4 × 48.3 cm, Alfred Stieglitz Collection, gift of Georgia O'Keeffe, 1969.835 © The Art Institute of Chicago, All Rights Reserved

Chapter 7

35: Brooklyn Museum of Art/Central Photo Archive

Chapter 8

39: Vatican Museums and Galleries, Rome/Fratelli Alinari/SuperStock   41: Otterlo, Rijksmuseum Kröller-Müller/Art Resource, New York

Chapter 9

51, 52, 53, 54, 55, 56: Illustrations from MUSICAL INSTRUMENTS OF THE WORLD: An Illustrated Encyclopedia by the Diagram Group, © 1976 by Diagram Visual Information Ltd., Published 1997 by Sterling Publishing Co., Inc., 387 Park Ave. S., New York, NY 10016, Reprinted by permission

Chapter 11

69: © Robert Washburn   70: © Robert Washburn

Chapter 12

75: Friedrich, Casper David, Staatiche Museum Berlin, © 2002, Bildarchiv Preussucher Kulturbesitz, Berlin   78: National Geographic Society/Lhasa Tokulhmandu, photo by Maria Stenzel

Chapter 13

85: © Dave Bartruff/Corbis

Chapter 14

89: © Bettmann/Corbis   94: © Peter Barton

Chapter 15

99: © Krzysztof Penderecki, Modulus Publishing House, Krakow   102: Sterling and Francine Clark Art Institute, Williamstown Massachusetts

Chapter 16

105: Courtesy of Tuskegee University Archives

Chapter 17

112: Popsie Randolf/Frank Driggs Collection   114: © Chris Brown   116: © Robert Washburn

Chapter 18

119: Smithsonian American Art Museum, Washington D.C./Art Resource, New York   122: © Archivo Icongraphico, S.A./Corbis   125: © Bettmann/Corbis

Chapter 19

128: © Robert Washburn   130: © Frank Driggs Collection

Chapter 20

135: A.K.G. Berlin/SuperStock   137: © Estate of Burgoyne Diller/Licensed by VAGA, New York, NY, Estate Represented by the Michael Rosenfeld Gallery, New York, NY, Courtesy of Michael Rosenfeld   140: Giraudon/Art Resource, New York

Chapter 21

144: © Stiftung Seebüll, Ada and Emil Nolde   147: Corbis/Bettmann

Chapter 22

150: Afro-American Symphony, First Movement by William Grant Still, © Estate of William Grant Still   151: © Bettmann/Corbis   152: The Sonata, by Marcel Duchamp, © Philadelphia Museum of Art/Corbis/Artist Rights Society (ARS), New York/ADAGP, Paris/Estate of Marcel Duchamp   153: © 2002 Artist Rights Society (ARS), New York/VG Bild Kunst, Bonn   155: © SuperStock

Chapter 23

158: Illustration from MUSICAL INSTRUMENTS OF THE WORLD: An Illustrated Encyclopedia by the Diagram Group, © 1976 Diagram Visual Information Ltd., Published 1997 by Sterling Publishing Co., Inc., 387 Park Ave. S., New York, NY 10016, Reprinted by permission   160: Copyright © Beth Bergman, 2002, NYC   168: © Tom Caravaglia, 1981   168, 169: "Satyagraha" by Phillip Glass, courtesy of Dunvagen Music

Chapter 24

170: Yale University Art Gallery, Gift of Collection Societe Anonyme   171: Woodcut by Hans Burgkmair, courtesy of Dover Publications   172: © Bettmann/ Corbis

Chapter 25

180: © Frank Driggs Collection   182: © Neal Peters Collection

Chapter 26

185: © Bettmann/Corbis

Chapter 27

190: © 2003 Estate of Pablo Picasso/Artist Rights Society (ARS), New York, Francis G. Mayer/Corbis   192: Jan Steen, Dutch, 1625/26–1679, The Family Concert, 1666, oil on canvas, 86.6 × 101 cm, Gift of T.B. Blackstone, © The Art Institute of Chicago, All Rights Reserved   193: © Archivo Iconographico, S.A./Corbis   195: Photo by Irene Young   196: © Christie's Images/Corbis

Chapter 28

198: © Noah Larson   200: Studie II (1954) Karlheinz Stockhausen, © Stockhausen-Verlag, 51515 Germany   201: Me and the Moon, by Arthur Dove, © 2002, The Phillips Collection, Washington, D.C.   203: The Sleeping Gypsy, 1897, Oil on canvas, 51″ × 6′7″, A.K.G. Berlin/SuperStock

Chapter 29

206: © Bettmann/Corbis   209: © Bettmann/Corbis   211: © 2003 Mondrian/Holtzman Trust, c/o Beeldrecht/Artist Rights Society (ARS), New York, Burstein Collection/Corbis

Chapter 30

215: © Frank Driggs Collection   216: © Frank Driggs Collection

Chapter 31

220: © 1962 by Warner Bros Inc. copyright renewed 1990 by Special Rider Music, All Rights Reserved, International copyright secured, Reprinted by permission   221: © Frank Driggs   222: © 1986 Watterson, Reprinted with permission of Universal Press Syndicate, All Rights Reserved   223: "Spinning Wheel", Words and Music by David Clayton Thomas, © 1968 (Renewed 1996) EMI Blackwood Music Inc. and Bay Music Ltd., All Rights Controlled and Administered by EMI Blackwood Music Inc., All Rights Reserved, International Copyright Secured, Used by Permission   224: © Corbis/ARS, New York

Chapter 32

228: © Frank Driggs Collection   232: "I Hope I Get It" music by Marvin Hamlisch, lyrics by Edward Kleban, © 1975 Marvin Hamlisch and Edward Kleban, All Rights Controlled by WREN MUSIC CO. and AMERICAN COMPASS MUSIC CORP., All Rights Reserved

Chapter 33

236: © Photofest   238: © Photofest

Chapter 34

244: © Bettmann/Corbis

Chapter 35

249: © Robert Washburn   251: © S.I.N./Corbis   252: © Chris Brown

Chapter 36

257: © Dave Parkhurst   258: Photo by Dan Rest

Chapter 37

263: Marc Chagall, French, born Russia, 1887–1985, America Windows, 1977, glass, Gift of the City of Chicago and the Auxiliary Board of the Art Institute of Chicago commemorating the American Bicentennial in memory of Mayor Richard J. Daley, 1977.938 overall view with light, © The Art Institute of Chicago, All Rights Reserved